LIVES A D WORKS

LIVES AND WORKS

Profiles of Leading Novelists,
Poets and Playwrights

Edited by Annalena McAfee
Portraits by Eamonn McCabe

Atlantic Books
London

First published in 2002 by Atlantic Books, on behalf of Guardian Newspapers Ltd.
Atlantic Books is an imprint of Grove Atlantic Ltd.

10 9 8 7 6 5 4 3 2 1

A CIP catalogue record for this book is available from the British Library

ISBN 1 84354 079 7

Printed in Great Britain by CPD, Ebbw Vale, Wales
Design by Helen Ewing

Grove Atlantic Ltd
Ormond House
26–27 Boswell Street
London WC1N 3JZ

Contents

Preface

Annalena McAfee

In an age of celebrity, when interviews are the staple of every newspaper and magazine, the *Guardian*'s Saturday profile claims a certain distinctiveness. Its first, most obvious characteristic is its size: at about four thousand words, the profile is more than twice the length of the most substantial newspaper interview. Then there is its depth: the epic form, as opposed to the haiku, affords a rare degree of detail. The profile portrait photograph also breaks newspaper rules and runs unflinchingly across two pages of the broadsheet Saturday Review section. Above all, the subjects of the profile must be figures of influence in their respective spheres, with a substantial body of work behind them. Newsworthiness is not enough.

Pop stars, sportsmen and sportswomen, soap actors and reality TV participants are generally covered elsewhere. Politicians have made several appearances on the profile pages (Jesse Jackson, Vladimir Putin and Barbara Castle, for example) as have scientists (Steven Pinker, E. O. Wilson and Sir Robert May) and many leading figures in the arts: theatre and film directors (Peter Brook and David Lynch); composers and conductors (Karl Heinz Stockhausen and Valeri Gergiev); and painters (Howard Hodgkin and Frank Auerbach). But the overwhelming majority of subjects have been literary. In the following pages, you can read a selection of our profiles of novelists, poets and playwrights, representing an overview of the vitality and diversity of contemporary international literature.

The standard newspaper interview, backed by a perusal of press cuttings, is by necessity swiftly produced and derived largely from an hour in the presence of the interviewee. *Guardian* Saturday profile writers are given time for preparation and are expected to be familiar with their subjects' work. Although the profile is built around a central interview, the interviewee's colleagues, critics, friends and foes are also canvassed and quoted. The life and the work should be covered with equal authority and seriousness, though humour is not discouraged. The result should be neither a hatchet job, nor fawning hagiography. The aim is to provide a considered, comprehensive, critical and biographical monograph.

Since the first profile was commissioned in 1998, a style has gradually evolved. The tone is broadly detached and the narrator invisible. The use of the first person singular is permitted only within the frame of quotation marks (though there are exceptions: the late poet and critic Ian Hamilton interposed himself in the two profiles he wrote for us, but the effect was characteristically illuminating rather than self-aggrandizing).

There should be no accounts of the journalist's difficulties in setting up the interview, no description of his or her subjective response to the interviewee, and above all no whimsical revelations about the journalist's personal life. This is not a celebrity interview, nor is it an exercise in the kind of journalism that promotes the interviewer as a celebrity. Unsubstantiated rumours or unattributed quotes are barred (exotic details of a subject's private life will be given only if on the record, or if the subject, or an associate who is prepared to be quoted, volunteers information supported by evidence). It is, finally, the significance and achievement of the work that is the focus of the Saturday profile.

But if this is an age of celebrity, it is also an age of biography. Our appetite for information about the way others live – philosophers and footballers, plutocrats and pop stars – seems limitless. It is not simply a matter of prurience and *Schadenfreude*. Empathy and healthy curiosity also play a part. The newspaper interview, as much as the vast publishing market in memoirs, feeds this appetite. In a more profound way, the writers profiled in these pages are engaged in the same project: they use their imagination and skills to help us understand the human condition. Through their work we can glimpse what it is to be someone else, and in the process, if we are receptive, we can learn something valuable about ourselves.

CHINUA ACHEBE
Storyteller of the savannah

Maya Jaggi

While Nelson Mandela was serving twenty-seven years in jail, he drew consola-
tion and strength, he says, from a writer 'in whose company the prison walls fell
down'. For Mandela, the greatness of Chinua Achebe, founding father of the
modern African novel in English, lies in his having 'brought Africa to the world'
while remaining rooted as an African. As the Nigerian Achebe used his pen to
free the continent from its past, said the former South African president, 'both
of us, in our differing circumstances within the context of white domination of
our continent, became freedom fighters'.

Mandela's tribute was videoed in honour of Achebe's seventieth birthday
on Thursday, and sent to leafy Bard College in upstate New York, where Achebe
is professor of languages and literature. The professor, born into the ten-
million-strong Igbo nation of eastern Nigeria, sat through a two-day celebration in the red fez-like hat of the Igbo elder. He was sent greetings from the
UN secretary-general, Kofi Annan, and Nigeria's first civilian leader in sixteen
years, President Olusegun Obasanjo, and homage was paid by fellow writers,
including three Nobel laureates: Toni Morrison, Wole Soyinka and, in absentia,
Nadine Gordimer. It is rare, Achebe remarked later with gentle irony,
to hear such concerted singing of your praises 'unless you're a Third World
dictator'.

Achebe has suffered for challenging just such strongmen in Nigeria. But his
present exile has a different cause. In March 1990, only weeks after attending a
gathering that anticipated his sixtieth birthday in the eastern Nigerian town of
Nsukka, a car crash on the country's lethal roads left him paralysed from the
waist down, and in a wheelchair. He was airlifted to Britain for surgery ('the
damage was so severe they didn't think I'd survive'), told he would never walk
again, and advised to move for therapy to the US, where he took up a profes-
sorship at Bard, in Annandale-on-Hudson.

'I thought I'd go home after a year,' he recalls in his clapboard bungalow on
campus. 'But home has simply got from bad to worse in terms of hospital facil-
ities. I've had severe infections, and you need proper antibiotics, not fakes.
When you say a country has broken down, that's what it means.' The annul-
ment of Nigeria's elections in 1993 by President Ibrahim Babangida militated
against his return. A subsequent coup by General Sani Abacha brought even
harsher dictatorship – marked by the hanging of the writer Ken Saro-Wiwa in
1995. Last year's return to democracy has scarcely begun to reverse the country's
decline.

This summer in the US, Achebe brought out a volume of essays, *Home and
Exile*, to be published in Britain in January. In it, he hankers for the homeland
where his fiction is rooted – 'where I could see my work cut out for me'. He

places his oeuvre within Salman Rushdie's notion of 'the empire writes back': postcolonial writers countering Europe's fictions by seizing the right to tell their own story.

Achebe is known across continents for his landmark first novel, *Things Fall Apart* (1958), a tale told 'from the inside' about the destructive impact of European Christianity on precolonial Igbo culture amid the scramble for Africa in the 1890s. Published on the eve of Nigerian independence in 1960 when its author was twenty-eight, it helped reshape literature in the English-speaking world, but it was not the first novel by an African: precursors included fellow Nigerians Amos Tutuola and Cyprian Ekwensi, South Africa's Peter Abrahams and, in French, Senegal's Ousmane Sembene and Cameroon's Camera Laye. It has sold more than ten million copies internationally and been translated into forty-five languages, making it one of the most widely read novels of the twentieth century. A biography by Ezenwa-Ohaeto was published in 1997 (published by James Currey).

For Soyinka, *Things Fall Apart* was 'the first novel in English which spoke from the interior of an African character, rather than portraying the African as exotic, as the white man would see him'. Nigeria's two literary giants are friends, though rivalry is often assumed: the critic Chinweizu deems Achebe superior in 'decolonizing the mind', while others judge Soyinka's politics more 'radical'. When Soyinka won Africa's first Nobel prize for literature in 1986, Achebe warmly congratulated him, but put the Swedish accolade in perspective as a 'European prize'. Last year they were billed with Derek Walcott at the Word festival in London's Hackney Empire as 'two Nobel laureates and a legend'.

Another Nobel laureate, Toni Morrison, says Achebe sparked her 'love affair with African literature' and was a major influence on her beginnings as a writer. 'He inhabited his world in a way that I didn't inhabit mine – the things he could take for granted – insisting on writing outside the white gaze, not against it,' she says. 'His courage and generosity were made manifest in the work; and that's difficult to do: to talk about devastation and evil in such a way that the text itself isn't evil or devastating.'

Achebe's arguments are delivered with force but in a deceptively soft voice. Though he can seem melancholic, his talk is punctuated by laughter and shafts of dry humour. As his birthday showed, he can bring together people who agree on nothing but their affection for him. Chinweizu, of a Nigerian school of critics known as the Bolekaja Boys (street slang for 'jump up and fight'), sat alongside Soyinka, whom they once pilloried as a 'Euro-assimilationist'. They were in turn put down as 'neo-Tarzanist primitivists'. Soyinka shared a platform with his intellectual sparring partner, the historian Ali Mazrui, as they declared themselves on their 'best behaviour'.

In *Home and Exile*, Achebe has stepped further into autobiography. 'Maybe that's what turning seventy does, though I don't feel any different; you tend to move in the direction of memoir. The ideas I wanted to pursue took an autobiographical turn because the final authority I could bring was that of my own experience.'

He was born in 1930 in Ogidi, an Igbo village near the Niger, four hundred miles east of Lagos. The fifth of six children, he was baptized Albert Chinualumogu, but 'dropped the tribute to Victorian England'. His father, Isaiah, was a Christian convert and evangelist, with 'gallows humour'. He and

Achebe's mother, Janet, were 'ardent followers, but not fanatical'; while the family sang hymns, Isaiah's relatives offered food to what he considered idols. 'An accommodation with the church developed after initial struggle,' says Achebe. 'Common sense and the strength of Igbo culture slowly reasserted themselves.'

His parents were 'extremely profound people, of few words but strong convictions; great believers in education'; with little resources, they sent their children to school. Chike Momah, a classmate, recalls Albert Achebe as a brilliant conversationalist – a trait shared with his father – and says his headmaster predicted he would 'make the rain that would drench us all'.

'We lived at the crossroads of cultures', wrote Achebe, who learned English at eight and whose passport declared him a British Protected Person ('an arrogant lie because I never did ask anyone to protect me'). He contrasts the slow, quiet education of his home village with the louder, formal education of mission school. 'I knew I wanted to understand the life of the society, the stories and masquerades,' he says. 'It's curious how brainwashed we were; quite a bit of my growing-up was discovering that fact.'

In a 1973 essay, 'Named for Victoria, Queen of England', he describes *Things Fall Apart* as 'an act of atonement with my past, the ritual return and homage of a prodigal son'. He says: 'It's that fascination with the scraps and pieces of information I could gather about my ancestors that developed into a desire to write my story. Colonial education was saying there was nothing worth much in my society, and I was beginning to question that, to see there were things that were beautiful even in the "heathen".'

Enrolled at Ibadan University to study medicine ('a false step'), Achebe switched to the arts. In the new essay 'Home Under Imperial Fire', he describes how he was spurred to write partly by being made to read Joyce Cary's 1939 novel *Mister Johnson*, with its 'bumbling idiot' of a Nigerian character: 'It began to dawn on me that although fiction was undoubtedly fictitious, it could also be true or false.' He explains: 'I'd read so-called "African novels" in school, by Rider Haggard and John Buchan, in which white people were surrounded by savages but managed to come out on top. But I didn't recognize them as relating to me until I read *Mister Johnson*: this book was not talking about a vague place called Africa but about southern Nigeria. I said: 'Wait, that means here; this is our story.' It brought the whole thing home to me: this story is not true, so is it possible the others are not either? It opened up a new way of looking at literature.'

That 'landmark rebellion' caught a wider moment. 'The fifties were also the time when the ferment for freedom was at its highest. India was independent, so it was only a matter of time for West Africa. The Second World War was fought for freedom; when they told us to collect pine kernels for the war effort, they said each one would put a nail in Hitler's coffin. Nigerians returning home from the war asked: "Where's the freedom we were told about?" So the two things were together: the political ferment and the revolution in the classroom.' Achebe credits Amos Tutuola's *The Palm-Wine Drinkard* (1952) with opening 'the floodgates to modern West African writing' in the fifties. 'It's as if this thing was waiting to be told; the time was ripe,' he says.

The precolonial society of *Things Fall Apart*, whose tragic hero Okonkwo mounts doomed resistance to encroaching European power, was far from idyllic. Achebe insists on 'an unflinching consciousness of the flaws that blemished our inheritance'. He says: 'Of all the things I remember, that was the clearest: I must not make this story look nicer than it was. I went out of my way to gather all the negative things, to describe them as I think they were – good and bad – and ordinary human beings as neither demons nor angels. I dare anybody to say these people are not human.'

Although arguments against using the language of the colonizer were gathering steam, he decided to write in English. 'It was part of the logic of my situation – like the inevitability of my writing at all – of countering stories about us in the same language in which they were written. Writing in English is a painful choice. But you don't take up a language in order to punish it; that language becomes part of you. And you can't use language at a distance; you introduce English and Igbo into a conversation, as they are in my daily life – that's fascinating.' The Igbo art of storytelling became central to the tale, since 'proverbs are the palm oil with which words are eaten.' Achebe, who writes poetry in both Igbo and English, says: 'I insist on both.'

For the critic Simon Gikandi, Achebe showed that 'the future of African writing did not lie in simple imitation of European forms but in the fusion of such forms with oral traditions.' Kwame Anthony Appiah, professor of Afro-American studies and philosophy at Harvard, says Achebe 'solved with deceptive ease difficult technical questions, such as how you represent the language of one society in the language of a very different one. His use of a variety of registers of English came to be seen as obvious; it set modern African literature in English on a certain path.' The Kenyan writer Ngugi wa Thiong'o, who in the eighties renounced writing fiction in English in favour of Gikuyu, believes 'Achebe created a third position out of the tension between Igbo and English, which becomes the base of his creativity; you feel there's an African voice in his work being rendered in English.'

After working as a radio producer, Achebe had come to London in 1957 to train at the BBC staff school. 'It was the first time I saw the great British Empire at close quarters, and it brought England a couple of pegs down: to find a white man in dirty overalls filling holes in the road was unbelievable.' He sent the longhand manuscript of *Things Fall Apart* to William Heinemann, where a reader pronounced it 'the best first novel since the war'. But at a time when many in the metropolis believed, according to the publisher James Currey, that 'an African could not reach the standards of an English publishing house', a modest two thousand hardbacks were printed.

Then, in 1962, Heinemann Educational Books launched the African Writers series with four novels, including *Things Fall Apart* and its sequel, *No Longer at Ease* – set on the cusp of independence, in the era of Okonkwo's grandson. It was an inexpensive paperback imprint that emulated the Penguin revolution down to its orange covers, while selling 80 per cent of copies in Africa and keeping titles in print. It proved that a readership existed, and was a signal for Africa's writers, says Achebe, who selected the first hundred titles.

He was able to do what was an unpaid job as series editor for ten years because he had jobs in broadcasting, and then academia. (The late Heinemann director Alan Hill recalled him as 'the very image of a modern Nigerian yuppie', with sharp suit, dark glasses and a Jaguar.) 'I thought it was of the utmost importance,' Achebe explains. 'People in England were sceptical, so I knew I was a conspirator. I was naive enough to think that if you do good work, you'll get your reward in heaven.'

For Kenyan writer Ngugi wa Thiong'o, Achebe 'made a whole generation of African people believe in themselves and in the possibility of their being writers'. The Somali novelist Nuruddin Farah says he learned his craft from him: 'He taught us a way of integrating what we know from being African with what we've become – hybrids of a kind.'

After travelling through southern Africa on a Rockefeller scholarship in 1960, 'the winds of change in my sails' (vexing the Northern Rhodesian authorities by sitting in the front of a segregated bus near Victoria Falls), Achebe became the first director of Voice of Nigeria, the state-run radio's external arm, where he remained till the eve of the Biafran war in 1966. He met his wife-to-be, Christie Chinwe, then a student, in Broadcasting House in Lagos, where she had a holiday job. She later became a professor.

The couple have two sons and two daughters (one of whom, Chinelo, is a writer), and two grandchildren. 'Christie saves my life every other day,' says Achebe. 'And she suffers my pain more than I do. When I had the accident, she left her classroom and never really got back.' Though she is now a psychology professor at Bard, she was forced to leave her field of education, a sacrifice Achebe feels keenly. 'When I was drifting in and out of consciousness I remember saying I wanted her to go with me – to England. That's been her life ever since.'

After his third novel, *Arrow of God* (1964), set in Igboland in the 1920s – which won the Jock Campbell *New Statesman* award – Achebe wrote a satire on corruption in a fictitious African country following the 'collusive swindle that was independence'. *A Man of the People* (1966) proved prescient about Nigeria's first attempted coup, which happened two days before its publication. Some thought the author complicit in the Igbo-instigated coup. He obviously wasn't. As massacres spread against Igbos in northern and western Nigeria, Achebe and his family went into hiding. They fled Lagos for Igboland, where Achebe took up a post at the university in Nsukka.

On the eve of the Biafran war of 1967–70, Achebe went on a peace-seeking mission to President Léopold Senghor of Senegal, founder-poet of the Francophone *Négritude* movement. 'I was sent by the government of Biafra because I was also a writer, in the hope of stopping the war,' Achebe recalls. 'We talked about Biafra for ten minutes and literature for two hours.' But as war broke out, Achebe served on more diplomatic missions for the breakaway Biafran republic. 'I was deeply disappointed with what was happening in Nigeria,' he says. 'I was ready just to go to my village, but I did whatever I was asked.'

The war was shattering for Achebe; his house was bombed and his best friend, the poet Christopher Okigbo, was killed. On the 'wrong side' when the secessionists were crushed, Achebe was refused a passport, but finally left in 1972 for professorships in the US, before returning to Nsukka as professor of English in 1976. He had first visited the US in the early sixties, when he met writers including Ralph Ellison and Langston Hughes. His unsentimental recovery of the dignity of Africa's past chimed with the notion of 'black is beautiful' among African-Americans brought up to see Africa as an embarrassment. John Edgar Wideman recalls the shock of finding 'language being refashioned from another centre I didn't know existed'.

Achebe embraced writers of the diaspora, calling Africa a 'spiritual phenomenon born of a painful history...which binds every Black person'. He launched the journal *Okike*, and later a bilingual Igbo journal. *Beware Soul Brother* (1971), which won the Commonwealth poetry prize, and *Girls at War and Other Stories* (1972) both reflected the trauma of the civil war. He also published children's books, essays and a heartfelt polemic, *The Trouble with Nigeria* (1983), when he became involved in party politics. But there was a gap of twenty-one years before his fifth novel.

Lyn Innes, professor of postcolonial literatures at the University of Kent, co-edited two Heinemann African anthologies with Achebe. In her view, 'his fiction was concerned with portraying a society, and Nigerian society was so totally destabilized, he found it difficult to write a sustained work – only fragments.' Achebe says: 'I don't think it damaged my work; it gave it a new direction for a while into poetry and short stories. I regard all of them equally.'

Achebe's friend James Baldwin savoured the elegance of Achebe's essays as 'not a mere pleasure but a benefaction'. The dissection in the essays of Europe's self-serving myths of Africa, and how they shored up slavery and empire, is a prelude to Edward Said's *Orientalism* (1978) and Toni Morrison's scrutiny of the black presence in American literature in *Playing in the Dark* (1992). In a famous lecture on *Heart of Darkness* in Massachusetts in 1975 (included in *Hopes and Impediments*, 1988), he described Joseph Conrad as a 'thoroughgoing racist', disputing that a novel that dehumanizes a portion of the human race could be called a great work of art (one American professor stalked off, saying 'How dare you?').

Achebe attacked the 'perverse arrogance' of reducing Africa to a 'setting and backdrop which eliminates the African as human factor'. In his view, 'Conrad saw and condemned the evil of imperial exploitation but was strangely unaware of the racism on which it sharpened its tooth.'

'I'm surprised it's gone on being controversial, but it has,' he says. Some still argue that to accuse Conrad of racism is anachronistic. Achebe responds: 'Long before Conrad, there were people who refused to be racist. Time does contribute something to what we think, but good people are never prisoners of their era.' As for Conrad's prose: 'It would have been better if the beautiful prose were used to unite the human race, rather than separate it. The best works, whether written or oral, seem to me to have an intrinsic morality; it's not Sunday school morality, but I've not encountered any good art that promotes genocide.'

Achebe's stand is sometimes misunderstood as censorship. 'I'm not Ayatollah Khomeini,' he objects. 'I don't believe in banning books, but they should be read carefully. Far from wanting the novel banned, I teach it.' By the same token, he advocates closer reading of V. S. Naipaul ('a new Conrad...purveyor of the old comforting myths of race') and Elspeth Huxley ('the griot [storytelling caste] for white settlers').

In his introduction, with poems, to *Another Africa* (1998, Lund Humphries), a collection of photographs by Robert Lyons, Achebe writes: 'The vast arsenal of derogatory images of Africa amassed to defend the slave trade and, later, colonization, gave the world not only a literary tradition that is now, happily defunct, but also a particular way of looking (or rather not looking) at Africa and Africans.' He warns against the enduring tendency to act for, or upon, Africa while failing to listen to its inhabitants.

In a 1998 lecture to the World Bank, he urged the cancellation of Third World debt, having told Western bankers in Paris a decade before: 'You talk about "structural adjustment" as if Africa was some kind of laboratory…But Africa is people!' Achebe has called himself a 'missionary in reverse'. Lyn Innes, who sat in on his classes in the US in the 1970s, says: 'Ill-informed students would ask outrageous questions about cannibalism, or from reading his work as anthropology not literature. But he was always patient and tolerant, trying to turn them around.'

Achebe's fifth novel, *Anthills of the Savannah* (1987), revived his reputation in Britain when it was short-listed for the Booker prize. Set in a military regime in present-day West Africa, it introduced a female intellectual, the journalist Beatrice, some say in response to criticism of his earlier work. 'Feminists would like to take credit; I've no objection, but I don't need anyone to scare me into realizing the paradoxical position of women,' says Achebe, who is working on a new novel with women at its heart.

'The female presence is there in all my novels. It seems as if it's not important – which is the reality of how it looks in Igbo society – till you get to a crisis that threatens survival. When the British came, that was a critical moment; the men fought and lost. But there were events in Igboland where women stopped the British in their tracks. That's been happening in my fiction: the incremental involvement of women in political matters. It's not straightforward: it's a struggle for power.'

Toni Morrison believes Achebe's early work leaves a lot of space for women, which was like a revelation to her: 'The notion here in America is that slavery was about the imprisonment and emasculation of black men. But with Achebe, I never felt the male claw grabbing up the entire canvas; there was feminine space where women existed without permission from the man.'

Others could step into that space. Nuruddin Farah, whose novel *From a Crooked Rib* (1970) was written from the point of view of a circumcised Somali woman, points out that the central consciousness, even of *Anthills of the Savannah*, is still male, but says his own writing was partly in response to the absences he felt in Achebe's oeuvre. He says it was important for someone to deal with the bigger quarrels of Africa and colonialism, 'but it left me free to cover quarrels within the community – between men and women'.

Last year Achebe visited Nigeria for the first time since his accident. His initial impressions of Lagos were 'confusing and very depressing; the place looked deserted, not well looked after, with potholes in the landing strip'. Only after a bitter quarrel was a wheelchair found to take him off the plane. 'I went incognito; I didn't want a red carpet. That's normally my style because I want to see the country as it is.' Pained, he murmurs the unthinkable: 'Maybe somebody wanted me to bribe them.'

In *The Trouble with Nigeria*, Achebe insisted: 'Nigerians are what they are only because their leaders are not what they should be.' He swiped at General Obasanjo for his 'flamboyant, imaginary' idea of a great Nigeria. On his recent trip, however, Achebe met the general, now civilian president, 'to encourage him'. Although Nigeria is 'sicker than we feared' (he identifies the Muslim sharia law as the greatest threat to the federation), Achebe clings to hope: 'Even Nigerians are not entirely immune from learning from their history.'

He had to steel himself for the four-hundred-mile car journey to Ogidi. 'You might suddenly find a ditch in the middle of the road. Life is so unsafe,' he says.

'Things had got much worse in nine years; for the first time you saw beggars camped out by the roadside. But I always return to the good things: the whole village had turned out and waited all day.' His arrival was hailed with an artillery salute. 'It was a tremendous experience. I almost found myself in tears; there are good things going on. My people deserve better than they've had by a long chalk.'

18 November 2000

Life at a glance

ALBERT CHINUALUMOGU ACHEBE

Born: 16 November 1930, Ogidi, Nigeria.

Education: Church Missionary Society primary school, Ogidi; University College, Ibadan (1948–53).

Married: Christie Chinwe Okoli (1961); two daughters: Chinelo, Nwando; two sons: Ikechukwu, Chidi.

Career: Editor, Heinemann African Writers series (1962–72); founding editor *Okike* (1971–); emeritus professor of English, University of Nigeria, Nsukka (1985–); Charles P. Stevenson Professor, Bard College, New York (1990–).

Select bibliography: Fiction: *Things Fall Apart* (1958); *No Longer at Ease* (1960); *Arrow of God* (1964); *A Man of the People* (1966); *Girls at War* (stories, 1972); *Anthills of the Savannah* (1987). Poetry: *Beware Soul Brother* (1971); *Another Africa* (1998). Essays: *The Trouble with Nigeria* (1983); *Hopes and Impediments* (1988); *Home and Exile* (2000).

Awards: Commonwealth poetry prize (1979); short-listed for the Booker prize *Anthills of the Savannah* (1987).

DOUGLAS ADAMS
Planet of the japes

Nicholas Wroe

Soon after *The Hitchhiker's Guide to the Galaxy* was published in 1979, Douglas Adams was invited to sign copies at a small science-fiction bookshop in Soho. As he drove there, some sort of demonstration slowed his progress. 'There was a traffic jam and crowds of people everywhere,' he recalls. It wasn't until he had pushed his way inside that Adams realized the crowds were there for him. Next day his publisher called to tell him he was number one in the *Sunday Times* best-seller list and his life changed for ever. 'It was like being helicoptered to the top of Mount Everest,' he says, 'or having an orgasm without the foreplay.'

Hitchhiker had already been a cult radio show and went on both television and the stage. It expanded into four more books that sold over fourteen million copies worldwide. There were records and computer games and now, after twenty years of Hollywood prevarication, it is as close as it's ever been to becoming a movie.

The story itself begins on Earth with mild-mannered suburbanite Arthur Dent trying to stop the council demolishing his house to build a bypass. It moves into space when his friend, Ford Prefect – some have seen him as Virgil to Dent's Dante – reveals himself as a representative of the planet Betelgeuse and informs Arthur that the Earth itself is about to be demolished to make way for a hyper-space express route. They hitch a ride on a Vogon spaceship and begin to use the Guide itself, a usually reliable repository of all knowledge about life, the universe and everything.

Adams's creativity and idiosyncratic intergalactic humour have had a perva-sive cultural influence. The phrase 'hitchhiker's guide to…' quickly became com-mon parlance and there have been numerous copycat spoof sci-fi books and TV series. His Babel fish – a small fish you can place in your ear to translate any speech into your own language – has been adopted as the name of a translation device on an Internet search engine. He followed up his success with several other novels as well as a television programme, book and CD-ROM on endan-gered species. He has founded a dot.com company, h2g2, which has recently taken the idea of the *Guide* full circle by launching a service that promises real information on life, the universe and everything via your mobile phone.

Much of his wealth seems to have been spent fuelling his passion for tech-nology, but he has never really been the nerdy science-fiction type. He is relaxed, gregarious and a solidly built two metres tall. In fact, he has more the air of those English public-schoolboys who became rock stars in the 1970s; he once played guitar on stage at Earl's Court with his mates Pink Floyd. In a nicely flash touch, instead of producing a passport-size photo of his daughter out of his wallet, he opens up his impressively powerful laptop, where, after a bit of fid-dling about, Polly Adams, aged five, appears in a pop video spoof featuring a cameo appearance by another mate, John Cleese.

So this is what his life turned into: money, A-list friends, and nice toys. Looking at the bare facts of his CV – boarding school, Cambridge Footlights and the BBC – it seems at first sight no surprise. But his has not been an entirely straightforward journey along well-worn establishment tracks.

Douglas Noel Adams was born in Cambridge in 1952. One of his many stock gags is that he was DNA in Cambridge nine months before Crick and Watson made their discovery. His mother, Janet, was a nurse at Addenbrooke's hospital and his father, Christopher, had been a teacher; he went on to became a post-graduate theology student, probation officer, and finally a management consultant, which was 'a very, very peculiar move', claims Adams. 'Anyone who knew my father will tell you that management was not something he knew very much about.'

The family were 'fairly hard-up' and left Cambridge six months after Douglas was born, to live in various homes on the fringes of East London. When Adams was five, his parents divorced. 'It's amazing the degree to which children treat their own lives as normal,' he says. 'But of course it was difficult. My parents divorced when it wasn't remotely as common as it is now, and to be honest I have scant memory of anything before I was five. I don't think it was a great time, one way or another.'

After the break-up, Douglas and his younger sister went with their mother to Brentwood in Essex, where she ran a hostel for sick animals. He saw his by now comparatively wealthy father at weekends, which was a source of confusion and tension. To add to the complications, several stepsiblings emerged as his parents remarried. Adams has said that while he accepted all this as normal on one level, he did 'behave oddly as a result', and remembers himself as a twitchy and somewhat strange child. For a time, his teachers thought he was educationally subnormal, but by the time he went to the direct grant Brentwood prep school, he was regarded as extremely bright.

The school boasts a remarkably diverse list of postwar alumni: Hardy Amies, the disgraced historian David Irving, TV presenter Noel Edmonds, home secretary Jack Straw and *Times* editor Peter Stothard were all there before Adams, while comedians Griff Rhys Jones and Keith Allen were a few years behind him. There are four old boys – two Labour and two Conservative – in the current House of Commons. In a scene that now seems rather incongruous in the light of Keith Allen's hard-living image, Adams helped the seven-year-old Allen with his piano lessons.

When Adams was thirteen, his mother remarried and moved to Dorset, and Adams changed from being a dayboy to a boarder. It appears to have been an entirely beneficial experience. 'Whenever I left school at four in the afternoon I always used to look at what the boarders were doing rather wistfully,' he says. 'They seemed to be having a good time and, in fact, I thoroughly enjoyed board-ing. There is a piece of me that likes to fondly imagine my maverick and rebel-lious nature. But more accurately, I like to have a nice and cosy institution that I can rub up against a little bit. There is nothing better than a few constraints you can comfortably kick against.'

Adams ascribes the quality of his education to being taught by some 'very good, committed, obsessed and charismatic people'. At a recent party in London he confronted Jack Straw on New Labour's apparent antipathy to direct grant schools, on the basis that it had done neither of them much harm.

Frank Halford was a master at the school and remembers Adams as 'very tall even then, and popular. He wrote an end-of-term play when *Doctor Who* had just started on television. He called it *Doctor Which*.' Many years later, Adams wrote scripts for *Doctor Who* itself. He describes Halford as an inspirational teacher who is still a support. 'He once gave me ten out of ten for a story, which was the only time he did throughout his long school career. And even now, when I have a dark night of the soul as a writer and think that I can't do this anymore, the thing that I reach for is not the fact that I have had bestsellers or huge advances. It is the fact that Frank Halford once gave me ten out of ten, and at some fundamental level I must be able to do it.'

It seems that from the beginning, he had a facility for turning his writing into cash. He sold some short, 'almost haiku-length' stories to the *Eagle* comic and received ten shillings. 'You could practically buy a yacht for ten shillings then,' he laughs. But his real interest was music. He learned to play the guitar by copying note for note the intricate finger-picking patterns on an early Paul Simon album. He now has a huge collection of left-handed electric guitars, but admits that he's 'really a folkie at heart. Even with Pink Floyd on stage, I played a very simple guitar figure from *Brain Damage* which was in a finger-picking style.'

He grew up in the sixties and the Beatles, he says, 'planted a seed in my head that made it explode. Every nine months there'd be a new album that would be an earth-shattering development from where they were before. We were so obsessed by them that when 'Penny Lane' came out and we hadn't heard it on the radio, we beat up this boy who had heard it until he hummed the tune to us. People now ask if Oasis are as good as the Beatles. I don't think they are as good as the Rutles...'

The other key influence was *Monty Python*. Having listened to mainstream British radio comedy of the fifties he describes it as an 'epiphanous' moment when he discovered that being funny could be a way in which intelligent people expressed themselves – 'and be very, very silly at the same time'.

The logical next step was to go to Cambridge University, 'because I wanted to join Footlights,' he says. 'I wanted to be a writer-performer like the Pythons. In fact I wanted to be John Cleese and it took me some time to realize that the job was in fact taken.'

At university, he quickly abandoned performing – 'I just wasn't reliable' – and began to write self-confessed Pythonesque sketches. He recalls one about a railway worker who was reprimanded for leaving all the points open on the Southern Region to prove a point about existentialism; and another about the difficulties in staging the Crawley Paranoid Society AGM.

The arts administrator Mary Allen, formerly of the Arts Council and the Royal Opera, was a contemporary at Cambridge and has remained a friend ever since. She performed his material and remembers him as 'always noticed even amongst a very talented group of people. Douglas's material was very quirky and individualistic. You had to suit it and it had to suit you. Even in short sketches he created a weird world.'

Adams says: 'I did have something of a guilt thing about reading English. I thought I should have done something useful and challenging. But while I was whingeing, I also relished the chance not to do very much.' Even his essays were full of jokes. 'If I had known then what I know now, I would have done biology or zoology. At the time I had no idea that was an interesting subject, but now I think it is the most interesting subject in the world.'

Other contemporaries included the lawyer and TV presenter Clive Anderson and the culture secretary Chris Smith. Smith was president of the Union, where Adams used to do warm-up routines for debates, though not because of any political interest. 'I was just looking for anywhere I could do gags. It is very strange seeing these people dotted around the public landscape now. My contemporaries are starting to win lifetime achievement awards, which obviously makes one feel nervous.'

After university, Adams got the chance to work with one of his heroes. Python member Graham Chapman had been impressed by some Footlights sketches and had made contact. When Adams went to see him, he was asked, much to his delight, to help out with a script Chapman had to finish that afternoon. 'We ended up working together for about a year. Mostly on a prospective TV series which never made it beyond the pilot.' Chapman at this time was 'sucking down a couple of bottles of gin every day, which obviously gets in the way a bit'. But Adams believes he was enormously talented. 'He was naturally part of a team and needed other people's discipline to enable his brilliance to work. His strength was flinging something into the mix that would turn it all upside-down.'

After splitting up with Chapman, Adams's career stalled badly. He continued to write sketches but was not making anything like a living. 'It turned out I wasn't terribly good at writing sketches. I could never write to order and couldn't really do topical stuff. But occasionally I'd come out with something terrific from left field.'

Geoffrey Perkins, head of comedy at BBC Television, was the producer of the radio version of *Hitchhiker*. He remembers first coming across Adams when he directed a Footlights show. 'He was being heckled by a cast member, and then he fell into a chair. I next came across him when he was trying to write sketches for the radio show *Week Ending*, then regarded as the big training ground for writers. Douglas was one of those writers who honourably failed to get anywhere with *Week Ending*. It put a premium on people who could write things that lasted thirty seconds and Douglas was incapable of writing a single sentence that lasted less than thirty seconds.'

With his dreams of being a writer crumbling around him, Adams took a series of bizarre jobs, including working as a chicken-shed cleaner and as a bodyguard to the ruling family of Qatar. 'I think the security firm must have been desperate. I got the job from an ad in the *Evening Standard*.' Griff Rhys Jones did the same job for a while on Adams's recommendation. Adams recalls becoming increasingly depressed as he endured night shifts of sitting outside hotel bedrooms. 'I kept thinking this wasn't how it was supposed to have worked out.' At Christmas, he went to visit his mother and stayed there for the next year.

He recalls a lot of family worry about what he was going to do, and, while he still sent in the occasional sketch to radio shows, he acknowledges that his confidence was extremely low. Despite his subsequent success and wealth, this propensity to a lack of confidence has continued. 'I have terrible periods of lack of confidence,' he explains. 'I just don't believe I can do it, and no evidence to the contrary will sway me from that view. I briefly did therapy but after a while, I realized it is just like a farmer complaining about the weather. You can't fix the weather – you just have to get on with it.' So has that approach helped him? 'Not necessarily,' he shrugs.

Hitchhiker was the last throw of the dice, but in retrospect, the timing was absolutely right. *Star Wars* had made science fiction voguish, and the aftermath of *Monty Python* meant that while a sketch show was out of the question, there was scope to appeal to the same comic sensibility.

Python Terry Jones heard the tapes before transmission and remembers being struck by Adams's 'intellectual approach and strong conceptual ideas. You feel the stuff he is writing has come from a criticism of life, as Matthew Arnold might say. It has a moral basis and a critical basis that has a strong mind behind it. For instance, John Cleese has a powerful mind, but he is more logical and analytical. Douglas is more quirky and analytical.' Geoffrey Perkins agrees but remembers there was no grand plan behind the project. 'Douglas went into it with a whole load of ideas but very little notion of what the story would be. He was writing it in an almost Dickensian mode of episodic weekly instalments, without quite knowing how it would end.'

By the time the series was aired in 1978, Adams says he had put about nine months' solid work into it and had been paid £1,000. 'There seemed to be quite a long way to go before I broke even,' so he accepted a producer's job at the BBC, but quit six months later when he found himself simultaneously writing a second radio series, the novel, the television series and episodes of *Doctor Who*. Despite this remarkable workload, he was already building a legendary reputation for not writing. 'I love deadlines,' he has said. 'I love the whooshing noise they make as they go by.'

Success only added to his ability to prevaricate. His publishing editor, Sue Freestone, quickly realized that he treated writing as performance art, and so she set up her office in his dining room. 'He needs an instant audience to bounce things off but sometimes this can weirdly backfire.

'There was a scene early in one book when he talked about some plates with, very definitely, one banana on each. This was obviously significant so I asked him to explain. But he liked to tease his audience and he said he'd tell me later. We eventually got to the end of the book and I asked him again: "OK Douglas, what's with the bananas?" He looked at me completely blankly. He had forgotten all about the bananas. I still occasionally ask him if he has remembered yet but apparently he hasn't.'

The writer and producer John Lloyd had been a friend and collaborator with Adams since before *Hitchhiker*. He remembers the 'agonies of indecision and panic' Adams got into when writing. 'We were on holiday in Corfu with three friends when he was finishing a book and he ended up taking over the whole house. He had a room to write in, a room to sleep in, a room to go to when he couldn't sleep and so on. It didn't occur to him that other people might want a good night's sleep as well. He goes through life with a brain the size of a planet and often seems to be living on a different one. He is absolutely not a malicious person, but when he is in the throes of panic and terror and unable to finish a book everything else pales into insignificance.'

However much the work was dragged out, it was extremely popular. The books all became best sellers and Adams was given an advance of over $2 million by his American publishers. He wrote a hilarious spoof dictionary with John Lloyd, *The Meaning of Liff*, in which easily recognized concepts such as the feeling you get at four in the afternoon when you haven't got enough done, were given the names of towns – Farnham being the perfect choice for this low-grade depression. In the late eighties, he completed two spoof detective novels featuring Dirk Gently.

For all his facility with humour, Freestone says she has been touched by how profoundly Adams's work has connected with some readers. 'In *Hitchhiker*, all you have to do to be safe is have your towel with you,' she explains. 'I heard about this woman who was dying in a hospice who felt she would be fine because she had her towel with her. She had taken Douglas's universe and incorporated it into her own. It embarrassed the hell out of Douglas when he heard about it. But for her it was literally a symbol of safety when embarking on an unknown journey.'

There are serious themes within his work. The second Dirk Gently novel can easily be read as being about people who are homeless, displaced and alienated from society. 'His imagination goes much deeper than just cleverness,' says Freestone. 'The social criticism is usually buried by the comedy, but it's there if you want to find it.'

Having been through such a lean period, Adams worked constantly until the mid-nineties, when he very deliberately applied the brakes. 'I had got absolutely stuck in the middle of a novel and, although it sounds ungrateful, having to do huge book signings would drive me to angry depressions.'

He says that he still thought of himself as a scriptwriter and only inadvertently found himself as a novelist. 'It sounds absurd, but a bit of me felt cheated and it also felt as if I had cheated. And then there is the money cycle. You're paid a lot and you're not happy, so the first thing you do is buy stuff that you don't want or need – for which you need more money.'

His financial affairs got into a mess in the 1980s, he says. He won't discuss the details, but says that the knock-on effect was considerable, so that everyone assumed he was wealthier than he actually was. It is possible to track the movement of Adams's life even between series one and two of the radio show. In the first there were a lot of jokes about pubs and being without any money. The second had more jokes about expensive restaurants and accountants.

'I felt like a mouse in a wheel,' he says. 'There was no pleasure coming into the cycle at any point. When you write your first book aged twenty-five or so, you have twenty-five years of experience, albeit much of it juvenile experience. The second book comes after an extra year sitting in bookshops. Pretty soon you begin to run on empty.'

His response to running out of fuel was to attempt some 'creative crop rotation'. In particular, his interest in technology took off, as did a burgeoning passion for environmental issues. In 1990, he wrote *Last Chance to See*. 'As is the way of these things, it was my least successful book but is still the thing I am most proud of.'

The book began when he was sent to Madagascar by a magazine to find a rare type of lemur. He thought it would be quite interesting, but it turned into a complete revelation. His fascination with ecology led to an interest in evolution. 'I'd been given a thread to pull, and following that lead began to open up issues to me that became the object of the greatest fascination.' A link at the bottom of his emails now directs people to the Dian Fossey Trust, which works to protect gorillas, and Save the Rhino. Adams was also a signatory to the Great Ape

Project, which argued for a change of moral status for great apes, recognizing their rights to 'life, liberty and freedom from torture'.

He was a founder member of the team that launched Comic Relief, but he has never been a hair-shirt sort of activist. The parties he held at his Islington home would feature music by various legendary rock stars – Gary Brooker of Procul Harum once sang the whole of *Whiter Shade of Pale*, including all the abandoned verses – and were peopled by media aristocracy and hi-tech billionaires. Slightly less orthodoxly – for an enthusiastic, almost evangelical, atheist – he would also host carol services every Christmas.

'As a child I was an active Christian. I used to love the school choir and remember the carol service as always such an emotional thing.' He adds Bach to the Beatles and the Pythons in his pantheon of influences, but how does this square with his passionate atheism? 'Life is full of things that move or affect you in one way or another,' he explains. 'The fact that I think Bach was mistaken doesn't alter the fact that I think the B minor Mass is one of the great pinnacles of human achievement. It still absolutely moves me to tears to hear it. I find the whole business of religion profoundly interesting. But it does mystify me that otherwise intelligent people take it seriously.'

This attachment to traditional structures, if not traditional beliefs, is carried over in the fact that his daughter, Polly, who was born in 1994, has four non-godparents. Mary Allen is one of them, and it was she who introduced Adams to his wife, the barrister Jane Belson. Allen says: 'In the early eighties, Douglas was going through some writing crisis and was ringing me every day. I eventually asked him whether he was lonely. It seemed that he was, so we decided he needed someone to share his huge flat. Jane moved in.' After several false starts, they married in 1991 and lived in Islington until last year, when the family moved to Santa Barbara.

Adams says the initial move was harder than he expected. 'I've only recently understood how opposed to the move my wife was.' He now says he would recommend to anyone in the depths of middle age 'just upping sticks and going somewhere else. You re-invent your life and start again. It is invigorating.'

His role in his dot.com business fits into this sense of invigoration. His job title is Chief Fantasist. 'I've never thought of myself in the role of a predictive science-fiction writer, I was never an Arthur C. Clarke wannabe. The *Guide* was a narrative device for absorbing all those ideas that spark off the flywheel, but it has turned out to be a very good idea. But it's early days,' he warns. 'We're still in a swimming pool and there is an ocean out there.'

Other new ventures are a novel (eight years late and counting), a Dirk Gently film project, the h2g2 website and an e-novel. 'I've been talking about how electronic books will come and how important they will be, and all of a sudden Stephen King publishes one. I feel a complete idiot, as it should have been me.'

The film project has been 'twenty years of constipation', and he likens the Hollywood process to 'trying to grill a steak by having a succession of people coming into the room and breathing on it'. He is surprisingly enthusiastic about this apparently antique art form. 'With new, more immature technologies there is a danger in getting excited about all the ways you can push them forward at the expense of what you want to say. It is therefore rewarding to work in a medium where you don't have to solve those problems, because it is a mature medium.'

After such a long fallow period, he wisely notes that many of these new projects and ideas will fall by the wayside. 'But I've been out of the mainstream of novel writing for several years and I really needed to take that break. I've been thinking hard and thinking creatively about a whole load of stuff that is not novel writing. As opposed to running on empty, it now feels like the tank is full again.'

3 June 2000

Life at a glance

DOUGLAS NOEL ADAMS

Born: 11 March 1952, Cambridge.
Education: Brentwood School, Essex; St John's College, Cambridge.
Married: Jane Belson (1991; one daughter, Polly).
Career: radio and television writer (1974–8); BBC radio producer (1978).
Select bibliography: Scripts: *The Hitchhiker's Guide to the Galaxy* (radio, 1978 and 1980; television, 1981); Games: *The Hitchhiker's Guide to the Galaxy* (1984); *Bureaucracy* (1987); *Starship Titanic* (1997); Books: *The Hitchhiker's Guide to the Galaxy* (1979); *The Restaurant at the End of the Universe* (1980); *Life, the Universe and Everything* (1982); *The Meaning of Liff* (with John Lloyd) (1983); *So Long and Thanks for all the Fish* (1984); *Dirk Gently's Holistic Detective Agency* (1987); *The Long Dark Tea-time of the Soul* (1988); *Last Chance to See* (1990); *Mostly Harmless* (1992).

Douglas Adams died on 11 May 2001.

JULIAN BARNES
Literature's Mister Cool

Nicholas Wroe

There is a scene in the novel *Bridget Jones's Diary* when Bridget unexpectedly finds herself standing in front of Julian Barnes at a literary party. Ms Jones, paralysed by Barnes's intimidating reputation for cool intelligence and languid wit, is struck dumb. The agonizing silence is eventually broken when, to her own horror, she blurts out: 'Do you know where the toilets are?' The resulting 'faint smile that hovered over his thin-but-attractive lips' ensured her humiliation was made complete.

The scene has been included in the film version of the *Diary*, which is currently in production in London. Although lots of real writers were gathered together by the producers to act as up-market extras, it was thought Barnes wasn't quite recognizable enough to a cinema-going audience to justify Bridget's level of mortification. So, while Barnes stands around holding a glass of warm white wine and muttering 'rhubarb', Salman Rushdie was parachuted in to precipitate the social catastrophe.

When Barnes tells this story, he goes through the motions of huffing and puffing at the lack of respect shown to him and the cavalier attitude to the text adopted by superficial film-makers. But far from complaining that he is not famous enough, in reality one senses that Barnes feels he has more than enough fame, meaning in this case celebrity, already. He might be adamant that he is not an autobiographical writer, but when the narrator of his novel *Flaubert's Parrot* at one point asks – 'Why does the writing make us chase the writer? Why aren't the books enough?' – there is little doubt that he speaks for Barnes.

None of this is to say he doesn't expect and appreciate the attention he gets as a front-rank journalist, essayist and most notably novelist. He is a wonderful prose stylist who has heeded Flaubert's dictum that words, like hair, 'shine with combing'. His work is both crowded with ideas and emotionally acute as he dissects with a coldly knowing eye the way we live and, most of all, the way we love. In so doing, Barnes has also pulled off the rare trick of producing work that is not only popular – it was as far back as 1996 that he sold his millionth paperback in Britain – but critically acclaimed. Graham Greene said *Flaubert's Parrot* was 'intricate and delightful'. Nobel laureate Nadine Gordimer called his novel *A History of the World in 10½ Chapters* 'funny, ironic, erudite, surprising and not afraid to take a dive overboard into the depths of sorrow and loss'. Carlos Fuentes 'saluted' him from Mexico, praising his work for being 'at the forefront of a new internationalization of British fiction'.

But the by-product of this success has meant his life has been periodically dragged into public view. 'In America, where all tendencies are admittedly exaggerated,' he says, 'you have to make the decision immediately whether to go down the route of Mailer or Vidal or go down the reclusive route of Salinger or Pynchon. Both of which seem to me to lead to madness. It's not quite that bad over here, but the question does remain.'

When the high-profile rift between Barnes and his former friend Martin Amis was recently rehashed in Amis's memoirs, Barnes maintained a characteristically scrupulous public silence. The row was precipitated when Amis changed literary agents in 1994. The agent he left was Pat Kavanagh, who is not only Barnes's agent but also his wife. Barnes still won't discuss the issue, but says the closest he came to joining in the fray came when he read a letter to this newspaper following the serialization of the memoirs. 'So, a bloke who writes books fell out with another bloke who writes books,' observed the correspondent. 'Then they swore at each other. Can someone explain to me why this is worthy of my attention in an already crowded day?'

'I thought, "Yes!" when I read that letter,' says Barnes. 'That's absolutely right. I nearly wrote to that man saying "I'm with you on this one." It seems that no sooner do you publish a book than everything from your bank account to your sex life become subjects about which the public have a right to know. I began to think that this wasn't in my book contract. I don't remember agreeing to all this.'

One source of aggravation for Barnes has been press fascination with an old affair between Pat Kavanagh and the novelist Jeanette Winterson. In fact, people close to the couple speak of their marriage as being particularly harmonious. 'They are actually a rather decorous couple,' says one friend. 'They really have terrific complicity and an extraordinary closeness,' says another. Yet such complications, added to the speculation that they appear as characters in other people's fiction, encourage the thought that Barnes must somehow be drawing on his own experiences.

'But I make things up,' he protests. 'After my first book [*Metroland*] I have not been an autobiographical writer. Martin in *Experience* was saying that fiction is the higher autobiography. I just don't agree. My novels divide into what are called novels of ideas and novels of the personal life. It is tempting, but ultimately fallacious, to think that they are about my personal life. It is observation and imagination. There is nothing easier to make up than a convincing private life. Much easier to make up a sexual life than a financial life.'

Hermione Lee, as a friend and a biographer, has an ongoing debate with Barnes about the impact of the life on literary work. 'He dislikes the travesty version of a life that gets into the public domain when you are gossiped about, which is not unlike the things he resents about bad biography. Someone like Philip Roth is clearly writing his own life over and over again. It is completely different with Julian. Obviously, he writes from his own state and habit of mind. His love of France is there and his visit to Eastern Europe went into his novel set in Eastern Europe, *The Porcupine*. But he's not writing novels about himself.'

Lee thinks this tendency to collapse the novels back into the life is particularly ironic in Barnes's case because he is so interested in 'imagining things and making them up and displacing himself into other characters and histories. Of course, he draws on his own emotions, but there is a difference between drawing on one's own life and writing autobiographical fiction. He is terribly interested in people's relationships and what happens to love and friendship.'

His new novel, *Love, etc*, carries on the story started in 1991 in *Talking it Over* in which Oliver, Stuart and Gillian talk straight to the reader about their intense and funny love triangle. In the new book, we meet them ten years on. Barnes was once asked in a newspaper questionnaire which novels should have a sequel. 'None' was his response, which begs the question. 'Fair cop,' he says. 'I do generally believe that.' But he was attracted back to the work because *Talking it Over* is the only book of his that people ask what happened to the characters afterwards. He also liked the idea of the characters speaking directly to the reader again. 'The membrane between the character and the reader is minimized.'

Love, etc is a much darker book than *Talking it Over*. Through its minute choreography, it unfolds the very Barnesian theme of what happens to love in a deeply mercantile society. 'I believe that the personal life is impinged on and has principles laid down by the general tenor and values of society,' he says. 'It can't not. When societies were primarily religious, what love was and what it was for were different. What people wanted in thirteenth-century France was salvation, and beyond that economic and social position. Love as we think of it was an add-on. Then, with the decline of religion and the rise of romantic individualism, love came to be assumed not only to be the ultimate good, but something that was somehow untainted. But it never is untainted, although it sometimes fools us that it is.'

'It is interesting that he meditates on love to such an extent,' says his friend, the writer Marina Warner. 'I don't know many novelists now who try to get to grips with it. How does one love well? How does one love so that one doesn't destroy or possess or inhibit?' She also says how wounding it has been to him to have his privacy violated. 'But he is part of a group that seems to exercise remarkable powers of attraction.'

In the mid-seventies, writers such as Amis and Ian McEwan began to impinge themselves on the public consciousness. Barnes, although a slightly later developer than his friends, was part of a group that not only had great talent, but were soon exercising considerable clout in the book world. Indeed, it seemed for many years that the only literary issue that mattered was whether Barnes, McEwan or Amis would ever win the Booker.

Martin Amis might have been born into this trade and been name-dropping since he first said 'dad'. But it was all new to Barnes. The only member of his family who had ever had anything published was his mother, who once wrote a letter to the *Evening Standard*. 'She complained about girl students getting themselves pregnant and then expecting the state to look after them,' he recalls.

Barnes says that even when he was a student at Oxford, the idea of being a writer was simply something that seemed off the radar. 'It was partly because I thought that art and literature were the supreme that I didn't think I could do it,' he explains. 'I used to go to the English Society and examine famous writers like Robert Graves and Stephen Spender who came to speak. I thought it must be wonderful to be a writer. But it was what other people did.'

That is not to say that Barnes had no expectation of achievement. His parents, both French teachers, 'weren't pushy in the sense that the fathers of girl tennis prodigies are pushy,' he says, 'but it was assumed everything would work out all right. There was no specific career advice as there was no sex advice.'

Barnes was born in Leicester in 1946, but the family moved to suburban west London six weeks later. His one older brother is now a professor of philosophy working in Geneva. His childhood provided the location for his debut novel *Metroland* – 'J'habite metroland', cynically proclaimed the young protagonist – as well as an intuitive understanding of the mores of a certain sort of middle-class English life. He didn't actually rebel against his upbringing, but remembers living though a 'furious and puzzled boredom. It was waiting for life to happen and fearing that it would not.'

He went to City of London School, which entailed an hour and a quarter each way on the train and six hours of 'quite intense' contact with other boys in-between. Barnes played rugby and cricket, and won a scholarship to Oxford. He says the family response to this achievement was typical. 'I got home from school and a letter was waiting for me. I opened it up and said: "I got a scholar-ship." My mother said: "Yes, I thought it was that." It was a classic dampening-down. Let's not get too excited.'

Outside of school, life was lived almost exclusively within the family unit, and he says both he and his brother suffered a 'phobic reaction' to this orthodoxy. 'After my brother went to university he virtually never came home again,' he says. 'He would stay up over vacations and things like that. I was fairly estranged from my parents, but did become closer to them in their later years. I was always very fond of my father, but my mother was a woman who I had to get away from for long periods.'

His brother Jonathan casually mentions that he has not seen Julian for 'a few years. We were chums when we were boys and I do always watch him when he is on French television. But we were never a close-knit family, thank God. We always thought that water was thicker than blood.'

Despite the distance between them, Jonathan Barnes says that his parents were proud of Julian's success and they had all his novels lined up on a shelf. 'My mother did say at one point that she couldn't read them because of the naughty bits,' recalls Jonathan. 'But she must have read them to some degree to get to the naughty bits.'

Barnes's friends speak of an extraordinary loyalty and kindness, and he acknowledges that he may have constructed a family out of his friendships. 'The advantage of friends is that you choose them and they choose you. Instead of with a family where they are a given. I suppose I have pointless regrets for not coming from one of those large warm, extended, open families that exist in the mythology of the family. But I've very rarely seen one.'

Although he and Pat don't have children, he has four godchildren and enjoys being with his friends' children. His brother says he was very supportive and kind to his nieces when they were studying in London. 'He's the perfect uncle. I'm sure he would have been a very good father.' In fact, his friend Jay McInerney has approvingly commented that the way the Barneses lead their life 'makes a great case for childlessness'.

They have a beautiful house and garden in north London. Barnes is by all accounts an excellent cook and they regularly travel together for walking holidays. A habit of collecting first-edition novels has now given way to collecting and drinking fine wine, and his friend, the wine writer Jancis Robinson, says Barnes drinks better stuff than she does. Some people see this cultivation of the good things in life as slightly too meticulous. One observer characterized Barnes 'as the sort of person who washes his hands too often', but Marina Warner says it is more 'a wise acceptance that his success means he can lead his life in an enriching way. He is a perfectionist with fantastic application.'

This meticulousness inevitably has a sharp side when confronted with the messiness of life, and Bridget Jones was probably right to display some apprehension. 'He has very high standards,' says Jancis Robinson, 'by which I don't mean he worries whether or not the napkins are folded correctly. He wants everything to be good quality, whether that is a decision or a moral stance or a hunk of beef.' Hermione Lee agrees that he can be very critical of 'some forms of behaviour: pretensions, sloppiness, showing off. You get on better with him if you behave well, which is different from behaving properly.'

It was all very different when Barnes went up to Oxford to study modern languages in 1964. He says he 'made a mess of the whole thing', and failed to get the first which would have allowed him to follow his brother into postgraduate work. The swinging sixties 'partly' happened to him: he bought the records – he is still a 'shameful' owner of a boxed set of Donovan LPs – but the drugs passed him by. 'People spoke about things like big H and little H, but you couldn't ask what they meant for fear of being uncool. I presume now it was heroin and hash.'

He also sidestepped the politics of the time. 'Other things seemed more interesting to me. The fact that I didn't understand one of Mallarmé's poems seemed more important than going to Grosvenor Square to protest against the Vietnam war.' Today he devotes time to the fallout from politics and is a patron of Helen Bamber's Medical Foundation for the Care of Victims of Torture. He has arranged a series of fundraising readings by writers including Jung Chang, Tom Stoppard, Ruth Rendell and Nick Hornby. 'Lots of people say they will help, and then life overtakes and other commitments come along and they don't fulfil,' says Bamber. 'But Julian, without any prompting, has kept this up year after year. It is hugely time-consuming and he is really willing to put himself out.'

After Oxford, he did the civil service exams, but instead of getting a position in the diplomatic service as he had hoped, he was offered a job as a tax inspector. 'It was humiliating, and as I was rather snobbish, I drew the line there.' Instead, he signed on the dole for a while and then landed a job on the *Oxford English Dictionary* on the 'sports and dirty words section'. While there, he made his first contacts in the literary world. He met the poets Craig Raine and Christopher Reid and even had a book accepted for publication, although this was a false start.

Barnes still has one copy of his *Literary Guide to Oxford*, but says it is 'dreadful'. He had been paid an advance, but after three years, it had still not been published. 'So I wrote a firm but fair letter saying they should give me a date for publication, and if they were not going to publish they should return the manuscript,' he says. 'Never did a manuscript come back so quickly. And, worse, it had been copy-edited up to about page 60 by someone who obviously hated it and hadn't got any further.'

After three years, Barnes came to London to read for the Bar. 'I was good at passing exams, but I was deeply unsuited to standing up in court with a wig on my head and thinking on my feet, as I was virtually mute at that time and very

self-conscious. I remember when I worked at the *New Statesman* we had a messenger who delivered all the internal mail, but none of the external messages. It
turned out he was agoraphobic. I was a bit like him in that I chose the profession for which I was the least suited.'

However, the move in to the law gave him two years' breathing space in
which he started writing book reviews. His first published piece was about the
restoration of old buildings and was printed in the *Times Educational Supplement*.
'I was sharing a flat with an architectural historian at the time and I just used
his knowledge.'

The architectural historian was Andrew Saint, now a professor at Cambridge,
who recalls the time as one of 'drifting around in that semi-privileged post-
Oxford languor'. He doesn't remember talking about books or about much else
to Barnes, whom he recalls as 'extremely taciturn. He really didn't speak very
much at all. He had this slightly saturnine smile so you didn't really know what
he was thinking. But having said that, when he did say something it was usually more friendly than you feared it would be.'

Barnes went on to pass his Bar finals, but by that time had realized he was
getting more pleasure from 'spending half the week working on a novel round-
up for the *Oxford Mail* than I ever would out of arguing Baker *v* Baker at the
Dalston crown court.' The die was cast and Barnes entered the rackety world of
jobbing literary journalism, where he began to meet journalists, writers and
editors.

To mark his arrival in Grub Street he bought a bottle-green velvet suit. At a
party someone asked him if it was his literary London suit. 'Not unkindly, but
as if I were sporting L-plates on my trousers.' Claire Tomalin was literary editor
at the *New Statesman*. She interviewed Barnes for a job. 'He was very funny,' she
recalls. 'I asked why did he want the job and he put on this wonderful show of
languor, saying that he gathered the literary life involved sitting around all day
and not doing much. Of course, he was very hard-working and a terrific hit with
readers from the start. He had such a sharp, cool wit.'

As a journalist, Barnes did high-class TV criticism for the *Observer*, having
accepted the apparently poisoned chalice of following Clive James in the job. In
the early nineties, his stylish essays as London correspondent for the *New Yorker*
were collected into a best-selling book. He started writing his first novel,
Metroland, after the debacle of the Oxford book. It wasn't published until nine
years later. 'I had a deep lack of confidence,' he says. This was presumably not
helped by the interventions of his friends. He showed the typescript to Craig
Raine and Christopher Reid. 'Craig said I should re-read *Great Expectations* and
put in a wanking scene. Re-read was a very nice touch, so I didn't tell him that
I hadn't read *Great Expectations* the first time. Christopher said put it away in a
drawer as I would feel differently about it in a year's time.'

By the time publisher Liz Calder saw the book it was 'almost perfect', she says.
'Its adolescent attitudes were so marvellously expressed I knew he was exactly
the sort of writer that would work at Cape.' The book went on to win the
Somerset Maugham award for a debut novel.

The year in which *Metroland* appeared, 1980, was immensely productive for
Barnes. Along with the literary journalism and acclaimed first novel, he also
published a thriller featuring a bisexual private eye written under the other family name of Dan Kavanagh. He bashed out three more Kavanagh books over the

next few years, taking a few weeks for each one. Liz Calder says they allowed him to use things like football and snooker from the laddish side of his life, but Barnes says they were never that successful and eventually ran out of steam. 'It got to the stage when Julian Barnes was subsidizing Dan Kavanagh rather than the other way around. It was ridiculous that *Flaubert's Parrot* was supporting these low-life thrillers.'

Flaubert's Parrot, Barnes's third literary novel, was published in 1984 and launched him into the first division of British writers. Liz Calder had already published *Metroland* and his next novel, *Before She Met Me*. She remembers that when she asked him what he was doing next, her 'heart sank'. The book is packed with arcane Flaubertiana and won an award in France usually given to collections of essays. 'I thought, "Why doesn't he just do another novel?"' remembers Calder. 'But when he sent in a few chapters I was completely blown away.'

Barnes says he was conscious that it was a departure. 'But it wasn't as if I was trying to follow up two international successes. I was following up two novels which had just stumbled into paperback and no one abroad wanted to buy.' *Flaubert's Parrot*, he says, was actually turned down by Penguin. 'They said they liked it, but thought it wouldn't sell any copies at all.'

The book became a worldwide bestseller and marked the point when Barnes changed from being a journalist who wrote novels to a novelist who did a bit of journalism. Two novels later, he wrote the even bigger-selling *History of the World in 10½ Chapters*, which sparked another is it/isn't it debate about whether it was a novel at all.

The critic James Wood has written that Barnes 'is a brilliant essayist inside whom a novelist is struggling to get out'. Barnes takes the line that 'I'm a novelist and therefore it is a novel.' He says: 'The lesson you learn is that you pursue the passion of the book in the form that it has to be made. People will follow or not, but you can't second-guess these things. It is liberating in that you write the book that has to be written, and it has success or otherwise depending on factors you absolutely don't understand. I'd rather someone say they enjoyed my book but didn't think it's a novel, than someone say they didn't like my book but it is absolutely a novel. But thankfully that's not the choice.'

Jay McInerney applauds Barnes's range and versatility. 'A lot of novelists set up a kind of franchise, and turn out a familiar product. But what I like about Jules's work is that he's like an entrepreneur who starts up a new company every time out.' His last two novels before *Love, etc* prove the point. *The Porcupine* was set in the ostensibly very un-Barnes-like milieu of post-communist Eastern Europe, while the Booker-shortlisted *England, England* was set in the more familiar Isle of Wight, but in the less familiar tone of a satire.

Barnes reveres truth and honesty, and seeks to express them in whatever form of fiction he needs. 'Fiction is telling the truth by telling lies, as opposed to telling less of the truth by telling facts,' he says. 'Even if you write something close to yourself, what you're aiming for is an objective construction artistically shaped. I admit that my early fiction was pretty close to my life, but then I learned to lie.

'You step off the land on to the ice and it doesn't give way. You start to skate and soon you aim for the double axel and the triple toe loop. When I read non-fiction, I am often aware that it is merely a masquerade of the truth. When you read the great and beautiful liars of fiction you feel that this is what life is. This is true, even though it is all made up.'

29 July 2000

Life at a glance

JULIAN PATRICK BARNES

Born: 19 January 1946.

Education: City of London School; Magdalen College, Oxford.

Married: Pat Kavanagh (1979).

Career: Lexicographer, *OED* (1969–72); contributing editor, *New Review* (1977); assistant literary editor, *New Statesman* (1977); deputy literary editor, *Sunday Times* (1980–82); TV critic, *Observer* (1982–6); London correspondent, the *New Yorker* (1990–95).

Select bibliography: Fiction: *Metroland* (1980); *Before She Met Me* (1982); *Flaubert's Parrot* (1984); *Staring at the Sun* (1986); *A History of the World in 10½ Chapters* (1989); *Talking it Over* (1991); *The Porcupine* (1992); *England, England* (1998); *Love, etc* (2000). As Dan Kavanagh: *Duffy* (1980); *Fiddle City* (1981); *Putting the Boot in* (1985); *Going to the Dogs* (1987). Non-fiction: *Letters From London* (1995).

Awards: Officier de l'Ordre des Arts et des Lettres (1995).

SAUL BELLOW

The worldly mystic's late bloom

James Wood

Lately, among Saul Bellow's keenest readers there had been somewhat emaciated expectations. It seemed that energy was fading. Bellow's first novel appeared in 1944, he had been writing for nearly fifty years, and it was perhaps time for his admirers to polish their gratitude for the earlier work and let things go.

In 1995, Bellow was poisoned by eating toxic fish in the Caribbean, developed pneumonia, and very nearly died in a Boston hospital. When he at last recovered, he was not strong enough to sign a cheque, had no idea of the day or month. His nervous system had almost been erased by the poisons, and he needed months of primitive tuition to reclaim it. When he published a novella, *The Actual*, in 1996, it was a feat to have written it at all. Unsurprisingly, it seemed a mere ricochet from a talent that had already hit many targets; it had an interrupted energy.

How extraordinary, then, that Bellow's substantial new novel, *Ravelstein*, written in his eighty-fifth year, should be so full of the old, cascading power, its prose displaying that august raciness one remembers from *Herzog* (1964) and *Humboldt's Gift* (1975), darting with metaphor and wit. The book's protagonist, Abe Ravelstein, is a lightly disguised portrait of Bellow's old friend, Allan Bloom, the conservative Chicago political theorist who became famous for his book *The Closing of the American Mind* (1987). Indeed, it memorializes a larger intellectual community at the University of Chicago, and tells the story of Bloom's death from Aids, and of Bellow's dance with death five years ago. Most of the recent events in Bellow's life find their telling in this new book.

But before one knows that, the novel's prose has to be reckoned with; it has an abundance and energy remarkable for a man his age, an overflowing quality that dissolves the book's biographical powders, and insists on its own autonomy. It tends to make irrelevant the usual questions of 'Who is X based on?'

Here are some of the many lustres to be found in *Ravelstein*. There is an angry cardiologist, who grips his stethoscope 'like a slingshot'. Or a man, seen with 'accordion pleats under his chin'. Or the neurologist who coaxes the poisoned Bellow-figure – the book's narrator – back from death, and is described thus: 'Dr Bax, like a skilful Indian scout of the last century, pressed his ear to the rail and heard the locomotive coming. Life would soon be back, and I would occupy my seat in the life-train. Death would shrink to its former place at the margin of the landscape.'

In these instances, one hears the sound of the Bellow of the 1960s, 70s, and

80s. He once said that, in old age, he had so little energy that 'you have your foot to the floor but you are only going twenty miles an hour'. Of course, his own habitual recourse to metaphor, even in this instance, suggested otherwise, and his new book entirely contradicts his own fatalism. Recently, he joked, unconvincingly, that 'maybe one reason that I have so much energy is that I'm so lazy, really. I preserve my energies.'

At present, they are doubtless stretched, because in addition to the media-flummery of bringing out a new book, Bellow has recently become a father. His wife, Janis, gave birth to a daughter, Naomi Rose, at the end of last year. He has been much more involved in the child's early months than perhaps he expected to be. He plays the recorder to her (he is an accomplished musician), and sings the 'Volga Boat Song', and various Yiddish tunes. 'I'm the kid's personal trouba-dour,' he laughs.

Janis Freedman, then a graduate student of Allan Bloom's, met Bellow fifteen years ago, at the University of Chicago. Bellow was estranged from his fourth wife, Alexandra Ionesco Tulcea, a Romanian astrophysicist. After marriages to Anita Goshkin, Alexandra Tschacbasov, Susan Glassman and Tulcea, and three sons, he has described himself as a serial husband, yet it is clear that in this fifth marriage an equilibrium and blessing have been found that he did not perhaps expect. He is aware of the rigidities in the writer's domestic life, and while no Tolstoy of matrimonial demand, has never hidden his past fail-ings and impossibilities. In his new book, he pays a fine tribute to Janis, to her intelligence and beauty, and writes that the narrator and his wife understand each other. That is certainly the particular vibration the Bellows' marriage sounds.

They have been living in Boston since 1994 – Janis teaches political theory at Boston University, and Bellow gives a statesman's course in the European novel – and their lives have a shapely, seasonal balance. In term-time they write and teach, and entertain in their large, unlavish home in a Boston suburb; and in the long summer they decamp to Vermont, where they have a house built to Bellow's specifications (he can lie in the bath and study the stars through a sky-light.) Until the Caribbean collapse, he rode a bike and swam in the local lake. They read Shakespeare out loud, sometimes auditioning village guests for other parts.

Janis, in her early forties, has a warm, shrewd, limitless quality, and a kind of wiry patience that suggests great reserves of strength. During his ordeal at the hospital in Boston, she did not leave his room for ten days, fearful that if she was absent even for a minute, he might die alone. Staff brought her infrequent meals. Bellow knows she saved his life, and continues to save it in some meas-ure. It was touching, last year, to see the couple when Janis was very pregnant, the great gourd of her belly making mobility difficult, and her much older hus-band, differently frail, tender and solicitous on her behalf. They are unwarily loving in public: it is one of those marriages that seems entirely right, the provider of its own nutrients.

Bellow seems unsurprised by, though grateful for, this late burst of creativity. But his biographer, James Atlas, rightly says that *Ravelstein* 'is an astonishing book, one of his strongest, and it comes, as you know, after a period of attenuation. Who are the other great writers who have done anything like this in their eighties? Tolstoy's late stories, I guess. Otherwise, I can only think of Thomas Mann, who created the character of Felix Krull, when he was, I think, seventy-nine.' And Bellow's old friend, Keith Botsford, who with him edits an irregular literary journal called *The Republic of Letters*, admits that he is 'amazed. The power is there; it takes a little longer.'

Bellow himself seems chiefly concerned that readers will ignore the book's fictive qualities, and consider it only as a memoir of Allan Bloom. 'There is a strange literalism that's become a habit in America,' he says. 'People only want the factual truth. Well, the truth is that Allan was a very superior person, great-souled. When people proclaim the death of the novel, I sometimes think they are really saying that there are no significant people to write about. Allan was certainly one. Yet I can't help being a fiction-writer. It's a curious process. Life is obviously feeding you, yet Ravelstein is a composite, taken from a hundred different streams, like all of my characters.'

This seems true, for one finds oneself treating Ravelstein as if he simply joins the room of large Bellovian comic characters, like Moses Herzog, or Tommy Wilhelm in *Seize the Day*, or Uncle Benn Crader in *More Die of Heartbreak*, or Victor Wulpy, in 'What Kind of a Day Did You Have?' (another powerful intellectual, yet one who 'wore his pants negligently', in Bellow's unforgettable phrase).

Bellow is celebrated for his powers of physical portraiture, of grotesquerie, which tend to make all of his characters old, whatever their actual age: they are seniors in moral struggle. One of the comedies of this description is that while Bellow insists on our free agency as intelligences and souls, he gestures at the same time toward the physical imprisonment of our bodies. We are all victims, physically, all helpless account-keepers. That is why his heroes are so often bearish, large, fat-chested, panting, clumsy men – yet with delicate sensitivities.

These men wear their moral age visibly, as a tree stump is ringed with years, and this in turn tells us something about Bellow's metaphysics. For he is not a psychologist, as novelists go. He does not go around unpicking his characters' selves, and truffling for motives. Instead, his people are embodied souls; they wear their stretched essences on their bodies, and it is Bellow's delight to, as it were, 'read' their souls through their surfaces, as a Victorian phrenologist might read the skull.

As in Dickens, Bellow's characters are flat, but they vibrate very strongly. The difference with Dickens, of course, is that Bellow writes often about intellectuals. Thus his people, paradoxically, are all mind and, simultaneously, all body. Typically, Ravelstein, in Bellovian mode, is large, flamboyant, and excessively clumsy. When he laughs, he throws his head back 'like Picasso's wounded horse in *Guernica*'. He loves fine clothes, Lanvin jackets, Zegna ties, but tends to spill food on them. Hostesses know to put newspaper underneath Ravelstein's chair at a dinner party.

At home, he wanders around in an exquisite silk dressing gown, chain-smoking. His apartment is stuffed with beautiful glass and silverware, with the finest Italian and French linens, and thousands of CDs. He reclines on a black leather couch, listening to Baroque music, is enormously learned, and given to oration on a thousand subjects.

Though Bellow does not say it, Ravelstein has more than a touch of Proust's Charlus, the brilliant, snobbish homosexual who loudly lectures Marcel as they walk along the Parisian boulevards. (Bellow is a careful reader of Proust.) Or closer to home, Ravelstein is a more refined version, perhaps, of Simkin, the lawyer in *Herzog*, who 'liked to lie down on the black Naugahyde sofa in his office, cover himself with an afghan knitted by his mother, listening to Palestrina, Monteverdi, as he elaborated his legal and business strategies.'

Ravelstein has become rich and famous with a popular book that has distilled to ordinary readers his conservative analysis of American decline. Now in the summer of his fame and influence, he likes to keep in touch with his former students, several of whom are in the US government. He is a shambolic gossip; the novel's narrator mentions a colleague who liked to joke that 'when I gossip it isn't gossip but social history'. He is loyally attended to by his boyfriend, Nikki. By all accounts, including Bellow's, this is Allan Bloom as his friends knew him.

Keith Botsford says that Bellow and Bloom, in addition to sharing a love of music, 'practised a kind of emotional shorthand together. Most of Saul's friendships have been like this. You have to be learned, to have read nearly everything, as he has done, and above all to enjoy it.' Bloom, Botsford continues, 'was an irresistible figure, especially to a novelist, whatever one's opinion about his politics. I remember sitting in Allan's apartment, and as usual he was wearing his beautiful silk bathrobe, somewhat opened so that you could, um, admire what was inside, and he went to get some CD or other to play. He had a fantastic collection of CDs. As he stood at the wall, he passed a map of Jerusalem that was hanging on it. "And that's a self-portrait," he said, gesturing towards the map. That was the kind of life-force he was.'

Bellow and Bloom taught together at the University of Chicago in the seventies and eighties. The university, which has always been a bulwark of a Great Books approach to learning, was perhaps at the height of its influence. Its committee on social thought allowed novelists (like Bellow), classicists, economists, and philosophers to draft their own courses. Milton Friedman (Thatcher's economics guru), Edward Shills and the great scholar of comparative religion Mircea Eliade were all at Chicago at the same time. 'Chicago was a place that loved irregular people,' says Bellow. 'Great scholars, most of them, but people with interesting streaks and histories.'

He has always been drawn to powerful intellects, in part because they offer an adequate match to his own powers, and also in part because their existence sanctions his own will-to-theory, his fondness for making use of speculation and scholarship in his fiction. Yet intellectuals are also a source of comedy because as scholars they are often labouring on quests for what is essential, but as private citizens their lives are full of the usual nonsense and superfluity. So their intellectual work seems to bring them no benefit, no relief, in domestic life. This is humblingly true of Moses Herzog, Bellow's most famous creation, a scholar of the Romantics who is undergoing a vicious divorce, and has taken to writing zany letters of plaint in his head to famous people, dead and alive: to Churchill,

Heidegger, Spinoza, Eisenhower.

But more generally, Bellow's work has as its theme the struggle to find what is essential amidst the piles of our emotional slack, and amidst the heap of trivia and gratuity that is the contemporary world. Allan Bloom seems to fit this mould, a penetrating intellect who soiled his ties. But Bellow was obviously attracted by more. There was a political agreement between the two men, a feeling that America was refusing to talk honestly about its problems, and instead hiding them under wish-fulfilment or meaningless jargon. For both Bloom and Bellow, America, in its materialism, its violence, its shallowness, embodied 'nihilism without the abyss'.

In his novel *The Dean's December*, written in 1982, his first after winning the Nobel prize in 1976, Bellow contrasted prosperous, capitalist America with punitive, communist Romania. In the Communist world, there was 'hard nihilism'; in America, there was 'soft nihilism'. Both dispensations incarnated a kind of cynicism about the possibilities of spiritual life. Bellow's complaint against America had been building since the 1960s, and *The Dean's December*, with its superb but unsettling descriptions of the Chicago ghettoes, was taken, by many, as a rancidly conservative book, even a racist one.

Bellow describes *The Dean's December* as a 'cri de coeur. I disliked the fact that people wouldn't talk about this stuff honestly, particularly the state of the ghettoes, the inner cities. But I don't know if anyone heard it.' Five years later, he embossed his reputation as a neo-conservative by writing the introduction to Bloom's book, *The Closing of the American Mind*, which wailed against the decline of the great universities, the destruction, as Bloom saw it, of the traditional literary canon, the sanctimonies of the left, the triumph of political correctness, and so on.

Some found his endorsement of what seemed a rather mediocre conservative squeal a diminishment. There are probably some who feel that Bellow's new valedictory to Bloom is a further political fall. One of Bellow's friends, Robert Boyers, the editor of the literary and cultural journal *Salmagundi*, explains: 'Bellow rapidly became anathema to left-leaning liberal academics. That preface marked his separation from mainstream American academic life. But it has probably not affected his reputation as a writer: it's mostly in the realm of PR or politics.'

What, I ask Boyers, did Bellow find so attractive in Bloom? 'He liked the courage of going against the grain of so many ideas dearly held by the academic world. Bloom had written the book that Bellow might have written had he the appetite to do it.'

Yet Bellow's preface is not especially political. Instead, it is largely an insistence, congruent with all his work, that the self should not be defined politically, nor even intellectually. Bloom, who was able to escape his clumsy body and his undistinguished origins by the power of mind, was probably attractive to Bellow because he was an example of the way the self flies beyond the nets that society wants to throw over it.

This liberation had an urgency at a time when, more strongly perhaps than now, academics and theorists were herding people into their ethnicities, sleeving them in racial and political data, arguing that we are always the ideology that speaks us, not the voice that sings over ideology. Singularity – if one wanted a word to define Bellow's ambitions for the self it would be this. In many ways, he is an Emersonian individualist. Moses Herzog recalls being a class orator at school, and reciting from Emerson: 'The private life of one man shall be a more illustrious monarchy than any kingdom in history.' This Emersonianism is then crossed with Russian and Jewish influences. It is hard not to hear Bellow in Martin Buber, when Buber writes that 'the uniqueness of man proves himself in his life with others. For the more unique a man really is, so much the more can he give to the other.'

Bellow's characters, especially his intellectuals, are people, like him, who grew up in straitened circumstances and discovered the expansions of thought in books, and then felt free to roam wherever they liked. He is something of a zealot for the freedoms of the soul. One of the more provocative contradictions of Bellow's enterprise is that he has been a late-modern novelist, writing in the age of Beckett and Bernhard (Beckett read Bellow with pleasure, and the two met once in Paris), who has yet prolonged the soul-pungency of the great nine-teenth-century Russian novelists. He is most like Tolstoy or Dostoyevsky in his determination to deliver his characters from the inessential.

Of course, Bellow was nearly born in St Petersburg, as Saul Belov. His family emigrated from Russia to Quebec, where he was born in 1915. But they moved to America, and he grew up in Chicago, 'clumsy, tender, stinking Chicago, dumped on its ancient lake bottom'. Chicago, as he has often said, was a fine place for a boy like him to educate himself. He took nourishment from the great books in the public libraries. In addition, traders came by with cheap editions of new work. 'You could get freethinkers like T. H. Huxley, along with Tolstoy's *Confession*, and selections from Hegel. It was a comprehensive education,' says Bellow.

And there was a thriving sensory world, of course. There were Jews and Poles, Germans, Italians and Russians, and Bellow was a keen observer. Much of this early life finds its way into the big novels like *The Adventures of Augie March*, *Herzog*, and *Humboldt's Gift*. Moses Herzog recalls receiving packets of worthless roubles from Grandfather Herzog, still in Russia. 'You held the glorious bills to the light and you saw Peter the Great and Catherine in the watermarked rain-bow paper.' This was almost certainly a family memory or story.

Bellow has been associated with Bloom, and with neo-conservatism, for over a decade now. He jokes that 'Allan had very serious enemies, and I came in for my share – a kind of agent's percentage cut.' But Bellow's sense of the world is finally religious, rather than political, and in this regard his new novel joins arms with his earliest work. Occasionally, one senses a tension between the Bellovian narrator and his metaphysical, even mystical impulses, and Ravelstein's atheistic materialism.

Bellow's new book is ghosted by death. His locomotive has raced past the death-sidings, full of friends like John Berryman, John Cheever, Ralph Ellison. One sometimes forgets that Bellow belongs to the generation of Robert Lowell, who died in 1977. He has been not only a greater writer than any of them, but one more steadily persistent. Allan Bloom's death perhaps seemed like a warn-ing: Bellow next. He writes, in *Ravelstein*, of Chicago (though the city is unnamed): 'On every one of the surrounding streets there were front rooms where friends had lived – and at the sides, the windows of bedrooms where they died... It was collection time for an entire generation.'

Partly to soften hard memories, the Bellows moved to Boston in 1994. I first met him, one of the few living writers I admired as I admired the august dead, ten years ago, in Chicago. In his mid-seventies then, he was vigorous, commanding, and planted solidly on his home turf: he offered to drive me around, and introduce me to his 'contacts' – the dry-cleaners, hotel-managers, policemen and local politicians who fund his fictional version of Chicago.

I met him again in 1996, not long after the Caribbean collapse, in Boston, and he was not strong enough to lift the salad-bowl. A gate had closed, one thought. Surely Bellow's style, so obviously indexed to his energy, a kind of intellectual virility, really, had died, too, was now as weak as the hand that had been so easily vanquished by the little salad-bowl, with its burden of greens. He had an old man's impatience at this dinner party, stiffly drumming his vine-like fingers, and eager for his bed.

In the past few years I have been lucky enough to witness Bellow's renovation, sometimes in Washington, more often in Boston. At times he seems weary or withdrawn, but more often one is struck by how intellectually speedy is his mind, still throwing out Bellovian enticements.

What is Bellovian? At a restaurant last year, a pompous dessert was served. The chef had placed little dots of red coulis around the rims of the bowls, each dot geometrically exact. It seemed that someone had measured the gap between each blob. 'Euclidean pimples!' Bellow said, raised his head, and offered his jointed, sluggish laugh.

When one thinks of a phrase from Bellow, it almost always has this kind of wit, and of course it is a metaphysical wit in the way that Donne or Shakespeare is: a metaphorical liveliness, yoking together apparent incompatibles. There is Valentine Gersbach, in *Herzog*, with his wooden leg, 'gracefully bending and straightening like a gondolier', or Mason, the young thug in *The Dean's December*, whom 'you had to study to find the humanity in. It was like looking for the mercury in a thermometer.'

It is not surprising that Joyce is one of Bellow's great pleasures, nor that he owns one of the Shakespeare and Company's editions of *Ulysses*, with the Parisian typesetter's errors. 'It was smuggled into America by a schoolfriend of mine.' In Joycean style, Bellow loves puns and word games. One of his jokes, which gets into *Ravelstein*, is to turn the Jermyn Street shirtmaker, Turnbull and Asser, into 'Kisser and Asser'. And this is not mere play, because it also contains a worldly judgment about Jews dressing as goys, kissing the gentile ass, as it were.

Bellow is a worldly mystic. His prose logs impressions with broken speed; his metaphysical engine then grinds through these images for what is essential. In *Herzog*, Moses is seen pausing on 'the metal doors of the sidewalk elevator,' and receiving 'the raised pattern of the steel door through his thin shoes; like Braille. But he did not interpret a message.' It could be said that the world presses on Bellow's characters like Braille for those who do not need it. Reality is both a code and a distraction, and the task is to sort out the necessary from the superfluous.

Although Bellow may be seen by some as a conservative, he has been constantly hospitable to American modernity, especially to the tumult of the city. He says that 'America contains all human types', and it is true of his books. It is this worldliness that allows him to be, as a stylist, both an aesthete and a pounding realist, so that he is very exquisite without being precious. He truly writes prose, but prose written at least as well as verse, and it is doubtless this combination of the worldly and the lyrical that has been such an influence not only on Philip Roth and Don DeLillo, but on the most interesting stylists in Britain, like McEwan, Amis, Rushdie.

And at eighty-five, astoundingly, he is still writing. One thinks of Henry James on his deathbed, the writing hand still moving involuntarily. Bellow will write to the end, no doubt, harnessed to the novel, that form he has sharpened again and again since the early 1940s. His biographer, James Atlas, says: 'He used to say, when he was in his seventies, "I'm not ready to be summed up yet", and I thought, privately, "Yeah, yeah." But you know what? It turns out he's right.'

15 April 2000

Life at a glance

SAUL BELLOW

Born: 10 June 1915, Lachine, Quebec, Canada.

Education: University of Chicago (1933–35); Northwestern University (1937).

Married: Anita Goshkin (1937, divorced; one son); Alexandra Tschacbasov (1956, divorced; one son); Susan Glassman (1961, divorced; one son); Alexandra Ionesco Tulcea (1974, divorced); Janis Freedman (1989, one daughter).

Career: Instructor, Pestalozzi-Froebel teachers' college, Chicago (1938–42); *Encyclopedia Britannica* (1943–6); University of Minnesota (1946–9); various teaching posts in USA and England (1950–).

Select bibliography: *Dangling Man* (1944); *The Adventures of Augie March* (1953); *Seize the Day* (1956); *Herzog* (1964); *Humboldt's Gift* (1975); *The Dean's December* (1982); *More Die of Heartbreak* (1986); *A Theft* (1989); *Ravelstein* (2000).

Awards: Pulitzer prize *Humboldt's Gift* (1975); Nobel prize for literature (1976).

JOHN BERGER
Contented exile

Nicholas Wroe

When John Berger won the Booker prize in 1972 for his novel *G*, he famously attacked Booker McConnell for their colonial past and gave half the prize money to the Black Panthers. No surprise there from the unflinching Marxist critic, whose already impeccable radical-chic credentials were further reinforced by the inevitable public furore.

'But while his speech was intense and angry and passionate', recalls publisher Liz Calder who was there that night, 'it was never a wild rant. He obviously has very deeply held convictions, but is also endlessly gentle and careful about explaining them.'

This combination of sternly unbending opinions and a highly conciliatory manner is an apparent paradox at the heart of Berger's life and work. Speaking at the home of sometime collaborator Nella Bieski in the outskirts of Paris, it is at first incongruous, not to say perverse, that this friendly, fit and ostensibly happy man sipping a glass of wine in this comfortable room should declare that, 'the world we live in is intolerable and our own time is an unprecedented dark age.' His speech is heavily accented after nearly forty years of living in France and littered with long – sometimes agonisingly long – pauses. 'But', he eventually continues, 'I also believe that life is a gift to be treasured. We all oscillate between these two perceptions and have to navigate them through life. You find exactly this dialectic in the first poetry of the ancient Greeks: life is a gift, but what happens in life is unbearably tragic.'

Over the years, this melancholic duoverse has conspired in the production of an extraordinarily rich life and an increasingly bleak body of work, particularly in his fictional output. He writes about exile and displacement, suffering and exploitation, the destruction of communities and the desperation of the powerless. His last novel featured a young woman with Aids and now his latest book, *King*, is set in the transience and degradation of a squatter camp.

At the root of his dark world-view is Berger's coming of age politically and philosophically during the horrors of the Second World War, but the slaughter at Ypres and Verdun during the previous European convulsion also played their part in shaping him.

John Peter Berger was born the first of two sons to Stanley and Miriam Berger. Although theirs was a comfortable and stable home, the lingering influence of the First World War still exerted a powerful psychological and emotional tug on the family. As Berger writes in a poem called 'Self-portrait', 'It seems now that I was so near to that war / I was born of a look of the dead / Swaddled in mustard gas / And fed in a dugout.'

Stanley Berger, the son of a Hungarian émigré merchant from Trieste 'who sometimes had quite a lot of money and sometimes had none', had wanted to be an Anglican priest before 1914, but four cataclysmic years as an infantry officer on the Western Front, where he was awarded the Military Cross, left him without faith or politics. 'He was a brave soldier but it indelibly marked him and for a while he was totally lost,' recalls Berger.

Like many former officers after the war, Stanley Berger tried his hand at a series of business ventures. They all failed and it wasn't until the mid-1920s that he established himself, first as the Secretary and then the Director of the inelegantly named Institute of Cost and Works Accountants, for which he was eventually awarded an OBE. 'For better or for worse,' says Berger, 'this Institute was the beginnings of what is today called management theory.'

Berger's mother came from a working-class family in Bermondsey, south London, where her father looked after brewery dray horses. Although both a vegetarian and a suffragette during the war, when she married she ceased any political activity, 'as women often did in those days'. It was left to the adolescent John to reintroduce radical politics back into the house when, in an early indication of both his continental and artistic tastes, he became an anarchist at the age of fifteen and started a correspondence on the subject with the art critic Herbert Read.

School was 'monstrous'. First the sinisterly Dickensian sounding pre-prep, Sunnydown, and then St Edward's in Oxford, at that time a school for the sons of officers and clergymen and, 'exactly like Lindsay Anderson's *If*. The whole system was absolutely bloody. Every Sunday afternoon there was systematic torture when the ruling gang of each age group would choose a victim for whatever reason, put him on a table and squeeze lemon juice into his eyes, stab the soles of feet with compass points, make him swallow cascara so he would shit for the next three days. I was never a victim and I never participated. I suppose I found a way of avoiding it by adopting this stance of being too crazy to be considered.'

Geoff Dyer, who has written a critical biography of Berger's work, says the reason he has never written about his school days is that 'the only aspects of his life that really interest him are those that he has in common with other people, not different from them. But I'm sure his terrible experiences did somehow contribute to him deciding to leave England.'

Berger has not maintained contact with anyone at the school since he left aged sixteen – 'I just walked out' – and enrolled at the Central School of Art. Two years later, in 1944, he was called up into the Oxford and Bucks Infantry. 'The army was very important for me, as it was the first time I was with young men who were working-class,' claims Berger. Although it was assumed that because of his background he would become an officer, he refused a commission and spent two years in the ranks stationed with a training battalion near Belfast.

The war also served to crystallize his politics, with the battle for Stalingrad moving him closer to the organized left, although he never became a member of the Communist Party. 'I'm sure people assumed I was, particularly when I wrote for the Communist press after the war, but I didn't join because I couldn't swallow the official party line about art. This was the thing I thought I actually knew something about, and although I was all for a social art, I couldn't accept the rigidity and obvious falseness of their position.'

After the army, Berger returned to art school, this time Chelsea, where his career as an artist and critic started in earnest. 'I was very happy and received a good art education. And equally importantly, with teachers around like Henry Moore, Ceri Richards and Graham Sutherland, there was a constant example of artists devoted to art.'

He continued to teach art and to paint, exhibiting in London, into the early 1950s, when he began to write weekly art criticism for the *New Statesman* and *Tribune* under the editorship of George Orwell.

The art critic Peter Fuller commended Berger's 'consistent testimony to a possible future other than a capitalist one', at this time of communist witch-hunts and cold war hysteria. Berger's Marxist critique made him both a hero and villain within and outside the art world as he famously dismissed Francis Bacon as 'a brilliant stage manager rather than an original visual artist', and entered into a prolonged series of spats with Patrick Heron. But it was with the publication of his first novel that the depth of feeling Berger was capable of arousing became apparent.

In *A Painter of our Time*, published in 1958, a Hungarian émigré returns to Budapest in 1956 where he disappears, and probably dies, in the chaos of the uprising. The novel ends with the narrator saying that he didn't know which side he took, but it was to be hoped that he took the side of the government against the counter-revolutionaries.

The book was almost universally savaged, with only a Jesuit writing in the *Tablet* giving it an enthusiastic review. It so outraged Stephen Spender that he wrote in the *Observer* that the novel stank of the concentration camps and compared it to Goebbels. Spender then, through the CIA-sponsored magazine *Encounter*, put pressure on publishers Secker & Warburg and the book was withdrawn from sale.

'It was obviously a difficult time for me', says Berger, 'but it was invaluable training for a writer in opposition. I don't mean any disrespect to dissident writers in the Soviet Union or many other countries, because after all, in reality I was risking nothing. But it was a fantastic exercise in making me tough as a writer.'

Within two years of the publication of *A Painter of our Time*, Berger had left England for good. He has given a variety of reasons over the years for his move, always ultimately describing it as 'a very personal decision'. He was by then divorced and claims to have been sick of the stultifying influence of the Home Counties middle classes. But mostly he was following a long-held continental bent – he had travelled widely both sides of the newly erected Iron Curtain – and he settled in France because he could continue to write and broadcast in England while benefiting from the culture that sustained writers he greatly admired, such as Camus.

'Although I am very much a voluntary exile,' he now says, 'as time has passed I have become more aware of what an absolutely characteristic experience of our time exile is. Globally the number of exiles increases exponentially every year.'

Before moving to France, Berger had been in on the ground floor of inde-

pendent television in Britain. While at Granada he worked on children's programmes about animals, and can still tell a string of very John Noakesian stories
about being scratched by chimps while on live television. But it was his arts cov-
erage, and in particular the 1972 BBC series *Ways of Seeing*, that made his name.

A Marxist riposte to Kenneth Clark's patrician *Civilisation*, it was described by
one art academic of the time as 'being like Mao's *Little Red Book* for a generation
of art historians'. The series and accompanying book developed the ideas of
Walter Benjamin's essay, 'The Work Of Art In The Age Of Mechanical
Reproduction', and opened up areas of cultural study to a mass audience that
had previously been confined to the academy. It addressed how unique works of
art are transformed into reproducible commodities, the sexist tradition of the
nude, the celebration of private possessions in art and the links between high
art and advertising.

'At first it was shown very late at night and excited little comment,' recalls
Berger. 'But then, to our great surprise, it began to have more and more influence. It's not that I'm unhappy with it, but a slightly incongruous thing has
happened. It was written very quickly to provoke people. But gradually over the
years it has become a sort of classic. I preferred it when it was a slap in the face,
but now people are a bit solemn about it. It's all a bit of a lottery, as I've written
other things which are much more serious and go further. But that's the way it
goes and I'm the last to complain, as during the seventies and early eighties,
when I found it difficult to earn a living, the not huge, but regular, royalty
cheques from *Ways of Seeing* kept me going.'

Photographer Don McCullin still credits Berger's series for helping people 'to
see beyond the tips of their noses. There is something nourishing about looking
at things carefully and so many people have such a narrowness of vision. He had
a way of addressing the subject and making it sympathetic. In that respect he
was a champion of the cause of all visual artists and I'm extremely grateful to
him.'

The same year Berger published *G*. A self-consciously modernist work full of
tricksy authorial interventions, it tells the story of a Don Juan-like figure travelling round Europe in the years before the First World War. In an unintentional
gesture of rapprochement to the Clark family, he acknowledges the use of Alan
Clark's First World War history *The Donkeys*, but mostly, like John Fowles's *The
French Lieutenant's Woman* of a few years previously, *G* drew heavily on developments in the novel from France and was equally loved and hated, with Auberon
Waugh calling it 'imbecilic'.

'I was totally flabbergasted when it won the Booker, but in those days you
were told two days before the dinner, which gave me time to think about how
to react,' he says. 'In the end I made the speech not because I'm against prizes,
but because I couldn't help making the connection back from literature to life
and asking where did this money come from? In the case of Booker McConnell
it came from trading interests in the Caribbean going back to the middle of the
last century.'

At a time when Lenny Bernstein was handing round canapés to the Black
Panthers in New York, Berger announced he would give half of the £5,000 prize
to a Caribbean branch of the Panthers in London and spend the other half fund-

ing a novel about peasant life.

'It wasn't difficult to get in touch with the Panthers, and one came along to the dinner with me and kept whispering: "Keep it cool man, keep it cool." When I first met them they were a bit suspicious, but after a while, they agreed to take the money and I was given a bank account number to pay it into. That was that really.'

The success of *G* and *Ways of Seeing* elevated Berger's radical chic celebrity status to its peak, and his move to his present home in a small village in the French Alps attracted a volley of sneering comments about middle-class Marxists playing at being peasants. Some of that feeling persists to this day, and one prominent art critic is still mystified by the rationale for his move. 'What is the difference between having to talk to Surrey philistines or to French peasants, if what you talk about is Ingres's portraiture?'

But those who know Berger better are less cynical and visitors speak of a rural existence that is neither contrived nor precious.

He celebrated this community, and others like it, in his novels *Pig Earth*, *Once in Europa* and *Lilac and Flag*, which comprise his trilogy *Into Their Labours*. These works mix storytelling with poetry and political essay in depicting the displacement of peasant communities and the destruction of peasant land. It has been said that you can learn to use a scythe from reading these books, and guests report how involved Berger is in the daily routine of farming life.

Berger does attract a huge degree of loyalty. A fellow founder-member of the Writers and Readers Co-operative, Berger's publisher until its collapse in the eighties, still talks in awe of how he ploughed back all his British royalties into the company. Another friend was given a leather jacket after admiring one belonging to Berger's son. But there have also been some dramatic disputes, most notably with the art critic Peter Fuller, who died in a car crash in 1990.

The iconoclastic Fuller had long respected Berger and the two men formed a close bond. 'Peter was very talented and very interesting to talk to. In a sort of way he elected me to become his father,' says Berger now of a relationship that became increasingly oedipal. Fuller often stayed at Berger's home in France, they occasionally wrote together and even took holidays together. But then, as part of Fuller's strange personal odyssey that had already taken in compulsive gambling, Marxism and psychoanalysis, he moved towards a sort of Ruskinian conception of a national art and began to break with Berger.

'He started accusing me of all sorts of things and I used to say, "Peter, cool it", but that only seemed to make things worse.' Fuller had written a book called *Seeing Berger* in which he praised the impact of *Ways of Seeing*. He now revised the title of the book to *Seeing Through Berger* and attacked his former mentor.

Fuller claimed that Berger's theories – in particular his perceived attacks on connoisseurship, museums and oil paintings – left an 'art-shaped hole' at the centre of art criticism and 'were indistinguishable from those philistine policies towards the arts followed by successive governments'.

In a characteristically idiosyncratic finale, Fuller announced that despite Berger's veneer of left-wing radicalism, in fact, 'in the 1980s Berger's most significant cultural ideas were implemented as policy by Mrs Thatcher and her ministers.'

'We didn't have a specific row, but it seems to me that politically he moved a lot to the right,' says Berger. 'Although I didn't really take his book very seriously in terms of his arguments, I did take it seriously in terms of the hurt it caused me. But of course I would also like to say that his death was terrible and that I forgive him and I have since dedicated an essay about the apes at Basel zoo to Peter and his memory because of the long conversations we had about evolution, which was a subject he was very interested in.'

That Berger should choose something so apparently off-the-beaten-track as an essay on apes to make such a moving gesture is typical of his unselfconscious approach to his hugely varied output. The seamless way he moves between forms and disciplines is a tribute both to his talent and the fact that he has had no academic education since he left St Edward's. He acknowledges that he just doesn't see the departmental walls between activities. Along with his fictional output and art criticism he has written and appeared in films; collaborated on theatre projects – most recently in an astonishing investigation of prehistoric cave drawings with Simon McBurney and Théâtre de Complicité, set in the disused Aldwych tube station; written political and cultural essays, reportage, medical philosophy, poetry, studies of photography; and continues to draw nearly every day. This month alone, he is publishing a novel, staging a play and is the subject of an exhibition in Switzerland that includes a whole room of his obsessional motorbike drawings.

'He's like a schoolboy constantly turning over stones on a beach,' says Don McCullin about his varied fecundity. Michael Ondaatje compares him to writers like Lawrence or Paz, 'who use every form to express themselves. When you look at his work you are looking at a map rather than a straight line or escalator going in just one direction. He's reacting to the real world, not just the literary world. All his books have broken the vessel they were written within in some way.'

Berger acknowledges that such diversity can be a disadvantage. 'If you are a gadfly, or a bastard, like me, there is a tendency for critics to say that you're not serious. But the freedom it gives me well outweighs the disadvantages.'

He goes on to reject the emphasis placed on the artist as an original creator. 'Of course there is some truth in it, but I think it has obliterated another aspect of being an artist – an artist of any kind – which is that of receptivity. Of listening and receiving, and then putting out again. What gives me the courage to go on, and it can be very lonely and quite an exhausting and haunting business, is the notion that what is being asked to be said, needs to be said.

'So for me writing a book is not to be original, but to say some small thing that belongs to human experience but hasn't quite been said before. And when people read it they are in some way able to continue the struggle of life with a little bit more energy. That's why I say that I'm a storyteller, not a novelist, although what I write often passes as novels.'

Author Tim O'Grady maintains that Berger is the most overlooked writer of the latter half of the century. 'In any sane world, a writer whose work was as various, humane and profound as Berger's would be a certainty for the Nobel prize.'

His previous fiction, *To the Wedding*, featured a woman about to be married who learns she has Aids. In fact, the book became semi-autobiographical for Berger when his own daughter-in-law died of an Aids-related illness, although he had begun work on the project before he knew she was ill. His latest book, *King*, subtitled *A Street Story*, is set in a squatter camp underneath a motorway on the outskirts of a Mediterranean city a bit like Barcelona. The book can be seen as growing out of a previous novel *Lilac and Flag*, the part of his trilogy set among peasants displaced to the city. *King* is narrated by a dog – or at least we think he is a dog – and covers twenty-four hours in the lives of a community of homeless people.

'This is a subject largely without a voice, although there are lots of sociological and philanthropic studies. But the subject demanded to be approached and I became obsessed by it. I'm not saying this to be brave or pathetic as I am an incredibly privileged person and I never forget that. But of all the books that I have written, for the first time having finished it, it was incredibly difficult to come back to myself and to my life. It took the best part of a year to find my way back.'

Berger has insisted that his name does not appear anywhere on the cover of the book. 'It isn't that I want to play coy or be modest, but it is a way of making this object a little different and maybe it will be read differently rather than immediately accommodated in the literary output of a guy called Berger.'

And seeing this guy called Berger, holding a glass of wine in this tasteful Parisian room, you can't help feeling that he looks a contented man. He beams when talking about his children: Katya, 37, a movie critic married to a Greek man – 'she is a wonderful swearer in Greek'; Jacob, 35, a television film-maker; and Yves, 22, who still lives in the same village as his father in the Haute Savoie.

Hardly the stock picture of the angry writer still railing against the injustices of this cruel world. 'Compare him to his near-contemporaries like Amis and Osborne,' says Dyer. 'Men who swung to the Right and eked out their last years in niggardly reaction. You would have thought that everything Berger stood for had turned to ashes with the death of Communism, but he remains happy and eager to embrace life and liberty in whatever form. He has not only literally outlived them, but spiritually outlived them as well. He's had the last laugh.'

So why does he still feel compelled to cast his gaze at horror, when he is so obviously by nature more attuned to seeing and appreciating beauty?

'I realize I am concluding my life's work as a writer in a way I did not foresee thirty or even ten years ago,' he says. 'I find myself writing only stories about people in extremis. Five years ago I wrote about a young woman who is told she is *séropositive* [has tested positive for HIV]. In Africa today, about a fifth of the population is *séropositive*, and for most of them, there is no prospect of any medical treatment at all. *King* is about the homeless. Last month, three hundred people in the streets of Europe died from the cold. The total amount of people in Europe who are homeless is at least three million, probably more. This choice of themes is not part of a personal predilection. Far from it. I prefer drawing exotic flowers with charcoal, riding long-distance motorbikes, going to Italian restau-

rants, listening to Gregorian chant. Yet more and more people in the world –
and they will soon be the majority if they are not already – are living in
extremis. And I cannot, as a storyteller, shut my eyes and close my imagination,
so I am bound to follow.'

13 February 1999

Life at a glance

JOHN PETER BERGER

Born: 5 November 1926, Stoke Newington, London.

Education: Sunnydown preparatory school; St Edward's, Oxford; Central
School of Art, London; Chelsea School of Art.

Family: Divorced from Liz Berger. With Anya Bostock, a daughter, Katya, and
a son, Jacob. With Beverley Berger, a son, Yves.

Select bibliography: Fiction: *A Painter of our Time* (1958); *G* (1972); *Into
Their Labours* trilogy (1991); *To the Wedding* (1995); *King* (1999); Non-fiction:
The Success and Failure of Picasso (1965); *A Fortunate Man* (with Jean Mohr)
(1967); *About Looking* (1980); Theatre: *Question of Geography* (RSC, 1987);
Poetry: *Pages of the Wound* (1994).

Art: Exhibited at Wildenstein and Redfern galleries in London.

Television: *Monitor*, *Ways of Seeing* (1972).

Awards: Booker prize *G* (1972).

ANITA DESAI

A passage from India

Maya Jaggi

Anita Desai has taken to stealing across the border from the US, where she teaches, into Mexico, where she rents a hideaway in the mountain village of Tepotzlan. 'It's such an Indian culture, it's the closest I can get to India when I'm in America,' she says, her enthusiasm masking traces of homesickness.

It's an apt paradox that, at sixty-one, the Delhi novelist, who has only recently found freedom in the life of the itinerant academic, should be escaping India – and rushing to embrace it. Salman Rushdie once described Desai's subject as solitude. Yet while her main characters tend to be isolates and outsiders – whether Indian or foreigners in India – her fiction probes the tensions between their desired privacy and detachment, and the powerful family and social ties that both stifle and sustain.

First published in the early sixties, Desai is widely praised as the finest of her generation of Indian writers in English, and one of few who had an international reputation, alongside R. K. Narayan, before the post-Rushdie wave of the eighties and nineties. She was twice short-listed for the Booker prize for the novels many think her best: *Clear Light of Day* and *In Custody* – the latter made into a film by Ismail Merchant. And thanks to the recommendations of the Macpherson report on Stephen Lawrence, Desai now has a place on the national curriculum beside the Nobel prize-winners Derek Walcott and Wole Soyinka.

Rushdie admires Desai's books as 'private universes, illuminated by her perceptiveness, delicacy of language and sharp wit'. Her subtle, unsentimental and elegantly structured novels pulsate with nature and sensuous imagery – from tropical blooms to betel-stained teeth. The illumination of her characters' inner lives has prompted comparisons with Virginia Woolf.

The fiction-writer and critic Aamer Hussein sees Desai's subject as 'the changing fortunes of the Indian middle classes – from Western-educated to struggling lower middle class – and the Western encounter with India'. But he cautions against mistaking her novels' elegant surfaces for their essence. 'People use the term "watercolour" about her work, but it can be expressionist. Beneath the calm surface, you sense the violence, with women on the edge, like widows who die of drink, or devouring characters like Nur, the decadent Urdu poet of *In Custody*. Professor Shirley Chew of Leeds University, who is writing a book on Desai, adds: 'The strong undercurrent of violence comes out through powerful imagery – of heat, bird cries, the brutal beating of a horse, or Nur surrounded by pigeons on the balcony, being preyed upon.'

Desai's demeanour suggests little of this turmoil. Softly spoken, she moved the

Times to remark on her first visit to London in 1965 that she belied the 'public image of female novelists [as] an intimidating and often unfeminine species' with her 'striking beauty, delicate figure and corresponding quietness of manner'. Though she commutes between Delhi, Boston – as creative writing professor at the Massachusetts Institute of Technology – and Cambridge, where she was a fellow of Girton College, she makes an unlikely jetsetter. There is a self-contained stillness about her in the house she has in a tucked-away Cambridge terrace.

Later, by the river Cam, in a summer dress, her grey bun neatly tied with black velvet, she is serenely immune to wind and rain. Describing how some of her MIT students ditch promising scientific careers to be writers, she says: 'Of course, one does everything one can to deter them.' Her mischievous smile tells another story.

Desai's 'earliest, freshest impressions' of the America that struck her, in a neat reversal, as 'exotic and bizarre' are there in her new novel, *Fasting, Feasting*. It casts a slyly ironic gaze at family life in provincial India and suburban America, with parallel symptoms of dysfunction erupting, from bride-burning to bulimia. While the American family is seen through the eyes of an Indian student, both families turn up carnivorous patriarchs and preening matriarchs whose force-fed values spawn vegetarian sons and convulsive or self-starving daughters.

'I've always been aware of food as an obsession,' says Desai. 'Indians love food. Family life turns around meal times: days are spent preparing and eating in an enjoyable way I never managed to share. America was a strange mirror image; the same obsession with food, but consuming it. I was staggered by the supermarkets, the cartloads of food. And curiously, people didn't want to enjoy it.' Teaching at Mount Holyoke, a women's college in Massachusetts, she became aware of eating disorders. 'It's strange in a land of plenty that there's also a fear of food.'

The American family converges not at the dining table but around the TV, its magnet not the stove but the freezer. 'The Indian family is still extremely closely knit; there's far greater individualism in America. Both have their ideal family, but the American family has a coldness at its heart because no one really believes in it any more. In India, the family is more a hearth or a fire: it keeps you warm, but it consumes you, too.'

Desai is a close observer of what she has called 'the web of [family] relationships, sticky and sweet, clinging and trapping'. But here she has unsheathed her rapier, skewering the lingering mores that make drudges of wives and unmarried daughters, or reserve education – like the choicest morsels – for sons. Nor is she too genteel to hint, say, at fathers lusting after their pubescent daughters. 'Leaving India frees one's tongue,' says Desai. 'Within India you hold back so much. And being part of that life, you're too involved to look with objectivity.'

The remark seems extraordinary from a novelist so praised for her cool gaze. As one reviewer wrote: 'Her achievement is to keep the shock of genuine freshness, the eyes of the perpetual outsider.' Or as an Indian critic wrote more perceptively: 'Insiders rarely notice this much; outsiders cannot have this ease of reference.'

Desai was born Anita Mazumdar in June 1937 in Mussoorie, a Himalayan summer retreat. Her Bengali father had met her German mother, a teacher, while an engineering student in pre-war Berlin. They married when it was still rare for an Indian man to wed a European woman, and moved to the 'neutral territory' of Old Delhi, then, Desai recalls, a 'sleepy, provincial place'. She grew up in its leafy lanes without an extended network of relatives. The youngest of three sisters with an elder brother, she describes hers as 'a small and intensely close family. My family was an oddity; it didn't belong where it was. Going to school, I became aware of its difference, of things that set us apart.'

They spoke German at home, and Hindi to friends and neighbours. She learned English at mission school ('It was always my literary language, my book language') and her father's language, Bengali, only after he died when she was eighteen, and the family moved to Calcutta. 'Growing up, I wasn't even aware of my mother's being a foreigner; she dressed in a sari and cooked Indian food.' But Desai adds: 'Everyone in India has close affiliations to state, home town, religion, caste – all the things missing from my life. That leaves one feeling free to invent whatever kind of home you want. I do have all the passions one's supposed to have for one's home country, but I know I'm not part of Indian society – it perplexes and amazes me. I find myself reacting sharply, as my mother would have. I don't think I'm sentimental about India.

'My mother's not being Indian was so little a conscious part of my life that when she died I went with my sister to cremate her, and immerse her ashes in the river. It was only on the way back, when we passed some English graveyards, it struck me, maybe she would have liked to be buried. It never occurred to me to ask, nor her to tell.'

Although her parents were effectively exiled from Germany and East Bengal by the upheavals of the Second World War and Indian independence, for which Desai's Bengali grandfather and uncle fought and were imprisoned, they recalled mythic homelands that predated their twin partitions. Her father, 'removed, remote and distant', spoke of Bengal as 'a wonderful green and fruitful land', while her mother, with her 'rich, warm, vibrant personality', quoted German nursery rhymes and tales of Christmas in Berlin.

As Desai notes ironically: 'We had beautiful pictures of both these countries very little tainted by history or world events, which we had to learn as we grew up.' While her mother never went back to Germany, Desai visited Berlin as a young adult. 'I couldn't recognize a single thing; my mother hadn't known how totally it was destroyed and rebuilt after the war. I felt a complete stranger, devastated at finding the dream didn't exist at all.'

Asked why she is repeatedly drawn to 'failures and wrecks' as characters, Desai says: 'I remember being very lost at school, not being popular or successful. It was always a great struggle to belong. It was an immense relief to come home to books, to be alone. I had a great need for privacy that was unusual for a child but not at all for a writer.'

She began to write aged six. While she recalls the 'remote literary triumvirate' of R. K. Narayan, Raja Rao and Mulk Raj Anand, and knows of isolated women writers – Attia Hosein, Kamala Markandaya, Nayantara Sahgal – she says: 'When I started I suffered from a great sense of being utterly alone. I would have loved the society of other writers, or even readers. I was working in a vacuum, turning out words with no echo.' But she met Ruth Prawer Jhabvala, whose mother was also German, her father Polish, and who had married an Indian architect who lived down the road. 'I saw you could live in Old Delhi and write books. She was very encouraging – a woman with two small children – while I was a schoolgirl.'

Jhabvala, now in New York and still a friend, recalls the eighteen-year-old she would go swimming with as 'absolutely beautiful, very quiet, tremendously well read and sensitive, and self-contained; she had a halo of perfection around her. I see Anita's writing, which is very exquisite and beautiful, as a reflection of her.'

Desai, who read English at Delhi University, met her husband Ashvin Desai, a businessman, at nineteen and married at twenty, moving to Bombay and bringing up two sons and two daughters. She wrote in term-time and put away her manuscripts in the school holidays. 'It was a very domestic life,' she says, and it remained so until her fifties, when she began to teach abroad. Jhabvala says: 'Her mother was a very cultured lady who encouraged her, but when Anita moved to Calcutta and Bombay, she was surrounded by more conventional social circles, where they tell you "writing is such a nice hobby".'

Desai has been compared to European women writers of the nineteenth or early twentieth century, hankering for a room of one's own. 'People are very threatened by the idea that you go away and in secrecy and silence do something mysterious,' she says. 'I don't think I felt like a writer till I first came to England, where people had read my books.' While family friends recall Ashvin as a proud and supportive husband, Desai insists: 'My writing career was entirely subservient to being a wife and a mother. I lived the life of the typical Indian housewife; wrote in the gaps and hid it away, kept it secret.'

Her early novels mirror tensions in her own life as a woman and a writer. Maya in *Cry, the Peacock* is driven to suicide after killing her stolidly insensitive husband by pushing him off a roof. In *Where Shall We Go This Summer?* Sita retreats into the past when she finds herself pregnant with her fifth child. Desai has long rejected these despairing narratives as sharing traits of the 'slipper-dragging' genre of tearful women's fiction. 'They were written by a different person; they're so overwrought I couldn't bear to look at them now.' She is equally harsh about her third novel, *Bye-Bye Blackbird*, set among Indians in Britain, which she calls 'out-of-date and irrelevant'.

The tensions between women and society also run through *Fire on the Mountain*, where the elderly recluse Nanda Kaul vainly seeks solitude in the hills after a lifetime of child-rearing, and *Clear Light of Day*, where the unmarried college lecturer Bim wrestles with family bonds while resenting her brother and sister who have both moved away. Desai's novels have been attacked for emphasizing the constriction of women's lives. Hussein says: 'They explore the position of the isolated within the family, especially an intelligent, sensitive woman lamenting lost creativity, or counting the cost of being creative. It might be held against her by feminists that her characters are constrained. But how many women do break out?'

Desai was taken to task for a 1990 essay in the *Times Literary Supplement* entitled 'A Secret Connivance', in which she claimed Indian women connived at their captivity by aspiring to the mythic role models of subservient Hindu goddesses that 'keep her bemused, bound hand and foot'. It was a polemical over-statement. Yet she insists: 'Indian women have made enormous strides into the professions and taking control of their lives since my generation and my mother's, but they have a long way to go.' Of the single working women in her books, she says: 'They have all paid a price; they're not, according to some, living happy lives. There's always a choice one makes.'

While her new novel is surely her most overt attack on the traditional limits placed on women in India, it hints at how US women, with their sun beds and supermarkets, are also in thrall to prescribed roles. 'Working women in America are weighed down and circumscribed by the ideal of the feminine that's not that different from India,' says Desai. 'The universal mother figure is idealized by every religion and every country.'

Desai, perhaps the first to acclaim *Midnight's Children* as a 'masterpiece', is often contrasted with Rushdie. Yet it would be wrong to set her books in a staid English tradition. 'My reading was so European: Woolf, D. H. Lawrence, Proust, Camus, Dostoyevsky, Chekhov – it had so little to do with the life I led,' she says. 'So I worked hard to bend the English language to bring in the sounds and tempo and rhythms of spoken languages around me, which are part of my world too. With English you can, it's so flexible and elastic, but you have to sharpen your ears, and not depend so much on reading.' She is also aware of how much of Indian life eludes that language. 'You're always having to select, to acknowledge your limits; you write only about those parts of life that have been affected by English.'

Hussein, who feels Desai's experiments with language have not been duly credited, says: 'Anita's work belongs to two traditions. Her sensibility is deeply rooted in Delhi's mixed culture, but she appropriated the language of English modernism and Woolf, as well as Japanese, Russian, and existentialist literature, to convey something very Indian. Now there's a multiplicity of voices, but then she was working pretty much alone.' As for her 'outsider's' eye, he adds: 'There's a whole class of people educated in a language that wasn't their parents', who see with detachment: there's always a process of translation going on.'

Desai was ten when India became independent. 'As a little girl I lived in a Delhi made up of three communities. The Hindu was dominant, but the skyline was full of Islamic monuments. Urdu literature was in the air – poetry recited, ghazals sung – and the British still had a presence, affecting me through school and the books I read. When I was ten these were all packed up and shipped away, gone. We were left with a new country to build. That sense of loss and drama have pursued me ever since.'

As have the Hindu-Muslim riots of partition. 'They're my most vivid memories of childhood, and the most violent and nightmarish. The British hauled down the flag and disappeared, and practically the whole Muslim population disappeared too, and were replaced with Punjabi refugees, who were foreign to us. Delhi has never been the same since.'

Clear Light of Day, Desai's masterpiece of familial attachments, and avowedly her most autobiographical novel, evokes this transition through an Anglicized family in Old Delhi in the forties. While Raja has fallen in love with a Muslim woman and left for Pakistan, and Tara has gone to the West as a diplomat's wife, the English lecturer Bim remains with her child-like brother Baba in a riot-haunted Delhi amid Chekhovian atrophy and decay. 'Perhaps I fused my sisters, both working women, one married, the other not, into one character, Bim,' says Desai. 'But what's mostly autobiographical is the atmosphere of that household and that house.'

In Custody is set in the sixties, the tragicomic tale of a small-town Hindi lecturer, Deven, sent to interview the legendary Urdu poet Nur. It also evokes a decaying culture, as Deven finds a drunken, gluttonous Nur surrounded by sycophants in the slums to which Urdu, the language of the Mughal court, has been relegated since partition. Desai describes this study of solitude and friendship, obsession and delusion, as 'the big break for me, moving to a male world I didn't know much about. I wanted to step out of the interior I'd been living in, a female, almost a purdah, world that was so enclosed and oppressive even to me; I wanted a bigger world.'

Yet even keeping the women in the novel peripheral makes a feminist point that Desai agrees was obscured in Ismail Merchant's 1994 film, for which she wrote the screenplay. 'I was thrilled to see it in Urdu,' says Desai of Shahrukh Husain's translation. 'But it's Ismail's vision. I saw it as a gritty, black and white, neo-realist film; the darkness and shadows became lost in all that technicolour beauty.'

By showing how Hindi has swallowed up other languages in a new imperialism, *In Custody* was prescient about the Hindu nationalist drive to extinguish Islamic history, razing mosques to resurrect temples. 'I'm not trying to idealize or romanticize the Mughal past,' the author says. 'There's a lot that's decadent, as well as beautiful. But it's wrong to pretend it never existed. It's reinventing history books in order to obliterate traces of the past that I want to make a stand against.'

Desai, who has admonished V. S. Naipaul for 'dangerously feeding the Hindu fundamentalist agenda', drew on communal violence against Muslims in India to re-imagine 1930s Germany and *Kristallnacht* in *Baumgartner's Bombay*, her first novel written outside India. 'I could only understand what was happening in Nazi Germany by recalling 1947,' she says.

Her most solitary character, the German-Jewish Hugo Baumgartner, is killed by a young German drifter whom he shelters. Desai, who remembers a tension in her home during the war, her mother (who was not Jewish) 'waiting for news that never came', uses her mother's German nursery rhymes to paint Baumgartner's idealized *Heimat*. But reality breaks into the myth: the curiously stilted letters from his mother are found to have been sent from Dachau. 'Myth is a romanticization of history, and Germany showed us what a dangerous thing it is,' Desai says. 'I don't know if we're not witnessing that in India now.'

The novel was also a response to the British vogue for the Raj. 'I wanted to write a totally non-exotic book about India, and Europeans in India, and to see the Raj from a different point of view than the British,' she says. Ironically, Baumgartner is interned in India along with non-Jewish Germans during the war. But the author disagrees with critics who object to his passivity. 'As a novelist you can only view history through individuals. But I see history as something that happens in spite of individuals; it gathers momentum and sweeps them away. What they choose to pick up when they flee, what they lose and what they take – that makes history real to me.'

Journey to Ithaca further explores foreigners' encounters with India through Matteo, an Italian ascetic and disciple of 'The Mother', and his more material-istic German wife, Sophie, who prefers sybaritic Goa to the ashram. Spanning India, Paris, Cairo, Venice and New York in the twenties of Sri Aurobindo – the Indian yogi and philosopher – and the seventies of Hermann Hesse-inspired hippies, it stages a conflict between scepticism and belief, but ends ambigu-ously.

Desai was interested in 'the non-political colonial view of India, of mystery, exoticism, the spiritual fascination. Indians take it for granted; it's as down-to-earth as eating and drinking. But Europeans approach it on a different level, so there's constant misunderstanding and distortion.' Yet she rejects the 'mediat-ing' role sometimes ascribed to her, insisting she has no answers. 'To me, fiction is exploring; if you felt you'd arrived, you'd give up.'

While Desai has expanded her fictional territory with each book, *Fasting, Feasting*'s return to the Indian family hearth has surprised even its author. 'I swore I'd never write about the past again, that sense of always being within closed walls,' she says. 'I was determined to open the door and break free – but it's the first thing I felt the urge to write in America. I've gone back to my roots; but then one doesn't really leave them behind. I could write about them for ever.'

While she still shares a house in Old Delhi with her husband, Desai spends most of the year abroad without him, mainly in the USA, where three of her children live. One of them, her youngest daughter, Kiran, has followed her mother into print. With her first novel, *Hullaballoo in the Guava Orchard*, pub-lished last year, Rushdie heralded 'the first dynasty of modern Indian fiction'. Desai is more than glad of the company: 'It's been wonderful that my daughter understands the writer's life, and we share it.' She adds: 'More and more, my closest friends are ones like me who move from country to country and don't feel they belong anywhere.'

Yet for many, Desai's finest and toughest fiction remains that set in India, a subject she still finds 'utterly overwhelming', and from which she withdraws, the better to shape it. 'I'm aware that I try to impose order on the chaos, espe-cially of Indian life,' she says. 'One does retreat from the noise and clamour into solitude. But India is always on the verge of toppling into violence, which gives it an immense tension. Just as if I wrote about powerful women who were in control, it wouldn't be truthful – if I wrote about a calm and benevolent place I wouldn't be telling the truth.'

19 June 1999

Life at a glance

ANITA DESAI (NÉE MAZUMDAR)

Born: 24 June 1937, Mussoorie, India.

Education: Queen Mary's mission school, Delhi; 1957 BA Hons English literature, Miranda House, Delhi University.

Married: Ashvin Desai (1958; two sons, two daughters).

Select bibliography: *Cry, the Peacock* (1963); *Voices in the City* (1965); *Bye-Bye Blackbird* (1968); *Where Shall We Go This Summer?* (1975); *Fire on the Mountain* (1977); *Games at Twilight* (stories) (1978); *Clear Light of Day* (1980); *In Custody* (1984) (screenplay, 1994); *Baumgartner's Bombay* (1988); *Journey to Ithaca* (1995); *Fasting, Feasting* (1999).

Awards: Winifred Holtby prize for *Fire on the Mountain* (1978); Sahitya Academy award (1979); *Guardian* children's fiction prize for *The Village by the Sea* (1982); Booker short-listed for *Clear Light of Day* (1980), *In Custody* (1984) and *Fasting, Feasting* (1999).

CARLOS FUENTES
The Latin master

Maya Jaggi

Mexico's greatest novelist is bemused, at seventy-two, to find he can still cause a scandal. According to the Mexican labour minister, Carlos Abascal, Carlos Fuentes' gothic novella *Aura*, first published in 1962, is corrupting to young women. Ridiculous though many in the Mexican cabinet find the complaint, it led to a woman being sacked for teaching the book at the convent school attended by the minister's teenage daughter in Mexico City.

'Abascal objects to a scene in which a couple make love under a crucifix,' Fuentes scoffs. 'But in Mexico most couples do that; there's always a crucifix above the bed. What's so shocking about that?' Though incensed by the sacking, he and Gabriel García Márquez – a close friend and fellow resident of Mexico City, whose fiction was also impugned by Abascal – have found reason to gloat. Sales of the offending works have rocketed. 'I'm willing to cede 10 per cent of my royalties to Minister Abascal,' Fuentes grins to an audience in downtown Los Angeles. 'He's the best literary agent I've ever had.'

He is in California to give a reading that is billed as being in English. But Spanish inexorably takes over, despite weak protests from a handful of outnumbered Anglophones. Though the multilingual author and one-time diplomat translates urbanely for the few monoglots, the scene illustrates one of his favoured themes: the Latino cultural 'reconquest' of Mexican territory lost to the United States in the nineteenth century. His oeuvre of some twenty novels, short stories, plays, essays and journalism has probed not only the history and identity of Mexico, but its shifting relations with the superpower on its border.

Fuentes was a leading figure – some would say the catalyst – of Latin America's literary 'boom' of the 1960s and 70s, when its writers became popular both in neighbouring countries and in Europe and the US. Alongside the Colombian García Márquez, the Peruvian Mario Vargas Llosa, the Argentinian Julio Cortázar and the Chilean José Donoso, Fuentes was one of the first Latin American authors who could live by their work. García Márquez's Nobel prize in 1982, Fuentes has said, marked the ascendancy of a whole region's literature.

Fuentes was pivotal not only as an innovative novelist, but as a cosmopolitan who has spent his life on the move. The US writer William Styron, a close friend, sees him as 'uniquely well positioned' to offer an 'extraordinary gift: an understanding of the relationship between the US and Mexico, and by inference, between Latin America and the rest of the world'. According to Jason Wilson, professor of Latin American studies at University College London, Fuentes has been a 'bridge between Mexico's view of itself and outsiders' views', Mexicans having been hostile to such foreign portrayals as those of D. H. Lawrence or Graham Greene.

Married since 1973 to his second wife, Sylvia Lemus, a television presenter in

Mexico ('She interviewed me, and has gone on interviewing me for twenty-seven years'), Fuentes spends about half the year in Mexico City and half in Europe, where they have a flat in Earl's Court, London. For a month each year, he is in the US, where he is 'professor-at-large' at Brown University, Rhode Island. 'Our careers don't collide,' he says. 'Wherever I go, Sylvia can follow, because she always finds someone to interview for her show.'

His globetrotting and expansiveness have spawned public friendships with writers, film stars and politicians, from Buñuel (with whom he collaborated) to Bill Clinton. He has remained close to García Márquez and Vargas Llosa (despite his two friends' mutual antagonism and opposing politics). He has also counted among his friends Norman Mailer, Shirley MacLaine, Arthur Miller, Philip Roth, Alberto Moravia, Milan Kundera, J. K. Galbraith and Claire Bloom. Critics of his autobiographical essays, *Myself with Others* (1988), resented what they saw as name-dropping, while Angela Carter, who admired his novels, noted in them an 'inexplicable streak of vulgarity'. Yet Fuentes, who hails from a 'periphery', has had the confidence to put his own country and culture on the map.

His novel *The Years with Laura Díaz* is published next week in English translation. It views episodes of Mexico's twentieth-century history, with leaps to Civil War Spain and the McCarthyite US, as though in a panoramic mural by Diego Rivera. The artists Rivera and Frida Kahlo (for whose diaries Fuentes wrote a brilliant introduction in 1995) appear as characters in the novel, which Fuentes sees as a 'monument to the horrible twentieth century, and to the place of my country and of Latin America in that world of strife, paradox and brutality'.

In it, he wrote of the death of a talented young artist, in part, he says, to ward off the illness of his and Sylvia Lemus's only son. (He has a daughter, Cecilia, by his first wife, the Mexican film star Rita Macedo, and another daughter, Natasha, with Lemus.) Born a haemophiliac, Carlos Fuentes Lemus died aged twenty-five, three months after *The Years with Laura Díaz* was published in Spanish in 1999. 'He knew his life would be short, so he worked a lot through the night, painting and drawing, writing poems. It's incredible the quantity of work he did in his short life.' He published not only poems but photographs, and had exhibitions in Madrid and Barcelona. 'We became extremely close. I guided him into films and novels and poetry. He guided me to rock music, of which I knew nothing. He had a dry, more phlegmatic sense of humour than a Latin, exuberant way of being; he corrected some of my excesses. Without him, life has become very sad for me and my wife. But I feel that when I write is when I have my son close to me, almost inside me, as though we were writing and living together at those creative moments.'

Every book written is an act of exorcism, says Fuentes. 'But exorcism can turn to prophecy. All the evils of Mexico City I tried to exorcize in *Christopher Unborn* [1987] came true with a bonus: pollution, crime, corruption.' Laura Díaz's elder brother and son draw on Fuentes' own relatives. It is as though, he says, the novel is 'bracketed by the deaths of two people in my family: my uncle Carlos and my son Carlos'.

Fuentes was born in 1928 to Mexican parents in Panama City. His mother, Berta, was watching a silent movie of *La Bohème* when her waters broke. His diplomat father, Rafael, took his family across the Americas, from Quito to Montevideo, and later became Mexico's ambassador to Italy and Portugal. 'I had the good fortune of having a happy, closely knit family. In diplomatic service, you have to stay close because you're constantly changing countries, schools, friends, languages.'

Fuentes' uncle was a talented poet who died of typhoid aged twenty-one. 'He left this legacy: my father named me after him and pushed me towards reading and writing as a homage to his brother. He guided me the way I did my son.'

He spent formative years, in 1934–40, in Washington DC, during the New Deal. 'That meant democratic values. I admired [Franklin D.] Roosevelt as a great statesman. He solved the same problems of the depression, unemployment, the financial crash that gave rise to fascist dictatorships in Europe, but through democratic and humane means. I lived through that time in the US, and that put me squarely on the left ever since. It made me lament every time the US fell into reactionary policies, especially in Latin America.'

Although Fuentes lived outside Mexico until he was sixteen, he remembers a 'great sense of being Mexican'. At ten, he saw a film in Washington, *Man of Conquest*, about the US-Mexican wars. 'During the attack on the Alamo, I couldn't restrain my patriotism. I jumped on the seat, screaming "Viva Mexico – death to the gringo!"' His father bundled him out of the cinema. That year, 1938, his popularity at school plummeted when President Lázaro Cárdenas nationalized the oil wells. 'There were blazing headlines: "Mexico steals our oil", "Communists take over American property." Suddenly I became a dangerous ten-year-old Red.'

Carlos and his younger sister, Berta, spent the summers with their grandmothers, 'keeping alive the Spanish language and hearing stories'. His father's ancestors had come to the Gulf state of Veracruz from the Canary Islands, and his paternal grandmother set up a boarding house in Mexico City. His mother's mother, a school inspector who campaigned for literacy in the 1920s, was the daughter of a German immigrant who founded a coffee plantation in Mexico. Fuentes calls *The Years with Laura Díaz* a homage to these women. 'Contrary to the macho culture of Mexico, both my grandmothers were very brave young widows. I was always very close to these hard-working, intelligent women.'

The annual journey to Mexico was instructive in other ways. 'There were signs in Texas restaurants saying: "No Mexicans or dogs allowed." Waitresses would say: "Stop talking that dirty lingo." There was tremendous racism and prejudice against Mexicans – which there still is. All of this shaded my childhood and shaped my sense of Mexicanness.'

During the Second World War, the family moved to a Chile 'governed by the Popular Front of communists and radicals. That was a revelation: that a Latin American country could have advanced social policies and also great poets, like Pablo Neruda.' He went to an English school in Santiago, but when they moved to Argentina in 1944, the schools in Buenos Aires were 'dominated by an anti-Semitic, pro-Nazi minister. I said "I won't go."' His parents conceded. 'At age fifteen I spent the most marvellous year, discovering [Jorge Luis] Borges, the tango and women. I owe the Argentine dictatorships at least three favours.'

Fuentes recalls the moment when he decided to become a writer. 'It was in Zurich, having dinner on the lake, when I saw Thomas Mann having dinner next to me. I was twenty-one years old.' Although he studied international law in Geneva, Fuentes turned down a key job with the International Labour Organization (ILO). The man who took it, Miguel de la Madrid, later became Mexico's president, but Fuentes has no regrets. 'I knew I would have ended up with a life I didn't want. My life is the life of a writer.'

His first novel, *Where the Air is Clear* (1958), broke ground in its urban portrayal of a metropolis in the making, harking back to the Mexico City of his childhood – famous, ironically, for its translucent air. The Mexican writer Elena Poniatowska saw then a 'sophisticated and cosmopolitan young man, eager to prove that he owns the world', while José Donoso was impressed by a Mexican who 'spoke perfect English. He had read every novel...and seen every painting and every movie in every capital of the world.'

While that novel prefigured the Latin American literary boom, Fuentes is anxious to share credit. 'The boom was a collective experience. We would not have existed without our forefathers.' He cites the Cuban writer Alejo Carpentier, the Uruguayan Juan Carlos Onetti, the Guatemalan Miguel Angel Asturias and the Argentinian Jorge Luis Borges. He also claims precedents in poets such as Neruda and the Peruvian César Vallejo – 'great fashioners of language'. But his guiding lights were Cervantes ('obviously'), Faulkner and Balzac. 'Balzac travelled between documentary realism and stories of the fantastic with the greatest of ease. I've written ghost and fantastic stories, and others on society and politics. I don't feel any contradiction.'

Fuentes has been called 'the Balzac of Mexico'. But for Maarten van Delden, the author of *Carlos Fuentes, Mexico and Modernity* (1998), he is 'heir to the great European modernists – Joyce, Woolf, Proust. *The Death of Artemio Cruz* was one of the first Latin American novels to use stream of consciousness. But what he takes from them, he applies to Mexican history and identity. Mexico is always his great subject.'

In *The Death of Artemio Cruz* (1962) a dying man looks back on the revolution with which he rose to power and wealth, but whose ideals were corrupted and betrayed. Fuentes calls himself a child of the Mexican revolution of 1910–20, which he sees as a political failure but a cultural watershed, a 'baptism'. The revolution, he says, 'promised many things and failed in many of them – democracy, human rights. But through it, Mexico saw itself as it really was; not as a fake, French facade with a Prussian-style army, but as an enormous country, extremely poor and illiterate, that had a rough and tough face – the face of an Emiliano Zapata and a Pancho Villa. Seeing yourself in a mirror is what the revolution was all about. From that sprang modern painting, music, poetry, film, novels.'

Mirroring Mexico meant unmasking it. 'Like all of Latin America, Mexico after independence in 1821 turned its back on a triple heritage: on the Spanish heritage, because we were newly liberated colonies, and on our Indian and black heritages, because we considered them backward and barbaric. We looked towards France, England and the US, to become progressive democratic republics.' He adds: 'The Indian past was masked by the Spanish conquest. Then there was the European mask. Then we put on a North American mask, which we're still wearing.' From 'Quetzalcoatl to Pepsicoatl', as he once wrote. 'Maybe that's the real face of Mexico: masks one on top of another.'

His monumental novel *Terra Nostra* (1975) reclaimed a Spanish heritage for Latin America, but a plural one. He credits Borges with 'reminding us that Spain was also the repository of great Jewish and Muslim traditions throughout the Middle Ages'. In his non-fiction work *The Buried Mirror* (1992) and a BBC series of the same name, Fuentes warned against using the quincentenary of Columbus's 'discovery' of the Americas (also the subject of his novel

Christopher Unborn) to castigate Spain.

'The conquest was catastrophic for the Indian peoples of the Americas,' he says. 'But it wasn't sterile. We became mestizo nations, of mixed European and Indian blood, then black also: mulatto. We gained the gold of the Spanish language. And in Spanish America, even atheists are Catholics. So we are what we are because of the Iberian conquests, and I, for one, will not suffer the false Atlantic division. Neruda and Lorca are poets of the Spanish language; they belong to all – which is an advantage we have over English-speaking peoples.'

The Zapatista leader, Subcomandante Marcos, is known to admire Fuentes, who welcomed the 1994 uprising in Chiapas for reminding the country of its suppressed Indian self. 'For me, the problem is not the Zapatistas but the state of Chiapas: oligarchs owning and running and corrupting everything, protected by armed guards that go around murdering Indians,' he says.

In the 1950s, before he published his first novel and began to live by his writing, Fuentes had edited Mexican literary reviews while working for the ILO, the UN and the Mexican foreign ministry. In 1974, he became ambassador to Paris. But he resigned in 1977 over the appointment as Mexico's ambassador to Spain of former president Gustavo Díaz Ordaz, implicated in the Tlatelolco massacre of hundreds of protesting students in 1968, which overshadowed the Mexico Olympics. 'Mexico never recognized the Franco regime. But after thirty-five years of non-recognition, when Franco died we sent our own local Franco as ambassador,' Fuentes fumes. In his view, the revolution 'came with a compact. Governments said: "We'll give you social reform but not democracy. We'll have a political monopoly, the Institutional Revolutionary party, the PRI, to defend ourselves against the backlash of the Church, dispossessed landowners and the gringos." That compact lasted till 1968, when the real children of the revolution demanded the freedom, equality and revolutionary ideals in the streets. The result was murder, and from that moment the compact was broken.'

Jason Wilson, author of books on the Nobel prize-winning poet Octavio Paz – who served as Mexico's ambassador to India – says Fuentes vied with Paz as the 'daring, outspoken Mexican intellectual'. Though the two had been friends since they met in Paris in 1950, they had a public falling-out in the late 1980s, when Paz's magazine, *Vuelta*, printed a vituperative attack on Fuentes' work. They never spoke again, creating a schism among their disciples that was unhealed at Paz's death in 1998. 'He never called me again; it was up to him to do it.'

According to Julio Ortega, professor of Hispanic studies at Brown University and co-editor with Fuentes of *The Picador Book of Latin American Stories* (1998), 'everybody in Mexico was waiting for Fuentes to fill the vacuum of power at the top of the cultural pyramid after Paz's death. But he's immune to the Mexican rituals of power. His politics are free of ideology or party lines. He sometimes overreacts, but always as an independent political voice with an instinct for social justice.'

Fuentes backed Castro's Cuban revolution of 1959, and the Sandinista revolution in Nicaragua twenty years later. He found himself harassed by US officialdom. Invited by NBC in 1962 to debate with the Kennedy administration's undersecretary of state for Latin America, he was denied a visa. 'The pretext was that I was a card-carrying communist. I said it was untrue, "But I'm going to become one thanks to your stupid policies – you're going to make communists of us all in Latin America."' He was barred from the US for much of the 1960s, till a ship he was on docked in Puerto Rico.

'This John Wayne character tore up my landing card, saying I was forbidden in American territory. I said: "Puerto Rico isn't American, it's part of Latin America, so fuck yourself." They reckoned without Fuentes' connections. He enlisted Vargas Llosa, Norman Mailer and American PEN, the writers' association, in a campaign, joined by Senator William Fulbright, to get him exempted from the list barring suspected communists (including Iris Murdoch, García Márquez, Graham Greene, Dario Fo and Simone Signoret) from the US. Fuentes attacked US foreign policy, 'not in the back yard, but right here, in the front yard' – the US.

From the early 1970s, he held a series of professorships at US universities. At the height of the US-backed Contra war in Nicaragua, he slammed the Reagan administration in a Harvard commencement speech in 1983. 'I said: "You fools, you behave like Dr Jekyll at home and Mr Hyde in Latin America. You're making a big mistake."' Caspar Weinberger, Reagan's defence secretary, was in the front row. In 1987, Fuentes became Harvard's first Robert Kennedy professor of Latin American Studies. Of what he calls the 'United States of Amnesia', he says: 'It's a country with a short memory. It has to be constantly reminded of its vices and virtues.'

Styron sees Fuentes as immensely influential among US scholars, with a 'purposely ambiguous approach to the US. Because he knows the culture so well, he neither panders to it, nor is he promiscuously critical. He's not an unqualified detractor like so many Latin American leftwing intellectuals.'

His novel *The Old Gringo* (1985), which became a film starring Jane Fonda and Gregory Peck, explored the US-Mexican border as a real and symbolic frontier. He returned to it in *The Crystal Frontier* (1995), a novel in nine stories in which Latinos cross the Rio Grande only to become invisible (terrain covered in Ken Loach's new film, *Bread and Roses*). Despite the brutal economic realities of a land frontier where the First World abuts the Third, Fuentes relishes the 'silent reconquest' of the Mexican territories lost in 1848. 'In the US, thirty-five million people speak Spanish,' he says. 'Los Angeles is the second Spanish-speaking city in the world after Mexico City – and before Madrid or Buenos Aires. These people are bearers of culture.' He believes the Latino presence will reshape US politics. 'The US has become a multicultural nation, which makes it stronger, not weaker – though it has difficulty accepting the fact.'

His novel *Diana: The Goddess Who Hunts Alone* (1994) forayed into autobiography with a thinly veiled portrait of Jean Seberg, the actress who committed suicide in 1979. Fuentes had met her at a New Year's Eve party in 1969, as his first marriage was breaking up. He and Seberg had a 'passionate location romance'. 'We went off together to the wilds of Durango where she was filming a tequila Western,' he says. 'She was brilliant, intelligent, beautiful – but I knew it would only last the time of the filming; she was married and had a son. She was a very hurt person; she'd been yanked out of the Lutheran Midwest unprepared to cope with fame. I think it disturbed her emotionally. But I can only be grateful for those two months – very grateful.'

That and earlier portrayals of women in his novels have drawn feminist criticisms. One of Fuentes' translators, Margaret Sayers Peden, feels his work is steeped in a 'Latin culture in which women are whores or Madonnas'. Alicia Borinsky, professor of Latin American literature at Boston University, views Fuentes as 'squarely in a tradition that places men at the centre of history'. Yet she adds: 'It wasn't a conspiracy of the boom writers, but the cultural and social context.'

Fuentes has since praised a constellation of women writers in what he terms the 'boomerang' generation that followed his own. He also wrote *The Years with Laura Díaz* as a 'counterpoint' to *The Death of Artemio Cruz*. 'I always felt a little worm inside me: 'Now you need to write a novel with a woman protagonist.'

While Fuentes remains prolific, some feel he is repeating himself. Ilan Stavans, professor of Spanish studies at Amherst College, Massachusetts, says his 'early novels transformed Latin American literature; they mesmerized an entire readership with a new view of the novel and how to perceive Mexico through it. But he got stuck in a vision of history and literature that belongs to the sixties *nouveau roman*. He's a very fluid and dynamic man, but he's lost touch.'

Fuentes has champions, however, among a new generation of Latin American writers, the 'junior boom', as he calls it, of the past three years. Born in 1968, the Mexican novelist Ignacio Padilla says: 'Fuentes is like our grandfather; he's the best example that you can be both local and universal, read both as a portrait of Mexico and as an epic of the world looking for its own identity.' Fuentes sees President Vicente Fox Quesada, whose election last year ended seventy-one years of PRI rule, as 'a breath of fresh air. A new Mexican democracy is testing itself, warily but surely. The problems are daunting, but a big step has been taken.' Democracy is changing what he sees as the role of the Latin American intellectual in speaking for the voiceless. 'Civil society has grown stronger; there are cooperatives, the feminist movement, gay rights groups, a free press. So a writer may still speak out – but as a citizen.' Yet, he says, responsibility remains. 'To maintain the vigour of language and the imagination – that's a role the writer cannot renounce.'

5 May 2001

Life at a glance

CARLOS MANUEL FUENTES MACÍAS

Born: 11 November 1928, Panama City.

Education: Schools in Washington DC and Santiago de Chile; Universidad Nacional Autónoma de México, Mexico City; Institute of Higher International Studies, Geneva.

Married: Rita Macedo (1959–72; one daughter, Cecilia); Sylvia Lemus (1973; one daughter, Natasha; one son, Carlos – deceased).

Career: editor, *Revista Mexicana de Literatura* (1954–8); Mexican ambassador to France (1974–7); Simón Bolívar professor, Cambridge (1986); Robert Kennedy professor, Harvard (1987).

Select bibliography: *Where the Air is Clear* (1958); *The Death of Artemio Cruz* (1962); *Terra Nostra* (1975); *The Old Gringo* (1985); *Diana: The Goddess Who Hunts Alone* (1994); *El Instinto de Inez* (2001); *The Years with Laura Díaz* (2001).

Awards: Mexican national award for literature (1984); Cervantes prize (1987); Légion d'Honneur (1992).

SEAMUS HEANEY
Son of the soil

Nicholas Wroe

When Shelley described poets as the 'unacknowledged legislators of the world', it is not too fanciful to imagine he had someone like Seamus Heaney in mind. Heaney's 1995 Nobel prize citation praised not only the 'lyrical beauty' of his work, but also its 'ethical depth'. His subtle probings of three decades of 'life waste and spirit waste' in Northern Ireland have provided rare shafts of illumination into the gloomy complexities of the province, and his intelligence and humanity have seen him venerated all over the world.

Poet Laureate Andrew Motion says of Heaney's translation of the Anglo-Saxon poem *Beowulf* that he has 'made a masterpiece out of a masterpiece. It's very interesting how his own defined Irishness approaches something that is generally considered to be a foundation of specifically English poetry. But the poem has not been appropriated by him. There is an inclusiveness about his translation which is something much more big-hearted, just as one would expect from him.'

'He has a very prolific talent,' says James Fenton, who followed Heaney as Professor of Poetry at Oxford. 'I saw him and Ted Hughes give a reading at the end of his time at Oxford that was undoubtedly the best poetry reading I have ever been to. Seamus has a marvellous delivery and is a tremendously attractive personality.'

It seems that while Shelley's line may be strictly applicable to Heaney – he is indeed unacknowledged 'as a legislator' – there is no getting away from the fact that the one thing Heaney has never lacked is acknowledgement. His life can be seen as a pageant of recognition from the age of eleven, when he won a scholarship and was transported from the family farm in County Derry to a prestigious Catholic boarding school, right up until the Nobel prize. In-between he was head prefect, claimed a first at university for which he was awarded the medal for academic achievement, and published a rapturously received debut collection of poems that set the critical tone for his subsequent output. He was elected to the Oxford post in 1989 and is currently Ralph Waldo Emerson Poet in Residence at Harvard. When the Nobel came, nearly everyone was delighted, but few were actually surprised.

Heaney has lived most of his adult life and all of his career under conditions of the most rigorous critical scrutiny and expectation. It was Clive James who first noted in the early seventies, with a commendable prescience, that 'some people are going to start comparing him with Yeats'. Since then, both the comparison and his status as the leading poet of his generation have been taken as read as much by his critics as by his supporters. James's prophecy was actually fulfilled a few years later by the American poet Robert Lowell, who baldly declared in a review of Heaney's 1975 collection, *North*, that he was indeed, 'the greatest Irish poet since Yeats'.

The critic, poet, and fellow Northern Irishman, Tom Paulin, recalls the impact the Nobel prize had on Heaney. 'He did a lot of travelling and lecturing, as I think he must have felt he owed it to people, instead of going into hibernation. And that's entirely typical of his extraordinary civic dedication. But what was really impressive was that he managed to survive it and he kept on writing.'

The publication of his *Beowulf* translation is the first fruit of this post-Nobel work. Heaney had picked at the project for fifteen years before finally committing himself to it in 1996. His translation will inevitably become the definitive school and college text for a generation. Discussion of *Beowulf* has previously been almost exclusively conducted inside academia, with the long-running row over its place on the English syllabus occasionally breaking out in rashes of erudite rancour. But Heaney's translation has pushed it into the mainstream. Fenton predicts: 'It will be everyone's Christmas book of the year, certainly everyone's Christmas poetry book.'

But perhaps more fundamentally, Heaney's translation has raised a slew of questions about the nature of the work itself: issues of cultural identity and ownership, nationalism and language have all been stirred up. The Irish farm boy has re-fashioned the rock-solid cornerstone of English literature and in so doing has amended the literary architecture not only of the present, but also of the past.

'As the years have gone on I have became increasingly devoted to the figure of Caedmon, the first Anglo-Saxon poet,' says Heaney, sitting in the kitchen of his comfortable but unprepossessing Dublin home fifty yards from the sea. 'The myth of the beginning of English sacred poetry is that this guy Caedmon was a worker on a farm attached to the abbey at Whitby. But every time the harp was passed at the feast, Caedmon would contrive to find a way not to be there because he thought he was not very good at chanting or singing with the harp. So he went out to the cattle in the yard, and one night when he was outside working, an angel appeared and said: "Caedmon, sing me the creation." And he obeyed and began to sing the first English poem about creation.'

The agricultural comparison is both attractive and apt. Heaney has said that he's read so many times that he was born on a farm called Mossbawn, the first of nine children, that he's stopped believing it himself, but this is where the road to Stockholm began. It was a happy childhood. Many of the day-to-day activities of the farm were subsequently co-opted into the poetry, as were family members and the muddy Ulster landscape itself. Heaney went to the local school, which was attended by Protestants and Catholics, and while there the 1947 Northern Ireland Education Act was passed, giving vastly increased access to higher education for children of poorer families. He won a scholarship to board at St Columb's College, a clerical-run school in Derry city.

The school was a remarkable powerhouse of emerging Catholic ambition and has produced a generation of leading figures in all spheres of Irish public life. His contemporaries included fellow Nobel prizewinner John Hume, writer Seamus Deane, playwright Brian Friel and journalist Eamonn McCann. 'I was extremely unhappy for the first couple of years because I was homesick,' says Heaney, 'but by the end I fitted it like a glove. I was head prefect and I enjoyed it. One of my Elysian memories is going out after night prayers on to the college lawn in the summer and practising for sports; the smell of new grass and so on. I don't think we were conscious of an ambition for the future, but there probably was a sense that we were being pitched out of the nest. I was the first in my family taking that path, and I know Seamus Deane was the first in his family. We were all sort of forging the path.'

Eamonn McCann was also the first from his family to receive such an education, but he was a dayboy who lived in the Bogside. 'We regarded the boarders with some pity because this was the fifties and we were hanging round ice cream parlours with girls, smoking and listening to rock'n'roll while they were locked up with priests and not allowed newspapers or even comic books.' But, says McCann, 'Seamus performed his role as head prefect with gusto. He was quite the disciplinarian, but that's OK because it's not everyone who can say they've been boxed round the ear by a Nobel prizewinner. And it's not everyone who can say they've been kissed by a Nobel laureate either. I played the female lead to him in a play and we kissed to the whoops and cheers of a packed school hall. My big line to him was: "Darling, I could tell you anywhere by the way you kiss." We couldn't do rehearsals for laughing too much, but we did it on stage.'

Heaney left for Queen's University, Belfast, where he read English Literature. He wrote 'a little bit of poetry' and was a star student. When he gained a first, he was offered the opportunity to go to Oxford. 'But it all happened so quickly,' he says. 'There was no family precedent and the only expectation was that I would proceed to a job. But I suppose that brush with the invitation to Oxford just jacked up my sense of what was possible. A veil had been lifted slightly, trembled a little.'

Heaney then took a job teaching in an intermediate school and enrolled for a postgraduate course back at Queen's. He also began to write poetry in earnest. 'I started discovering a voice and discovering animations. It was a life-turning point. I think I really came alive to myself through poetry and young energy.'

The deeply moving poem 'Mid-Term Break', about the time he was called home from St Columb's after his four-year-old brother Christopher had been killed by a car, was written at this time, and poems were published in the *Belfast Telegraph* and the *Irish Times*. 'It was a magical transition to move from the speechless and needy and hopeful, although you are not quite sure what you are hopeful for. In yourself, you feel "Yeah, something happened there" and that is ratified by the world and the mystery of editors, and you move into a textual life as it were. And then the next confirmation is the actual publication of your book, where you read about yourself in the third person and your name is detached from you. I don't think anything ever equals the sense of change and gift that comes from young poetry.'

In one sense, he says, 'the Nobel is just another prize; it changes something but it doesn't change your being the way your first writing does. You usually have something of veteran status by the time it arrives and you should be able to handle it. But you can't handle that first sense that you have written something, except with joy and surprise and narcissism and yodelling.'

By this time Heaney was part of a set of young Belfast poets called the Group, assembled by Philip Hobsbaum, a lecturer at Queen's who had been taught by Leavis and was an admirer of Ted Hughes. Hobsbaum organized sessions of reading and discussion attended by Heaney, Derek Mahon, Michael Longley and James Simmons, among others.

'Admittedly I was the first of the gang to get published,' recalls Heaney, 'and there was a sense of the flutter around that, but I think Derek Mahon and Michael Longley would have been more securely established in their own minds as having a poetic call, so there wasn't any sense among us of a head. There was a sense of energy and difference, and, I suppose, competitiveness. But I guess between 1962, when I left the postgraduate school and started to teach, and 1965, when my book was accepted, a hell of a lot happened.' Three of his poems had been bought by Karl Miller for the *New Statesman*; he published a slim volume called *Eleven Poems*; and in 1965 he married teacher Marie Devlin.

'Digging', one of the poems chosen by Miller, opened Heaney's debut collection, *Death of a Naturalist*, published by Faber & Faber in 1966. It is still one of his most famous poems and, knowing what we know today of how his career progressed, it is a remarkably bold statement that has been utterly justified by time and achievement. In it he describes how naturally and expertly his father and his grandfather handled a spade, whether digging potatoes or peat, before bemoaning that 'I've no spade to follow men like them. / Between my finger and thumb / The squat pen rests. / I'll dig with that.'

Death of a Naturalist attracted astonishing reviews for a first collection. Christopher Ricks called it 'outstanding' in the *New Statesman* and Alan Ross said it was 'a book of enormous promise' in the *London Magazine*. Tom Paulin remembers reading the book at school. 'It was a big public event. This was his plenary work – it set everything going. The pastoral and nature poems carry all sorts of things that were opened out in later collections. He extended into public territory, into politics later, whereas it was all encoded in his first volumes.'

Heaney acknowledges the scale of his early success. 'Yeah, the stakes were raised. From the beginning, I felt myself under scrutiny in a special way because in those days Faber's was an elevation, it wasn't just a publisher. My book was accepted in 1965...As far as I was concerned, Faber was the home of Wallace Stevens, T. S. Eliot, Ezra Pound, W. H. Auden. They weren't human creatures, so being published by Faber's, I felt I was under scrutiny. It wasn't until I did *North* in 1975 that I really thought: "OK, that's fine, you've paid your way, now proceed."'

The years between 1965 and 1975 saw life in Northern Ireland transformed by the Troubles. Heaney has been criticized, by both sides, for being too detached from events on the ground, but in the late sixties, already a public figure, he was 'necessarily' involved in some of the marches. 'And then the interviewing began in earnest,' he says. 'All the journalists who arrived in Belfast would go to the young scribblers, so that sense of being called upon to represent was there. I think anybody that didn't feel that would have been pretty insensitive. But then the question is, what do you do with this access?'

James Fenton says it has been difficult for Heaney to manage this access and expectation to comment. 'He's been criticized a lot along the lines of "If you're not with us you're against us", but he has managed to rise above that to be true to a kind of nationalism which isn't corrupted by the Provos.'

Heaney concedes that 'things changed radically once the Provos started. That changed the safe moral high ground that the majority of Catholics occupied up to internment in 1971. And gradually, once the bombing started from the Republican side, it wrong-footed righteousness; victim culture couldn't promote itself so readily.'

Andrew Motion notes: 'On the whole, over here he gets a very warm welcome, but we don't quite see the range of responses he has to deal with in Ireland.'

Eamonn McCann explains, 'The Catholic middle class take great pride in him and, let's face it, if anyone won the war in Ireland over the last thirty years it is the Catholic middle class. There is no other section of the population whose position has so improved, and Seamus is their poet. His work is perceived to be rooted in the clammy soil of Northern Catholicism and these people used to be stained because they came from the bogs, and now he has fashioned from the bog a new image and new reputation which has fanned out around the world.' It's slightly different for the Republican community, which tends to be more urban, says McCann.

'But in Gerry Adams's awful, sentimental memoirs there was a scene when he was on the run, of course, sitting on this bus when the troops came looking around. He kept his head down in this book he was reading and the local pro-letariat silently protected him by not giving a flicker of recognition or interest in him. It's too perfect, but what other poet would he be reading but Seamus Heaney? So he is a bit of a talisman, but real Republicans, as opposed to posing Republican leaders, would regard him as being very stand-offish and not engaged.'

This apparent lack of engagement is equally criticized by those who feel he should be far more censorious of violence. The Belfast Catholic writer Robert McLiam Wilson poked fun at a Heaney-esque figure in his novel *Eureka Street*, and launched a blistering attack on him following the award of the Nobel prize. 'Those who would maintain that in writing about hedges and blackberries, Heaney has actually treated the manifestations of political violence in a different manner are entirely fraudulent. Anyone who has actually read Seamus Heaney's work can only conclude that, in the main, he has left out that unpoetic stuff, that very actual mess. Some of Heaney's adherents might claim that this is because he rises above the fray. To which one might profitably enquire why a writer would want to attempt such an ascension.'

In the early seventies, Heaney made the decision to leave Ulster for good. 'Ian Paisley was very vigorous in the late sixties – people forget that. There was a lot of sectarian energy there.' Heaney received death threats but they were only part of the reason he left. 'There was no sense of being specially selected. There were phone calls to everyone's house and you would have felt deprived if you hadn't got one. But, of course, there was tension and anxiety. But that was Belfast. Belfast is a very tense place at the best of times.'

The Heaneys moved to a cottage in Wicklow in 1972. 'In one way it was leaving and hiding in the country, but in another way you were exposing yourself to yourself. And also, as a couple, exposing ourselves to ourselves. I think we started again and I started again with a definite sense of dedication in a different way.'

He's never seriously considered moving back north. 'I am still at home in the North, it's just that a change occurred. I was more grown up in myself and I moved into a life that wasn't a given life, it was one that I invented and discovered. I always think of my 1979 book, *Field Work*, as a bonus of the change. It was an expression of an adult experience. Something was verified by the move and my home is here now.'

He has, he says, always had a sense of being an outsider. 'From the moment I started college, I was a slight stranger at home. I was the eldest, I was away from home. And living in Belfast, I felt on the edge, not alienated, just separated. Here there is a sense of being completely at eye-level with life.'

In the years after he moved south he truly became a superstar poet, and so his decision to object to his inclusion in Andrew Motion and Blake Morrison's 1982 *Penguin Book of Contemporary British Poetry* was particularly controversial. Heaney wrote a pamphlet which included the lines: 'Be advised, my passport's green / No glass of ours was ever raised / To toast the Queen.'

'I completely respect what he did,' says Motion now, 'but it does need a little effort to put it back into context. Our anthology came out at a time when people were crucially getting involved with these issues more or less for the first time in recent history, and in a sense I'm pleased for him that our anthology was a convenient peg for him to hang this argument on.'

James Fenton says that a lot of people will always think that Heaney is British. 'He was born in Northern Ireland and they think he belongs to us. In fact, whether he likes it or not, he is our leading poet. He has been taken to people's hearts, and if what defines the community is the language, he is in the tradition of English poetry.'

In the early eighties Heaney took up a teaching post in Harvard for one term a year, and it was his time in America that led to the *Beowulf* project. 'I was very deliberately listening to a more open-weave kind of writing, much more conversational. I read a lot of John Ashbery. It's the opposite of the European pattern for poetry, which is back to the echoing of the first deposits. He was more Dante and Disney together – very American. Anyway, I was asked to do *Beowulf* and I prescribed it to myself as a counter-course to keep some connection with the ground-base of my language and of the noises in myself.'

After seven or eight years of indecision, he says, the publisher decided to finally call it off. 'And it was very interesting – I didn't want to yield it up, so I just headed into it. Then in the October the Stockholm business struck, and that discombobulated me for a while. So I was very glad to have it as a kind of steady day job.'

Heaney is genuinely self-effacing about his award and hedges round the subject with phrases like 'the Stockholm business' and even the 'N word' rather than saying 'Nobel prize'. He was on holiday in Greece when it was announced. When he arrived back in Dublin, he was met as a national hero at the airport by the prime minister. Heaney now wears the mantle of Ireland's leading private citizen lightly. 'I wrote a piece for the 1994 ceasefire, when John Hume and Trimble got the prize, and I wrote something when the Belfast agreement was signed. That's all good citizen work. But I stay off talk shows, as I have no gift for that. I don't have many opinions. I just nod, "Yeah, yeah, yeah", and wait for something to really happen. The greatest thing is not to believe your own prophecies, and the guard against that is to have a set of fast and sceptical friends, where your language is always tested against the verity of vigilant intelligences. That's the best vaccination.'

As well as the *Beowulf*, he has translated the libretto of a Janacek song-cycle that will be staged in Dublin and London this autumn. But he says there is a sense of retrospect in his current work, 'rumination, chewing-the-cud poetry'.

It was Auden who claimed a poet's hope to be 'like some valley cheese / Local, but prized elsewhere'. It's a hope fulfilled by Heaney. He belongs to Ireland, Britain and the rest of the world. Like the other yard boy Caedmon, he was surprised by his poetic gift, but with his pen has dug deeper than he could with any spade.

9 October 1999

Life at a glance

SEAMUS HEANEY

Born: 13 April 1939.

Education: Anahorish School (1945–51); St Columb's College (1951–7); Queen's University, Belfast (1957–61); St Joseph's College of Education (1961–2).

Married: Marie Devlin (1965); three children: Michael, Christopher, Catherine Ann.

Career: Teacher at St Thomas Intermediate School (1962); teacher at St Joseph's College of Education (1963–6); lecturer at Queen's University, Belfast (1966–70); visiting professor at University of Berkeley, California (1970–71); head of English at Carysfoot College (1975–81); Professor at Harvard (1981–96).

Select bibliography: Non-ficiton: *Preoccupations*, essays and articles (1980); *Government of the Tongue*, essays (1988); *The Redress of Poetry*, lectures (1995); Poetry: *Death of a Naturalist* (1966); *Door into the Dark* (1969); *Wintering Out* (1972); *North* (1975); *Field Work* (1979); *Sweeney Astray* (1983); *Station Island* (1984); *Haw Lantern* (1987); *The Cure at Troy* (1990); *Seeing Things* (1991); *The Spirit Level* (1996); *Beowulf* (1999); *Electric Light* (2001).

Awards: Nobel Prize for literature (1995); Commandeur de l'Ordre des Arts et Lettres (1996); Whitbread book of the year award for *Beowulf* (2000).

P. D. JAMES
Murder, she wrote

Emma Brockes

Although she didn't publish her first novel until she was forty-two, P. D. James had been writing about the world since childhood. The young Phyllis discovered there were ways of making trivia meaningful. 'I commented on everything to myself,' she says. 'For example: "She got up in the morning, put on her slippers and went downstairs." I commented on life as it continued. It was one long story, of which I was at the heart.'

As she got older, her reflex narrating found more eventful territory. As a twenty-two-year-old Red Cross nurse during the Second World War, she attended a lecture in which a plucky volunteer was fed solution through a tube in her nose. 'I thought: "Now if I were writing a detective story, that would be a very good way of killing someone."' She had powers of dissociation, an inclination to study her own reaction to things. She knew from the start that she was a novelist.

Phyllis Dorothy White (James is her maiden name) is eighty and about to publish her seventeenth book, *Death in Holy Orders*, the twelfth to feature Commander Adam Dalgliesh. She lives in Holland Park and welcomes visitors with a gusty wrench of the door and a jubilant 'hello'.

Her demeanour – wide features, plain dress, a quickness to exclamation – has long been used to diminish her authority as one of Britain's most popular crime writers. 'The sweet little lady who now wears Agatha Christie's crown', is how one tabloid introduced her to readers after eight successful novels, and James is often referred to in terms similar to those adopted for the title of her 1972 bestseller, *An Unsuitable Job for a Woman* – someone who, by virtue of her appearance, is judged too mimsy for the butch world of her chosen profession. Two years ago, in a joint interview with Ruth Rendell, the writers were asked by a *Daily Telegraph* reporter 'how two respectable, middle-class ladies' could be involved in the 'sordid world of crime fiction'.

In her autobiography, *Time to be in Earnest*, James refers to herself as 'an elderly grandmother who writes traditional English detective fiction', although not, one senses, without a little irony.

In fact, the 'sweet little lady' of the cosseted middle classes had withstood two major encounters with mental illness, the first when her mother was hospitalized, the second when her husband, Connor, returned from the war irreversibly damaged. For thirty years, she had worked her way up the civil service. For ten years, she was a senior administrator in the forensic science service at the Home Office and the police and criminal law departments, harvesting details for her books while consolidating a substantial career.

Curiously, James identifies indolence as one of her chief shortcomings. She is very bad in the afternoons, she says and tasks that bore her, like letter-writing and paperwork, are only grudgingly and belatedly attended to. For the past ten years she has been helped in these labours by her assistant, Joyce. But for twenty-five years, she not only worked full-time, attended night school to qualify as a medical record-keeper and cared – albeit with the aid of her parents-in-law – for two daughters and an incapacitated husband, but also rose every morning at 6 a.m. and wrote for two hours before work, all of which she puts down to necessity. 'My most valuable trait is tenacity,' she says, 'but what got me where I am now is courage.'

It is for this reason that friends defend James as a novelist first, and as a writer of detective fiction second, an odd distinction necessitated by the general sniffiness towards crime writing, and the peculiar contempt reserved for its female practitioners. 'She is like the Dickens or the Trollope of the genre,' says Frances Fyfield, fellow crime writer. 'She is the weight, the ballast, and she has dragged detective fiction kicking and screaming into the twenty-first century.'

'People can see detective fiction as an easy way into getting published,' says Joan Smith, journalist and author. 'There are certain rules to be followed, a template, and that means much of it can be not very good. The fact is that P. D. James is a very good writer. Some detective fiction is OK to read on the plane, but doesn't give you anything to think about afterwards. She uses it to explore bigger themes.'

James's vehicle is Adam Dalgliesh, a chief inspector on his first outing in *Cover Her Face* (1962), now a commander at the Met aided by two detectives, Kate Miskin and Piers Tarrant, characters through whom James has tried to modernize her gentle depiction of the police force.

Dalgliesh is a frustrated poet, a graduate capable of the sort of introspection that, for the last three books, has been offset by the more modish preoccupations of Kate Miskin. For the purposes of balance, Miskin was brought up on a predominantly black council estate in south London after being abandoned by her mother.

'If I was starting now, I would almost certainly have a woman professional police officer [as the main character],' says James, 'and that would be perfectly logical. But when I began, in the late fifties, it was a very different world. Women in the police force mostly dealt with issues concerning women and children. I don't think they were even in the detective force, so I had no choice about sex.'

In keeping with the tradition of English crime fiction, she could have made her protagonist an amateur sleuth rather than a professional officer. The books she most admired, those by Dorothy L. Sayers, featured an amateur detective. But James was aiming for realism (one of her favourite compliments, she says, came from the head of a regional murder squad, who told her Dalgliesh was a 'good cop'), and she thought it would be better served by a professional officer. Borrowing the name Dalgliesh from her old English teacher, Miss Maisie Dalgliesh, she attached him to the Met, where she thought he would come across a wider range of investigations than a rural detective.

'I gave him the qualities I admire because I hoped he might be an enduring character and that being so, I must actually like him. I can't help thinking that logically, he would have been a musician. There's something about him that reminds me of my more musical friends. But I don't know enough about music to make this credible, whereas I do understand the poetic imagination, so I thought, all right, I'll make him a poet.'

He wasn't to be distracted by a family, so she killed off his wife in childbirth and had Dalgliesh throw himself into work as a way of escaping the loneliness. 'Dalgliesh is probably the most intelligent officer in modern detective fiction,' says Ruth Rendell, author of the Inspector Wexford novels and James's closest rival. 'He is the sort of person readers like to think the police might be like – sensitive and elegant, not elitist like Dorothy L. Sayers's Peter Wimsey. He is the sort of person you wouldn't mind being interviewed by.'

None the less, accusations of elitism have occasionally arisen. During a radio interview five years ago, James attempted to explain how contrast is at the root of good crime writing by arguing that middle-class murderers make better characters, because the contrast between their ugly deeds and their urbane environment has a more dramatic effect. This was seized on, in some quarters of the crime-writing world, as covert advancement of the theory that the middle classes are more capable of making moral choices than the lower.

One of the critical voices was Mark Timlin, creator of the fictional detective Nick Sharman, who, as a drug-using, university dropout, is as far from Dalgliesh as the dimensions of the genre will allow. 'Phyllis is talking a lot of nonsense,' he said in an interview at the time. He said that James's criminals were far removed from 'the reality on the streets of south London' and rounded on the Crime Writers Association as 'snobbish and stuffy', thanks largely to her and those like her.

Rendell leaps immediately to James's defence. 'She writes about all sections of the community – you don't have to be upper-class to feature in her books.' And this is true, although James's original premise ensures that her novels tend to be set in colleges and hospitals – environments in which most of the characters are highly educated. 'But she writes intelligently about crime,' says Fyfield. 'She was one of the first detective writers to put pain into crime fiction – compassion, real suffering.'

There is no emotional squeamishness in James's fiction. *Death in Holy Orders* is set in a theological college, and James doesn't flinch from dumping a body in the church or tackling, alongside the momentous occasion of Dalgliesh's first flirtation, mental illness, suicide and a gamut of ugly human emotions. Neither is she a prude. The novel includes sympathetic portrayals of an incestuous couple and, more controversially, a priest with a conviction for child abuse.

'For a detective story,' she insists, 'the contrast between respectability and planned brutality is of the essence. I think contrast does intensify horror. If you have appalling and violent events happening in a civilized place, it's a great deal more horrific. I think it was W. H. Auden who said: "The single body on the drawing-room floor is more horrific than the bullet-riddled body on Raymond Chandler's mean streets." And Auden felt that very strongly – that you want a contrast between order and hierarchy and apparent goodness and the horror of the deed.'

There is a difference, says James, between the public's interest in real-life crimes and the popularity of the detective fiction genre. 'With the detective story there is horror – I think one needs to make the murder realistic. But I think the main attraction isn't the horror, it's the puzzle, the bringing of order out of disorder.'

She is intensely interested in and repelled by violence, and has confessed to a disproportionate fear of intruders. 'I don't agree with Ruth Rendell that motivation is more interesting than the act of murder. The physical act of killing a human being has an awesome and horrible fascination. All that flesh to dispose of, all that blood to be washed away, so many lies to be told.' Which, for P. D. James, is where the story begins.

Phyllis James encountered no physical violence during her childhood, but there was enough emotional disturbance to leave her with the impression that the world was an unreliable place. She was born in Oxford in 1920, the eldest of three children each born eighteen months apart. Her father Sidney was an Inland Revenue official and remote from his children. Her mother Dorothy suffered from a mental illness that might be treatable at home today, but in the thirties confined her to hospital.

James says: 'In one sense, I was very lucky – I've always felt at home in the world. But yes, I did feel that in some ways it was a frightening place and those two things don't seem very easy to reconcile. I was a child of a not very happy marriage and therefore I think it was a childhood of some apprehension, living in a sense with fear, that things might erupt, that things might go wrong.' Her mother's illness, she says quietly, ensured that she grew up prematurely.

The insecurity is apparent still in James's lingering fear of violence, and more obscurely in her dislike of the distorting effects of great pressure. She will not accept money in advance of writing, since the burden of having to earn it back – even at this advanced stage in her reputation – will, she says, interfere with getting the job done. 'Suppose I took a huge advance for the next two books?' she has said. 'Will they be any good? Will the publishers like them? Will they wish they hadn't given me that huge amount?'

For years after becoming a published author, she continued to work full-time for the Home Office and to insist that she was not a 'professional' writer. Writing was never something she did under duress, but because she chose to.

It was clear from the beginning, however, that writing was one of the few constants in her choppy existence. Her happiest childhood memories are of books. 'I read from a very early age. My mother used to buy us comics every week: the *Rainbow* and one called *Tiger Tim*. She read them to us when we were three or four. And then, one day, I suddenly discovered I could read it. I was probably helped by the pictures. But I remember that moment of thinking: "I don't have to wait for her! I can read it myself!"'

It was a moment paralleled forty years later when she heard that her first novel had been accepted by Faber. 'It was certainly one of the great moments of my life,' she says. 'I remember dancing for joy.'

Her education was short: she left school at sixteen, armed with a thorough knowledge of Shakespeare and the Bible, which for the purposes of becoming a writer she found quite adequate. She is scandalized that today's school curriculum pays such scant attention to the Bible. 'This is so much part of our history and our literature that one would suppose that the King James Bible would be a set book. One was brought up listening to some of the most wonderful English prose. The cadences stayed with me. It's amazing that we can so neglect it.'

In retrospect, James thinks that had the money had been available, she would have liked to go to university and become a barrister. As for the police force, she would have found the administration irksome, but reckons she has a talent for sniffing out the truth. 'I imagine, without being conceited, that I would have been a good detective for two reasons: people do tend to tell me things, quite astonishing things sometimes, often on quite short acquaintance. And I do seem to have an idea when people are lying.'

In the end, however, the career she took up fed as much into her writing as she would have got from anywhere (the nursing demonstration with the tube was used to dispatch a character in her fourth book, *Shroud for a Nightingale*). In 1949, James moved to London and joined the NHS, where she was responsible for the administration of psychiatric outpatients (details were used in *A Mind to Murder*, 1963).

She stayed in the civil service for thirty years, accruing enough qualifications to enter the Home Office in 1968 and work first as an administrator for the forensic science service (*Death of an Expert Witness*, 1977), and then in the criminal law department. 'I couldn't bear not to be a success at the job. I am ambitious. Inevitably, I qualified myself for promotion. Whether it's a matter of personal pride, if I'm doing it, I want to succeed at it.' Knowing of her desire to write, her mother suggested she turn the experiences of her first job into 'a cheerful book about all these lovely people in hospital, where a nice nurse falls in love with a lovely doctor'. James suspects that her mother always knew that 'within the first chapter there'd be a dead body in the sluice room and the nice nurse would probably have done it'.

Through her twenties and early thirties, James waited for a convenient moment to begin her writing career, but none came. Her life at home in London was not easy. Connor Bantry White was an Anglo-Irish doctor whom she had married at twenty-one, after meeting him at the Festival Theatre in Cambridge. They had three happy years together before he went off to war with the Royal Army Medical Corps and returned with his mental health broken. Their two daughters, Clare and Jane, who went on to become a midwife and a teacher, were largely cared for by James's parents-in-law at their home in Ilford, Essex. Connor White was admitted to hospital for psychiatric treatment, where he adopted the name Ted and played eccentric games of football with the other patients. It was not unknown for the goalkeeper, distracted by voices in his head, to stand immobile while the ball shot past into the net.

'One suffers with the patient and for oneself,' writes James of her husband's illness, in her autobiography. 'Another human being who was once a beloved companion can become not only a stranger, but occasionally a malevolent stranger.' After years in and out of psychiatric hospitals, Connor died at home in 1964, aged forty-four.

During this time, it occurred to James that a convenient moment to start her writing career would never present itself and that if she didn't hurry, she would wind up 'unfulfilled as a human being'. At thirty-five, she began her early morning regime. Detective fiction was an obvious choice, since it reflected her own interests and, she thought, had a good chance of being published. 'It's a kind of instinct, really,' she says. 'I read a lot of classical detective stories when I was a girl – it was my light reading. So to an extent, it seemed to come about naturally. The novel is a way in which the writer's own enthusiasms, interests, compulsions, maybe even neuroses, are rearranged in a form that he or she hopes will be compelling and attractive to the reader.'

There were two principles on which James was immovable: that the intricacy of a plot could never make up for poor writing ('I find with my own reading, that it doesn't matter how exciting a book is: if it's badly written one just can't be bothered with it'); and that an author must always write with the reader in mind, and not the publisher or the book market.

James talks about this with a sort of belligerent modesty. 'At the end of a book, I want to feel "Well that's as good as I can do – not as good, perhaps, as other people can do – but it's as good as I can do." There are thousands of people who do like, for their recreational reading, a classical detective story, and I think they are entitled to have one which is also a good novel and well written. Those are the people I write for. They don't want me to adapt to what I think is the popular market. They want a good novel, honestly written and I think they are jolly well entitled to it.'

'Some modern detective fiction can be very didactic, used as a vehicle for a lecture,' says Joan Smith. 'But James never does that to her readers. The story comes first.'

After experimenting with Phyllis James and Phyllis D. James, P. D. James was chosen because she thought it would look enigmatic on a book spine. It didn't occur to her that she would be mistaken for a male author, and when someone pointed it out, she did not see it as a particular advantage. It is rare, she believes, for readers to reject a book because they dislike the sex of the author, especially in crime fiction.

Before writing, she constructed a chart to keep track of who was doing what, where and with whom, planning and structure; this took a whole year. After five years of early mornings, she sent an agent *Cover Her Face*, a detective story in which Adam Dalgliesh investigates the murder of Sally Jupp, a parlourmaid found dead in mysterious circumstances on the day after the church fête.

James finds the book dated now, confined to the cosy, domestic setting of an English village in the shadow of its Elizabethan manor, that puts it very much in the Agatha Christie mould. In the forty years since, her novels have had to keep pace with great advancements in modern policing. DNA testing has caused her some trouble, since it leaves no room for doubt and could solve a crime in the first chapter. In *Death in Holy Orders*, it is introduced into the storyline only at the last minute, after more traditional policing has been exhausted. The book also contains references to the Macpherson report into racism and the latest policing methods. It is important to her to remain contemporary.

Cover Her Face was a critical success, but it was *The Black Tower* (1975), in which Adam Dalgliesh, grown disillusioned with the force, investigates the death of a friend at a care home in Dorset, that Kingsley Amis called 'almost Iris

Murdoch with murder in it'. Financially, the breakthrough was *Innocent Blood* (1980), one of the few novels not to feature Dalgliesh, in which an adopted eighteen-year-old girl discovers the identity of her murderous true parents. The paperback rights went for £380,000, the film rights for £145,000, which was more than she had earned in ten years at the Home Office. She happily retired.

'I started out as more of a cult writer. The one that broke through here was *Shroud for a Nightingale*. Then the huge international bestseller was *Innocent Blood*. At the beginning of the week I was relatively poor and at the end of the week I wasn't.'

Did they make an enormous fuss of her at the Home Office? James laughs. 'No dear, the Home Office doesn't make a fuss. Just occasionally people would come up at Christmas and say: "We want to give the Home Secretary one of your books, would you mind signing it?" Otherwise, no. I was Mrs White there, you see. They knew I was a writer, but there was a general feeling that you don't encourage people in hubris. It was very funny really.'

It was while writing the opening scenes of *Devices and Desires*, her twelfth book, that James had the most powerful sense of her own duality, of being someone who both experienced things and stood aside and watched them, a self-consciousness that she believes might only be lost during extreme agony or the death of a loved one. It is the closest she comes to delineating the process of her writing: 'A girl is on a lonely road and begins to remember that there's a psychopathic serial murderer loose. And we know she's going to be killed, because the book opens with a reference to her as the fifth victim.

'It's a terrifying opening. Now when I was writing it, I was, of course, that girl. But with another part of my mind I was thinking, well, I wonder if I ought to have a moon, or whether that's going a bit far? What have we got on each side of the road? We must have lots of bushes so you can feel that people might be lurking. And I think I'll have a car coming past, because that will seem reassuring, but obviously, it goes past at speed and there's no help there. You think: "How do I increase the menace?" You feel the emotion of the girl and at the same time wonder how best it can be conveyed.'

James does not know if there is another book in her. She always waits for an idea to possess her, usually inspired by a particular location. Her great regret is that she didn't start writing sooner, although if *Death in Holy Orders* turns out to be her last book, she won't complain. With the promise of a relationship between Dalgliesh and Emma Lavenham, a Cambridge academic, hanging in the air, however, she is pretty sure there is another one coming. 'I want it to be quite subtle; I don't want to have buttocks heaving everywhere. They are both private people.'

If another book doesn't arrive, she has plenty to occupy her. Afternoon indolence notwithstanding, there is a briskness to P. D. James that shows itself in her enthusiasm for public duty: she has served as a governor of the BBC, a board member of the British Council and is president of the Society of Authors. In 1991, she was created a Tory life peer, Baroness James of Holland Park. The pick-your-ideas-up, anti-dogma of old-style Conservatism has always appealed, and she is a regular guest speaker at local party level. She has told her daughters that in the event of a debilitating illness, she doesn't want to linger but would prefer to be 'put out of my misery'. In April, she flies to Texas for a book tour. 'It has been a very busy life,' she says, with a touch of defiance. 'But a busy life by compulsion.'

3 March 2001

Life at a glance

PHYLLIS DOROTHY WHITE, BARONESS JAMES OF HOLLAND PARK

Born: 3 August 1920, Oxford.

Education: Cambridge Girls' High School.

Married: Connor Bantry White (1941, died 1964); two daughters: Jane, Clare.

Career: Administrator, NHS (1949–68); Principal, Home Office police department (1968–72); criminal policy department (1972–9).

Select bibliography: *Cover Her Face* (1962); *A Mind to Murder* (1963); *Unnatural Causes* (1967); *Shroud for a Nightingale* (1971); *The Maul and the Pear Tree* (with T. A. Critchley) (1971); *An Unsuitable Job for a Woman* (1972); *The Black Tower* (1975); *Death of an Expert Witness* (1977); *Innocent Blood* (1980); *The Skull Beneath the Skin* (1982); *A Taste for Death* (1986); *Devices and Desires* (1989); *The Children of Men* (1992); *Original Sin* (1994); *A Certain Justice* (1997); *Time to be in Earnest* (autobiography, 1999); *Death in Holy Orders* (2001).

Honours: Life peer, 1991.

ELMORE LEONARD

Get Elmore

Lawrence Donegan

In the Squad Seven room at 1300 Beaubein beats the dark heart of American crime. The fifth-floor office in downtown Detroit, with its battered green metal desks and wooden school chairs, is where the city's 'whodunnit?' murders are investigated. 'All we start with is a body,' drawls Monica Childs, a hard-boiled homicide detective in a yolk-coloured trouser suit. Across the desk, a weary-looking male detective is flicking through a pile of Polaroids. 'Look at this fuckin' freak,' he says, holding up a picture of a twenty-stone male murder suspect dressed in a black leather mini-skirt and a red cashmere sweater with two medium-sized coconuts stuffed down the front. 'Is that supposed to be a fuckin' disguise?' The two cops are competing for attention. Monica points at two white cardboard boxes over by the office computer. 'That's part of the Purple Gang files [the Purple Gang was a Mafia mob which terrorized Detroit in the forties and fifties]. The smaller box is Rico Jones's. He killed five people, four of 'em children. Jumped out the window of the interrogation room next door.' Did he die? 'Walks better than you. Went feet first. That's when we knew he was trying to escape. Head first? Now that would've been suicide.' Fans of Elmore Leonard will recognize such a scene: the undercurrent of violence, the humour, the hip dialogue. The Detroit-based crime writer spent three months hanging out in the Squad Seven room in 1979 on assignment for the *Detroit News*. The resulting piece, 'Impressions of Murder', is a brilliant exposé of police methods and attitudes and of the mayhem that earned Detroit the title of America's capital of crime.

The piece provided Leonard with the raw material for his 1980 novel, *City Primeval: High Noon in Detroit*, the story of a detective, Raymond Cruz, who sets out to nail a psychopath called Clement Mansell for the murder of a crooked Motown judge. It is his best novel to date. Like all of his books, it is written in 'scenes', each told from the point of view of the different characters. No one is ever 'telling', they are always 'doing'. There is no message, no explaining and no metaphysics. The dialogue is ligature tight and alternates between brutal and funny.

City Primeval revolves around Mansell's efforts to steal a bag of money from a rich Albanian boyfriend of a girl he's screwing but – another feature of Leonard's novels – the plot is only called upon in the most dire of narrative emergencies. The fact is, no one reads Leonard's books for the plots. You read them because they make you laugh, because they describe a world of psychos, drug-crazed sickos, loan sharks, bent judges, and go-go dancers that you'd like to visit (but only in the comfort of your armchair), because the good guys are flawed and the bad guys have redeeming qualities.

'I think he is an excellent writer. He makes everything so real. Areas, locations, crimes. He ain't exaggerating, y'know,' says Monica Childs. 'The only problem is he doesn't really ever have women detectives in his books.' With that last statement, she gains entry to a very exclusive club: those who have a critical word to say about Elmore Leonard. By contrast, the list of his admirers stretches across all of American society, including the Nobel laureate Saul Bellow, who is said to have several Leonards on his shelf. The venerable American political commentator George Will dishes out signed first editions of Leonard's books as Christmas presents.

Time magazine has described him as the 'Dickens of Detroit', suggesting that he is perhaps the closest there is to a 'national writer of America'. (This in a country which can boast Bellow, Updike, Mailer and Ford.) Our very own Martin Amis, when he was writing brilliant journalism rather than pastiche Elmore Leonard novels, once described the American as 'a literary genius who writes re-readable thrillers'.

Amis leads the army of literary luminaries who consider Leonard to be one of the best American writers of the twentieth century in any genre. 'Saul Bellow and I agreed that for an absolutely reliable and unstinting infusion of narrative pleasure in a prose purged of all false qualities, there is no one quite like Elmore Leonard...[his] prose makes Raymond Chandler look clumsy,' he said recently.

Meanwhile, the librarian at a prison in Connecticut wrote to Leonard that 'while you ain't caught on with the crack and cocaine heads, you have got a following amongst the heroin crowd'. And in a university somewhere in Florida, there is a gentleman professor writing a book about the 'patterns of imagery' in his books.

Leonard affects indifference to all this attention – 'Patterns of imagery? What's he talking about?' – but friends say he is quietly and rightly thrilled.

Last and most lucratively, Hollywood loves Elmore Leonard. To date, he has written thirty-five novels. All but two have been bought outright, optioned or turned into a movie. *Out of Sight*, a $60 million film starring George Clooney of his last but one book, is released in the US this month. ABC Television is about to begin showing a ten-part series of *Maximum Bob*, based on Leonard's novel about a skirt-chasing Florida judge. Quentin Tarantino has already made *Jackie Brown* (based on *Rum Punch*) and has bought the rights to three more Leonard books. The Coen brothers are currently writing the screenplay of *Cuba Libre*, Leonard's new novel, just published here and set in the Spanish-American war of the last century.

'Elmore has this ability to write books that seem like treatments for movies,' says Walter Mirisch, legendary producer of *The Magnificent Seven* and *West Side Story* and the proud possessor of the film rights for Leonard's novel *LaBrava*. 'That's why he's so popular here.' There is another reason: Barry Sonnenfeld's 1995 film version of Leonard's satire on Hollywood, *Get Shorty*, starring John Travolta, Danny DeVito and Gene Hackman, was a big critical success. It made over $200 million.

The 359-page manuscript of Leonard's latest (unpublished) work, *Be Cool*, has just thumped onto the desks of studio executives. The book tells the story of what happens when Chilli Palmer, the loan-shark-turned-movie-producer in *Get Shorty*, joins the music industry as the manager of a band fronted by a female singer recruited from a Spice Girls tribute group. (Yes, Leonard can name the Spice Girls; his favourite is Posh.) Those who have read the book describe it as his best and funniest. Negotiations with the studios have started, with the

Leonard manuscript cast as the object of desire. This time it is the bags of money that are doing the chasing: the figure being bandied around is $5 million plus.

'I don't want to get drawn into any of that,' says Leonard's literary agent, Michael Siegel, as he battles to swallow a smile. 'Hubris is our biggest enemy.' In the flesh, Elmore Leonard looks like the man who pulled a .45 on hubris and shot it stone-cold dead. He is cool in the burning Detroit sun, dressed in khaki shorts, a white Discus Athletic T-shirt and a pair of greying Reebok trainers that have caught the fashion wave second time round. The brown skin on his neck is beginning to hang a little, turkey fashion. The voice is a midrange, Midwestern drawl.

'These figures,' he says, lifting his hand to pluck fruit from an invisible tree. 'Nothing to do with reality.' As you might expect from such a stylish writer, studied cool is Leonard's stock demeanour. He is friendly and forever wandering off into his vast home in the northern suburbs of Detroit to search for dog-eared magazines that will piece together his early literary career. Telephone numbers of friends are helpfully faxed over, all of whom are delighted to assist. However, Leonard himself doesn't give much away. Read through cuttings of his interviews and it's clear he has planed down the story of his life and work. Anecdotes are recycled down the years (the prison librarian's letter made its first appearance in a 1991 BBC documentary). Fresh information has to be chiselled out.

Is it true that he failed the eyesight test for the paratroops? 'Yeah,' he replies with a 'how-d'you-know-about-that?' look.

Perhaps he no longer feels he needs to give too much away. Why should he? He's seventy-two, rich beyond any writer's dreams, and has Martin Amis licking his boots. Or perhaps it is because he is 'shy' and 'reserved'. Both adjectives are frequently used by friends to describe Leonard, along with 'droll', 'hysterically funny', 'loyal' and 'a very social person'. Everyone speaks in admiration about his Stakhanovite work ethic (nine to five, six/seven days a week, four pages a day, one book every year).

Then there is his ability to turn the mundane anecdote told over the dinner party table into racy prose. 'He's the greatest listener I've ever come across,' says Balthazar Korab, the renowned architectural photographer who turns up as a Hungarian anarchist in *Freaky Deaky*, just one of the many long-time Leonard buddies whose names are attached to characters in his novels. Peter, Leonard's eldest son, recalls an incident where a friend of his told Leonard a story about leaving his jacket in a restaurant and when he went back for it, the jacket was gone. 'Six months later the story turned up as the start of *Get Shorty*,' Peter laughs.

Leonard's sister, Margaret Maday, says he was 'a wonderful little boy, lively, intelligent, always interested in what was going on around him and always telling stories. I had a wonderful relationship with my brother. I used to read to him all the time.' It appears to have been a Waltons-esque existence. The two Leonard children were shielded from the worst effects of the Depression by their father's job as an executive with General Motors. The family lived in cities all over – Dallas, Oklahoma, Memphis – before finally settling in Detroit in 1934. Elmore was nine. He has a blown-up picture taken around that time showing him wearing an over-sized white cap and pointing his finger like a gun. 'That was around the time of Bonnie and Clyde, Pretty Boy Floyd and John Dillinger – I think that's where I got my interest in gangsters from,' he says.

He certainly didn't get it at the University of Detroit High School, a strict, Jesuit-run establishment in the northwest of the city where middle-class

Catholics sent their children. There, Leonard made more of an impression as an athlete than as an academic. 'He played quarter-back in the football team,' recalls schoolfriend Dan McCarthy. 'He was small, y'know, but good for his size. Tough. Didn't mind taking on fellas bigger than he was.'

Leonard was bright enough to be accepted for university, but the Second World War got in the way. Bad eyesight consigned him to the Construction Battalion – the SeaBees – as a store manager. He spent most of his time on a South Pacific island dishing out beer to combat troops. Back from the war, he enrolled at the University of Detroit, majoring in English. It was only then that he started to show some signs of literary promise. He entered a couple of short-story competitions, finishing in the top ten in one and second in the other. 'I only entered because the teacher said you would get an automatic "B" if you did.' He already had a job at a Detroit-based advertising agency called Campbell-Ewald when he graduated in 1950. By then, he'd decided he wanted to make his living from writing. 'I think discovering Ernest Hemingway was a big moment in Elmore's life,' says his long-time friend and attorney, Bill Martz. 'He loved the dialogue, y'know. He would take one of Hemingway's books and write his own story the way Hemingway might do it. Once he made his mind up about being a writer, he was very methodical about it, figuring out how he could break through, about what kind of writing would sell. He had a commercial approach to writing.' Leonard acknowledges the debt. 'Sure, I'd open *For Whom the Bell Tolls* anywhere and start reading for inspiration. I loved his work – the short dialogue, all that white space, his constructions, his use of participles. I realized that I didn't share his attitude. He took himself too seriously. I didn't.' Westerns were what sold in the early 1950s, so that was what Leonard wrote. His earliest attempts were rejected by the dime Western magazines. 'I decided I'd better stop making it up and find out what cowboys actually wore, what Apaches wore, what a canyon really looked like. I subscribed to the *Arizona Highways Magazine*. If I needed a canyon, there it was – it was like being there.' The drive for authenticity still plays a very important part in his fiction. He has his own full-time researcher, Greg Sutter, a 47-year-old gumshoe with the vocabulary of a Goodfella. Sutter is devoted in equal measure to his boss's writing and surf bands. He considers himself to have the world's number one job, hanging around on the fringe of seedy America. He has been to Cuba (for *Cuba Libre*), Atlantic City (for *Glitz*), Florida (*Riding the Rap* and *Out of Sight*). He set up home in Los Angeles last year to research *Be Cool*. 'Elmore wants everything in his books to be right. He wants a sense of realism about them,' Sutter says.

Leonard's first published work of fiction, a short story entitled 'Trail of the Apache', appeared in *Argosy* magazine in December 1951. Within days, he was contacted by an agent, and within a couple of months she had sold another five short stories to the pulp magazines. 'As fast as I could write 'em, she sold 'em.' He wrote his first novel every morning between 5 and 7 a.m. before going to work at Campbell-Ewald, where he wrote advertising copy for Chevy Trucks – 'a whole new approach to truck durability and ride!' It was not a happy time. 'It was hard to get passionate about a Chevy truck,' he says. 'But I had to stay at the company for seven years to get my profit share.' *The Bounty Hunters* was published in 1953. Four more novels and thirty short stories appeared over the next seven years. Two of the stories were made into movies. The first, *The Tall T*, starred Randolph Scott and premiered at the Broadway Capitol in downtown

Detroit. 'Eight of us went to the screening at this 2,500-seater theatre. There were about 60 people in all, most of them asleep or drunk,' says Dan McCarthy. 'Randolph Scott came on stage and said how delighted he was to be back in Denver.' Leonard was paid $5,000 for the film rights to *The Tall T* and the same for *3.10 To Yuma*, basically a small-town siege movie starring Glenn Ford and Van Heflin, released in 1957. This was nowhere near enough money to enable him to become a full-time writer. His son Peter remembers early morning visits to the damp basement of the family home, where he would find his father behind his desk, surrounded by discarded balls of yellow paper. 'I must have been about ten years old when the two of us were standing in the kitchen and he said to me "That's it, I'm going to make my run for it",' he says.

This was 1960. Leonard had just finished writing *Hombre*, another kind of siege story given an extra dimension by its shrewd observation of race prejudice. The book was later chosen by the Western Writers of America as one of the twenty-five best Westerns ever written. At that time, however, Leonard couldn't sell it: the market was saturated. There were thirty Western series running on television – all of them terrible, according to Leonard. 'Especially *Bonanza*. All those guys hanging around in hats.' He managed to find a buyer a year later, but his price was dropping: $1,250. It was his last published work for five years – the least creative period of his life. He started drinking heavily. Jack Ryan, best man at Leonard's first wedding, to Beverly, recalls: 'We were always drinking. I remember being pissed on a beach in Florida, dreaming up this idea for a movie. It was about this giant penis rampaging across America eating everything in its path.' The Leonards had five children. To pay the rent, he wrote scripts for 25-minute educational films at $1,000 a throw. Relief came in 1966 with the sale of the film rights to *Hombre* for $10,000. Paul Newman played the white boy raised by Indians who dies to save a group of besieged travellers. The money gave Leonard freedom to write fiction again. This time he used crime instead of the Wild West as his backdrop, again, a purely commercial decision: crime novels were big in the late sixties.

His next book, *The Big Bounce*, was passed to the legendary Hollywood agent H. W. Swanson, whose clients included Hemingway, Scott Fitzgerald and Raymond Chandler. 'He called me a couple of days later and said: "Kiddo, did you write this?" I said I did. He said: "Kiddo, I'm going to make you rich."' *The Big Bounce* was rejected eighty-four times. 'I read it again and realized it needed a plot,' Leonard says, as if this was a mere oversight for a novelist. In the end, it sold for six figures.

The next decade saw his reputation soar. His tight, dialogue-driven prose, free of metaphor or simile, caught the eye of critics, who began to compare him favourably with Chandler and Dashiell Hammett. His marriage to Beverly began to fall apart, partly because of his prodigious work rate, though mostly because of his drinking. He joined Alcoholics Anonymous and, like most AA members, the date of his 'last drink' is committed to memory – 9 a.m., 24 January 1977. Friends say he was a hilarious, pleasant drunk, but that he changed after becoming dry – more introverted, less vocal. His work shows a deep understanding of alcohol and its effects on his characters.

Two years later, divorced from Beverly, he married a neighbour, Joan Shephard, whom friends describe as the greatest influence on his life. She was stronger than Leonard, his intellectual equal. Unlike Beverly, she took a keen interest in his work. She read his manuscripts, suggested changes, urged him to develop his female characters into more than ornaments. The result was a spell-binding series of books: *City Primeval, Split Images, LaBrava, Stick*.

Joan died suddenly from cancer in 1993. A few months later he married Christine, a forty-nine-year-old master gardener who caught his eye when he was gazing through the study window. He liked the way she hung her clippers from her belt. 'He was devasted about Joan,' says one friend. 'But the thing is, Elmore doesn't like to be alone.' He didn't make an appearance in the best-seller lists until 1985, with *Glitz*, but by then his popularity among movie executives had never been greater. 'There was a stage when the family would be sitting down to watch a football game on television and the phone would go and it would be Clint Eastwood or Steve McQueen or someone like that wanting to talk to Elmore,' says Peter Leonard.

If Hollywood were ever brought up on a charge of murder, the prosecution would open with the case of Elmore Leonard's collected works. *Get Shorty* was a success, critically, artistically and financially. The jury is split on *Jackie Brown*. As for the rest, most of them have been dreadful, says one critic. '*Stick*? Terrible. *The Big Bounce*? I left after 15 minutes. '*52 Pick-Up* had some good bits but over-all, not very good.' That critic is Elmore Leonard himself, who has long been immune to the fact that the movie industry's enthusiasm for his books is in inverse proportion to its ability to make decent movies from them. 'They like my books because they are easy to read in scenes, full of characters and dialogue. They love dialogue. But you take a 350-page manuscript and turn it into a 120-page screenplay and most of the good stuff will be gone. Then they always want to change things – why pay a million dollars for something then go change it?' The classic example of Hollywood's uncanny skill in ruining Leonard's work was *Stick*, which starred and was directed by Burt Reynolds. Another screenwriter was brought in to add machine-guns and scorpions to Leonard's tale. 'Terrible. I said to the guy after the screening: "Hey Joe, you don't have a credit. I insist that you have a credit."' Leonard shrugs. 'What's the point in worrying? It's only a movie.' Such insouciance in a writer is admirable, even when it is shored up with the knowledge that the cheque won't bounce if the movie stiffs. But it's a fascinating question: if you pay a million dollars for a story why on earth would you change it? Is it just the studios' insatiable desire to tinker, to re-draft, to cre-ate work, or does it point to something more fundamental in Leonard's work? Hollywood being Hollywood and studio politics being shiftier than one of Leonard's bad guys, the answer you get depends on who you ask. 'What pro-portion of movies that are made do any good?' asks Walter Mirsch. 'Five per cent. If you take the number of Elmore's stories that have been made into movies and then turned out to be successful he's got about the same strike rate as anyone else.' Michael Siegel quietly suggests that some of his client's stories may have ended up in the hands of actors 'showing up near the end of their careers'. One screenwriter, who preferred to remain anonymous, said: 'No plot. His books don't have stories and in the movies you need a story.' He is right in that Leonard's books have no plot when he sits down to write them. He starts with a character and sees where it takes him. *Be Cool* begins with Chilli Palmer having lunch with a music industry executive. The guy gets shot. 'Who shot him? I got 90,000 words to find that out,' says Leonard. 'If you don't know what's going to happen next, better things happen.' In the hands of a less relaxed or less-established writer, this method leads to abandoned manuscripts and a rapidly curtailed career.

Even the Dickens of Detroit sometimes can't escape from dead-ends of his own making. *Rum Punch* had its redeeming qualities but not even Leonard's best friend would describe it as coherent. The reason was simple. 'A hundred pages in, I realized the main character, the bail bondsman, wasn't the main character. The air hostess was,' he says.

There have been a few other mishaps along the way. The principal character in one book was cast aside on page 200 because he was always complaining. 'I didn't like the guy.' His new novel *Cuba Libre* was an everyday tale of gunrunning in nineteenth-century Cuba until George Will called for a chat one day. 'Ah, crime in Cuba,' Will said when his friend revealed what he was working on. Only then did Leonard realize that the book didn't have a crime, and introduce the staged kidnapping of the heroine.

For a spell in the late eighties and early nineties, Leonard's reputation in Hollywood dipped. Executives still bought his stories, but only after they appeared on the best-seller list, or received rave reviews in the *New York Times* books pages. His price fell to $25–50,000 for an option. There was a new breed of executive who considered Leonard to be yesterday's man. Until *Get Shorty*.

Ironically, Barry Sonnenfeld's adaptation stuck more rigidly to Leonard's original story than any previous film versions of his work. It finally proved that his books could be made into good movies, that it was more a question of touch and humour rather than plot, according to Michael Siegel. 'The film premiered at Mann's Chinese Theatre the day after Elmore's birthday,' Siegel says. 'When it ended, he leaned over to me and said in his sweetest, most modest way: "I hot!"' Typical Elmore Leonard. Even when he's hot, he's cool.

6 June 1998

Life at a glance

ELMORE JOHN LEONARD

Born: 11 October 1925, New Orleans.

Education: University of Detroit High School; University of Detroit.

Married: Beverly Claire Cline (1949, divorced 1977; three sons, two daughters); Joan Shephard (1979, died 1993); Christine Kent (1993).

Select bibliography: *The Bounty Hunters* (1953); *Hombre* (1961); *City Primeval* (1980); *Glitz* (1985); *Freaky Deaky* (1988); *Rum Punch* (1992); *Get Shorty* (1990); *Maximum Bob* (1991); *Out of Sight* (1996); *Cuba Libre* (1998).

Movies include: *Stick*; *The Big Bounce*; *Rum Punch* (as *Jackie Brown*); *Get Shorty*; *Out of Sight*.

Awards: *Hombre* chosen as one of the best twenty-five Westerns of all time. Received Mystery Writers of America Grand Master Writer award for life achievement (1993); North American Hammett prize for best crime book of the year *Maximum Bob* (1991); Edgar Allen Poe Award *LaBrava* (1983).

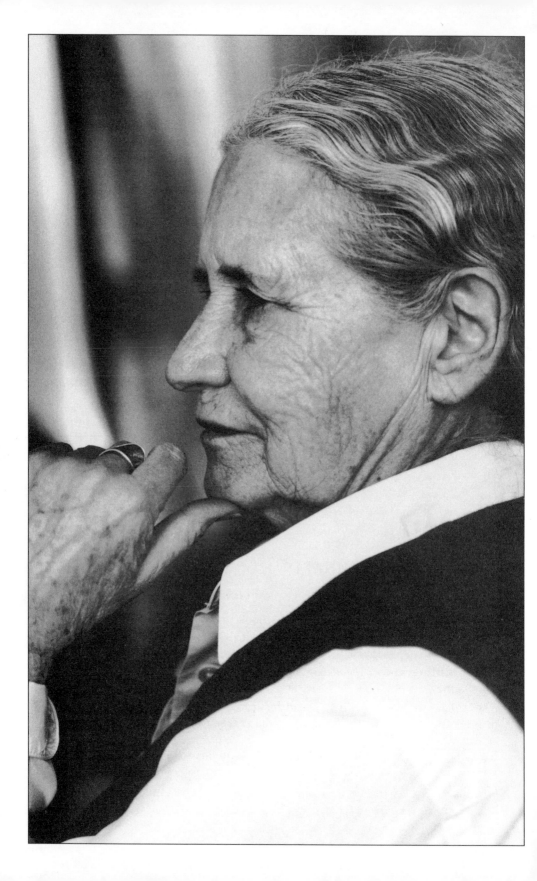

DORIS LESSING
A singular survivor

Emma Brockes

It was in a café in Bulawayo, Southern Rhodesia, that Doris Lessing received her first, rather clumsily delivered death threat. This was 1956, and her debut novel, *The Grass is Singing*, about a relationship between a white woman and a black man, was incensing colonial Africa. A large, blond, South African man approached her at a table one afternoon and after hesitating for a moment, handed over a white feather dipped in tar.

'What are you,' she asked drily, 'the Ku Klux Klan?' Like a child fulfilling a dare, he gabbled a warning about putting ideas into the blacks' heads, before losing his nerve and leaving. The following year, the Rhodesian government named her a 'prohibited immigrant' and she was banned from the country she grew up in, until the old order crumbled and it turned into Zimbabwe in 1980.

Lessing is not a woman easily intimidated. By the time she was thirty, she had survived successive waves of bullying, from an embittered mother, from a regime of unhinged nuns, from a bigoted husband. Above all, she had survived the punishing cycle of drought and thunderstorm that characterizes the African bush, where children must learn to conquer their fear of snakes, scorpions and poisonous insects.

'What influence does African culture have on your work?' asked a witless member of the audience at the Hay-on-Wye literary festival some years ago. Lessing blinked at her with undisguised irritation. Africa, she pointed out, is not like 'the Isle of Wight or Long Island'. Its cultures are unquantifiable, its influence on those who grew up there too intrinsic to analyse. 'Whatever I am, I have been made so by Central Africa,' she wrote in *Going Home*, her journalistic account of Southern Rhodesia. 'The fact is, I don't live anywhere. I never have since I left that first house.'

She is nearly eighty now and has been based in London for fifty years, first in Notting Hill, then in Earl's Court, now in a winding street of mansion blocks in northwest London. Her house is cluttered with books, throws, sheepskin rugs and a black and white cat called Yum-Yum ('after the Mikado'), whose smell is everywhere.

In snub-nosed shoes and a plain smock, Lessing is a formidable figure – what in South Africa would be known as a 'buller': a tough nut, a hard case, who even at seventy-nine looks as though she could do you some serious damage in a rugby tackle. Her hair is parted down the middle and drawn into a low bun, giving her the outline of a Russian doll – appropriate for a woman whose life comprises phases so contradictory that they are often studied as independent parts of a too-complex whole.

'Her whole career is very interesting as a map of imaginative survival for the last fifty years,' says Lorna Sage, an academic who has known Lessing since the 1970s. 'She's got a kind of talent for mobility.'

'She descended on a gloomy Britain and became one of the great observers of its culture,' says Malcolm Bradbury, Lessing's friend for over thirty years. 'She is one of a group of writers who really sparked post-war fiction at the end of the fifties.'

She is an outsider, a 'difficult' woman whose old comrades from the Communist Party still smart from her brisk re-evaluation of the movement as a figment of their own 'mass psychopathology'. One suspects that she referred to her phenomenally successful book, *The Golden Notebook*, as a 'failure' and an 'albatross' partly to piss off the feminists who took it up as their manifesto. She more than justifies her reputation for scaring people.

Just now, however, she is excited, because I have said how much I enjoyed her new book, *Mara and Dann*, a science fiction adventure set in Africa after the next ice age. It is a treat to read, a novel with a storming plot that pursues two adolescent siblings as they flee up the length of Africa with the fires of global warming licking at their heels.

'Thank you, that really is a great compliment,' she says energetically, the Rhodesian accent worn down into a slightly clipped English. 'They were always asking me to write a book for children and I never have, because if I deliberately try to do something, it will be dead. But the kids like it very much, which really pleases me.'

She makes no concessions to a younger readership. The book is written in her usual, arid prose, free of the humorous nips and tucks authors sometimes deploy to make readers feel they are in on a private joke. Lessing delivers the occasional blast of dry humour, but it is her intellectual honesty, her ability to say the unsayable, which has made her famous.

None the less, her publishers have a problem with *Mara and Dann*. Lessing's previous works of science fiction, the *Canopus in Argus Archives* series (sample titles: *The Making of the Representative for Planet 8* and *Documents Relating to the Sentimental Agents in the Volyen Empire*) were met with horror by some critics, who regarded her switch from 'real' literature to the geek market as a sort of brain fever.

Friends swallowed and called it 'brave'. 'It was certainly radical for a "serious" novelist to go anywhere near science fiction,' says Malcolm Bradbury. 'But she is not, really, one of the great team of science fiction writers.'

Lessing regarded the controversy with amusement. It appealed to her playful side, her particular brand of irony which she expressed in 1981 by submitting one of her manuscripts – *The Diary of a Good Neighbour* – under the pseudonym Jane Somer, and delighting when it was rejected by two of her main publishers. ('I have never really been forgiven for that,' she says.) Her point? That books are judged less for the quality of their writing these days, than for the reputation of the name on the dust jacket.

In this sense, *Mara and Dann* does not conform to the Doris Lessing brand name. 'My publishers don't know how to market it. It has been out in the States for six weeks now and readers don't know what to make of it. It's a straightforward adventure story and they want to find deep messages in it, but I don't think there are any, really.' Students of her work will still pick out familiar themes: disintegration, flux, the redeeming power of storytelling. 'What did you see?' ask the main characters, again and again, so that it becomes a motif. Why 'what did you see?' and not 'what did you feel?'?

'Now that really is a question – "What did you feel?"' says Lessing, scathingly. 'A woman who has just seen all her kids die in a fire: "What did you feel?" What you see is much more important. If a child was asked: "What did you feel?" they wouldn't learn anything. "What did you see?" – now that's the beginning of learning everything.'

What the young Lessing saw and learned is recorded to the last pore in *Under my Skin*, the first volume of autobiography she wrote four years ago to thwart inaccurate biographers. It won the James Tait Black prize, but was still received by some critics as almost hurtfully factual: the tone snappish, the refusal to flirt with the reader's expectations of personality taken as a snub.

'It is not a likeable work,' ran one unfavourable review, 'containing little humour or tenderness or modesty. Even her self-criticism has an arrogant finality about it.' Perhaps this revealed more about her than anything else: that here was a woman not afraid to be disliked.

'She has a great air of self-containment,' says Lorna Sage. 'It can make one feel very trivial and restless by comparison. I have seen her in lecture halls and she does not perform in any grand way, but she answers people's questions with sometimes scary directness. She is very unaffected, unselfprotected, which I think impresses no end.'

She has been upbraided for being too serious, but friends insist that, though she may sound like a guru, she is often only teasing.

'I would like to have been an explorer,' Lessing says, smiling a little now, for that is in many ways what she is. 'A friend of mine has just been in Mongolia looking for lost cities and dinosaur bones. Off they went, into the heart of the Gobi desert, where they ate two bowls of noodles and an apple a day and it was very cold. That is what I would like to have done.'

Lessing was born in Persia to middle-class English parents, and spent the first years of her life in Kermanshahan, where her father, Alfred Taylor, was branch manager of the Imperial Bank of Persia. Like many veterans of the First World War he was deeply disillusioned with Britain and, to her mother's regret, never felt able to live there again. After his stint in the bank, they moved to a farm in Southern Rhodesia, which brought them nothing but misery.

'I can't convey the horribleness of Southern Rhodesia as a country,' says Lessing. 'Quite apart from it being a tiny white minority, it was the most provincial, boring place you can imagine. I mean it was unspeakably boring. No one ever talked about anything but sport or the problem of the natives.' She squirms at the recollection.

Unbeknownst to her, Muriel Spark was experiencing similar frustrations not far away. Spark writes in her own autobiography, *Curriculum Vitae*: 'Some miles away lived Doris Lessing, then a young girl like me, still in her teens. How I would have loved to have someone like Doris to talk to.'

While Lessing's brother, Harry, settled into a life of stolid conformity, she rebelled, graduating from a junior school run by nuns who had been out in the sun too long, to a high school which she left when she was fourteen. Her adolescence, largely spent roaming about the bush, was not without its pleasures.

'The world had unused places then,' she wrote in *Under my Skin*. Exploring them gave a sense both of independence and of physical pride: 'It never occurred to me to be ashamed of what I had, even when in a plump phase. I used to stand among people, knowing my body was strong and fine under my dress, and secretly exult.' Away from the influence of social mores she was free, for a little while, to define herself.

It didn't last. For a young woman there was little to look forward to but morning tea parties and evening sundowners. At nineteen she married a civil servant called Frank Wisdom, ten years her senior, and by her early twenties had two children, John and Jean.

'The war atmosphere was so hectic and unreal. Everyone was getting married. I was like a fish in a shoal, I did what everyone else was doing. But of course, it wasn't what I wanted to do. I wouldn't have survived if I'd stayed.' Where did it come from, this belief that there was something better out there for her? She doesn't know. Not from her parents, who wilted a little more each year under the burden of failing crops and physical hardship. Not from solidarity with her brother, Harry, who would grow up to be a sort of Colonel Blimp figure and die in the colony.

'My brother was innately conservative. I don't think it ever crossed his mind to disagree with authority. He was racist to the extent that the word becomes meaningless. And the word sexist? You just have to laugh.'

Her mother, a capable and vigorous woman, longed for a social life beyond the narrow, unsophisticated circles of white settlerdom and when she didn't get it, put all her energies into criticizing her daughter. If Lessing inherited anything from this deeply disappointed woman, it was the no-nonsense stoicism English matrons are parodied for.

Her own resilience has shortened her patience with others. Young women are upbraided in *Walking in the Shade*, the second volume of her autobiography, published last year, for their lack of mettle: they 'scream or swoon at the sight of a penis they have not been introduced to, feel demeaned by a suggestive remark, and send for a lawyer if a man pays them a compliment.' Young writers are put off too easily when they don't win big contracts for their first manuscript. 'It was a different attitude then,' she says, coolly. 'We just got on with it.'

This is more than retrospective bravado or old-biddy chauvinism of the 'Young people? They don't know they're alive' variety. It is rooted in Lessing's essential capacity for cutting her losses, jettisoning allegiances and hauling herself into the next phase of her life. Lorna Sage says: 'She is a figure of great mobility and restlessness and that is her representativeness. It's about moving on.'

For a while, she 'got on' with her marriage, socializing with thick-necked men in polo shirts and women for whom she says no other word but 'lumpen' will do. 'While I was married, I was going along with everything very efficiently: being a good housewife, going to morning tea parties. I did it all and I did it well. And then I thought, what am I doing in this awful country?'

She wasn't the only one. The Communist Party in Rhodesia was, at that time, viewed by its sister party in South Africa as rather amateur. But it was culture, not politics, which drew Lessing to the group of dissidents and intellectuals – one of whom she would marry – who made up the only group of white people in the colony to openly oppose minority rule. In 1942, at the age of twenty-three, her education really began.

'I suddenly met people who had read books and took it for granted that the political system was not going to last,' she says. 'It was absolute bliss to be able to talk about ideas.' She began chewing through the great, literary classics of nineteenth-century realism that would provide a foundation for so much of the work that followed.

Over fifty years later, Malcolm Bradbury recalls witnessing the fruit of this education burst out into a lecture hall: 'I have been on reading tours with her and seen her address audiences with fire in her eyes. On one occasion she went round to sixth formers, pressing them: "Read! Read!" It is a great passion of hers, because she is one of those people for whom reading was the great transforma-tion, the absolute centre of her education. That is one of her striking features.'

For a while the two existences, colonial wife and political activist, ran in par-allel. 'I was going between this very heady atmosphere back to being a civil ser-vant's wife where you had to be careful of what you said because the husband's career was at stake.' Something had to give.

In 1943, she left her first husband and two children to marry fellow comrade, Gottfried Lessing. The marriage was only built to last the duration of the war. 'He really was a very narrow man and went on being all his life, so I'm told,' she says. In 1949, they parted and Lessing came to London with their young son, Peter.

It is a decision which has pursued her ever since. 'How could you?' interview-ers have asked time and again, grappling with the inconsistency of a woman known for her humanitarian spirit, leaving her two young children to move thousands of miles away with a third.

'Now, I know that it was about the most intelligent thing I ever did,' she says. 'But at the time I was doing it, it was awful; dreadful.' She believes that if she had stayed, the misery would have turned her into an alcoholic. Does it anger her that she has been penalized for leaving her children in a way that a man would not have been? She looks annoyed.

'It doesn't anger me, it was inevitable.' There is a pregnant pause. 'Of course it's worse for a woman to do it than it is for a man.' And she narrows her eyes in suspicion at what feminist piety might argue otherwise. 'I became friends with the children when they got older and that was OK, but it didn't make it any better. It is far worse for a mother to leave her children than a father.' She got on with it.

The London that Lessing found in 1949 was drab, shell-shocked, class-ridden – 'it saved me, having a child. If it hadn't been for him, I would have gone to bed and put the blankets over my head' – and it wasn't until the mid-1950s that things started looking up.

Lessing's friend and agent, Jonathan Clowes, was in London at that time and recalls the excitement of feeling they were living in a new meritocracy. 'There were a lot of people like me – jumped-up working-class people who had come up through the grammar schools, who somehow seemed to be running everything.'

'About halfway through the fifties, a new generation arrived that didn't want to talk about the war,' says Lessing. 'They opened coffee bars, the police got all excited about the sin that was going on. I liked that all very much.'

In keeping with the age, her house became a drop-in centre for troubled youngsters, and she, a kind of 'housemother'. It was in this frenetic atmosphere that she broke off from the serial novel she was working on – part of the *Children of Violence* series that charted the progress of an Afrikaner girl across five volumes – to write *The Golden Notebook*, her experimental novel dissecting the life of a sexually liberated woman. The book ran the full gamut of female unmentionables – menstruation, clitoral orgasm, frigidity – and transformed Lessing into an icon for women's liberation. To some female readers, however, her frankness was an unwelcome and unpalatable exposure of their 'secrets', a straw that broke more than one camel's back.

In a 1962 issue of *Vogue*, Siriol Hugh-Jones, the magazine's former features editor, unleashed a tirade of abuse on that triumvirate of women writers: Iris Murdoch, Muriel Spark and Lessing.

Murdoch was culpable for 'an endless flow of bizarre and usually enormously disagreeable people involved in meaningless and heartless events'. Spark, though commended for her 'witty care for words', ultimately boiled down to 'a lonely, Roman Catholic prankster whispering little dry and lethal jokes about peculiar school mistresses'.

But it was for Lessing that the author reserved her most indignant disapproval. Here was a woman, 'dismal, drab, embarrassing', sodden with 'self-pity', who in *The Golden Notebook* had single-handedly set back the women's movement 'a good long way'.

'Mrs Lessing leaves one with the really terrible impression of a woman – shrewish, naggy, self-righteous and impossible to live with.' Hugh-Jones could only marvel that the gentlemen reviewers of Fleet Street were chivalrous enough not to have finished her off in a way her fellow females were happy to.

The Golden Notebook, first published in Britain in 1962, didn't make it to France or Germany for fourteen years because it was considered too inflammatory. When it was republished in China in 1993, 80,000 copies sold out in two days. 'It took realism apart from the inside,' says Lorna Sage. 'Lessing threw over the conventions she grew up in to stage a kind of breakdown – to celebrate disintegration as the representative experience of a generation – when what you should have been doing is getting the act together.' She challenged the put-up-or-shut-up culture of an uptight nation; it was all very un-English.

The Golden Notebook became so widely and endlessly talked about that Lessing grew to regard it as a distraction from the rest of her work and particularly to resent how the hype overshadowed the book's intellectual content. But she shrugged off the press attacks with relative ease. After all, she had been writing in a climate of disapproval since the early days.

'When *The Grass is Singing* came out, nobody liked it. The whites hated it, my dear comrades hated it. When it did well, it annoyed a great many people. But if you want to be a writer and you haven't got some kind of stubbornness, you've had it.'

'Yes, there was a lot of to-do over *The Golden Notebook* at the time,' says Clowes, 'but I think she was a bit surprised by it all. She couldn't understand why everyone was making such a fuss. She's never bothered too much about reviews because she says that, historically, they are often shown to be totally wrong.'

Besides, the Communist Party had taught her to observe a certain nobility in suffering; a forbearance under siege. When she later came to analyse these feelings, she identified them as a hangover from the war. The 'elite of suffering', as she called it – a sort of 'nobody knows the trouble I've seen' romanticism, bred in the trenches – was a truth so hard it made people wince when referred to in public talks.

'The Communists were elite because they were alone in their bravery. It took a long time for me to say, hang on, this is the same attitude that the soldiers had in the Great War: the civilians don't understand us, the government sold us out, we stand alone. And I thought, my God, it has probably fed into Communism.'

It wasn't until 1956, when Khrushchev 'came clean' about Stalin's crimes at the party's famous twentieth congress, that Lessing terminated her membership. For many western Communists, this event destroyed the last vestiges of their belief in what Lessing now calls a political 'nonsense'.

Some old comrades were so appalled they committed suicide. The extremity of the fallout still intrigues her.

'The question is, why did people refuse to recognize the truth for so long? In the early 1960s, when everyone was leaving the Communist Party, a man who had been tortured in a Soviet prison came to my house to tell the comrades in the West the real truth about Russia. There were a lot of people there who had been Reds. The man was waiting for us to say: "Ah, comrade, at last you have told us the truth!" But nobody did. I don't understand it to this day.'

But others who survived the political climate at that time question the slant of Lessing's appraisal. Professor Jane Miller lived in London through the same period and shared Communist friends with Lessing. 'I suppose I questioned the claim that her experience of the party was representative,' she says. It was a 'partisan' account of the time, she believes, 'lopsided and over-generalized', and in an essay Miller wrote for an American academic journal, she casts a sceptical eye over Lessing's dismissal of the movement as a sort of mass delusion. 'To gather retrospectively an entire generation's ideological commitment into a single, idiosyncratic *mea culpa*, smacks of another kind of ideologue, even a scourge.'

Lessing concedes that she was only ever a 'real' communist in Rhodesia – 'I had never invested my whole self in it the way a lot of people had' – and has been quick to highlight the movement's more ridiculous aspects: 'The typical Communist was an unsmiling little tyrant served by a bevy of gasping women.'

Still, she implies, if she is betraying the spirit of the time by refusing to re-evoke the sentiments that drove it, then it is because one cannot revisit strong feelings without poisoning them with nostalgia or retrospective bitterness. The best one can hope for is a clinical evaluation. 'I think the tragedy was that the Socialist parties of the West allied to the Soviet Union in their minds. They identified with failure, with brutality and I am sure this is what has corrupted social-ism in our part of the world.'

Does she worry that today's younger generation is dangerously politically apa-thetic? 'When I look back and see what all that moral fervour did, no.' Did noth-ing good come out of it? 'What was attractive was the accomplishment that went with it: people were very brave.'

And does she still think that literature has the power to destroy empires? 'Yes, it probably does, in countries where you've got a tyranny. Of course, some writ-ers can't wait to have a tyranny to work on. But it is very nice to be living in a time when there aren't passionate beliefs.'

She continues to lend her name to local campaigns, however, for better read-ing in schools, for the preservation of the trees in Hampstead Heath, and, reveal-ingly, to pursue a faith in Sufism, a mystical branch of Islam which she studied for years under the tutelage of Idries Shah. Its origins are in seventh-century aes-thetics, and followers of Sufism aim to achieve direct union with God. They grew in number after the publication of Shah's book, *The Sufis*, in 1964. 'It was as if I had been waiting to read that book all my life,' Lessing has said. 'It is a cliché, but the book changed my life.'

She has a granddaughter studying at Oxford and another doing architecture in Cape Town, where her daughter Jean has settled. Peter lives in London; her other son John died of a heart attack in 1991, a casualty of farming in Africa. 'She is a very clear, firm-minded person,' says Bradbury. 'She used to be much more light-hearted than she is now, but that is part of the peril of ageing, that people lose some of their *joie de vivre*.'

'I do find the world less and less convincing as I grow older,' she has said, unconvincingly. Since finishing *Mara and Dann*, she has completed a sequel to *The Fifth Child* in which, with characteristic optimism, the *enfant terrible* of the first volume grows up to parent a decent child.

She is now working on another book, taking the total to over eighty. 'I think it's her wisdom that distinguishes her,' says Clowes. 'And her amazing capacity to surprise. We'll talk about a book she might write, then suddenly she rings up and says "Oh, I've started something else." It is extraordinary.'

The day before we meet, she has had a new experience. Lessing is posing for a portrait commissioned by the National Portrait Gallery and has endured the first, hour-long sitting. She is anticipating the others with dread. 'It is incredibly hard work,' she says with a sly grin. 'I am always moving.'

24 April 1999

Life at a glance

DORIS MAY LESSING

Born: 22 October 1919, Kermanshahan, Persia (now Iran).

Education: left school at fourteen.

Married: Frank Wisdom (1939, divorced 1943; one son, one daughter); Gottfried Lessing (1945, divorced 1949; one son).

Political affiliation: joined the Communist Party in London, 1951, left 1956.

Select bibliography: *The Grass is Singing* (1950); *In Pursuit of the English* (1960); *The Golden Notebook* (1962); *The Memoirs of a Survivor* (1975); *The Good Terrorist* (1985); *Under my Skin* (1994); *Mara and Dann* (1999); *Ben, in the World* (2000).

Awards: Somerset Maugham award (1954) for *Five*, a collection of short stories; W. H. Smith Literary award and the Mondello prize for *The Good Terrorist* (both 1985); James Tait Black prize for *Under my Skin* (1994); nominated for the Bad Sex award in the *Literary Review* (1996); Companion of Honour (1999).

CHRISTOPHER LOGUE
Classic upstart

James Campbell

There is a long workbench in Christopher Logue's study, in addition to the desk, and pegs on the wall on which hang scissors, knives, and various kinds of tape. For more than forty years he has been engaged intermittently on *War Music*, an idiosyncratic account of Homer's *Iliad*, that he works on lengths of continuous computer print-out paper to which he sticks Post-It notes, building up detail upon detail, image after image. A draft page for a section of *War Music*, therefore, can be five metres long. Portions of it get nailed to the wall above the bench, to establish what Logue calls a 'flow chart'. When the first small part of what is now a very long poem was published in 1962, Henry Miller wrote to Lawrence Durrell: 'Just tumbled on Chris Logue's extraordinary rendition of Book XVI of the *Iliad*. I can't get over it. If only Homer were anywhere near as good.'

At the same time as reworking Homer, and producing a steady flow of poems and plays, Logue has kept up a performance as a literary maverick. He wrote the script for Ken Russell's film *Savage Messiah*, and played the role of Cardinal Richelieu in the same director's version of *The Devils*. He was the Player King in Jonathan Pryce's *Hamlet* at the Royal Court in 1980. He can lay valid claim to having invented the poster poem, with the help of artists such as Derek Boshier and Michael English. One example hangs in the bathroom of his house in Camberwell: 'Apollinaire said: Come to the edge... / So they came, / And he pushed, / And they flew.' Logue has designed others himself.

Faber and Faber have just issued all of Logue's Homer in one volume, for the first time in Britain. It is not intended as a birthday present, though it so happens that he turns seventy-five on 23 November. He is small and wiry, with a walleye that sometimes floats disconcertingly. Many people who know Logue speak of his laughter – a big haw-haw-haw laugh – or his mischief-making, or sense of fun. 'We did have so much fun', says Doris Lessing, recalling Logue on the Aldermaston CND march, Logue at the Royal Court, Logue the pornographer, Logue at *Private Eye*, Logue setting out to conquer Homer's *Iliad* with an army of modern effects. Lessing describes him as 'an enormously witty and entertaining man, with a peculiar line in black humour. He's got a sort of ribald quality of enjoyment that contributes to any gathering.'

Yet many people meeting Logue come away nursing a savaged ear. One admiring young poet, who is also a poetry editor, approached to pay public homage only to have his stuttering flattery dismissed. Joan Bakewell was hectored for several minutes at a party, after she had cheerfully informed him of a programme she was making about the sixties. He recently knocked a hole in the wall of his study while banging with the heel of a shoe in protest against a noisy neighbour. 'She's an awfully nice girl, really', he says, tickled at his own fury. 'Christopher's someone who's always spoiling for a scrap,' says his friend, the American poet August Kleinzahler. 'There's something subversive about him. He thrives on upsetting the applecart.'

Logue shows little concern for his social reputation. He volunteered the names of people who might provide uncomplimentary remarks about him: 'Al Alvarez was never very keen on me.' Later, he suggests A. N. Wilson as a source, 'since he wrote such an unpleasant review of my memoirs'. In the course of this review, in the *London Review of Books*, Wilson wrote: 'This is a book that makes me think not merely that poets are shits, but that I really hate left-wing people.' Logue, he said, had painted himself as 'extremely unlovable – a snob, a social climber, a neglectful friend, a layabout', and somebody who frightened the audience when Wilson invited him to an *Evening Standard* literary lunch.

The memoir, *Prince Charming*, now reissued in paperback, records that Logue was born near Portsmouth in 1926, and raised there and in Hampstead Garden Suburb. 'The less expensive part,' he says. 'Better make that clear.' The only child of middle-aged parents, he was indeed a little prince, charming or not. His grandfather was an Irish Catholic from Coleraine, who made a career in the British Army. 'I think, though I'm not sure about this, that my father was born in Fort George, in Perthshire. He worked all his life in the Post Office, eventually becoming paymaster in London. It was a service of which he was extremely proud.' Logue recalls how, as a small boy, he identified more with the Sheriff of Nottingham than with Robin Hood. At school, he invented a game called Heaven and Hell, in which 'St Peter (me) condemned the smaller boys to Hell'. Nowadays, in the living room of the fine terraced house in Camberwell, south London, which he shares with his wife, the writer Rosemary Hill, there stands a statuette of Napoleon. 'A nice likeness of Christopher, that,' guests have been heard to quip.

The Roman Catholic boarding school he attended in Southsea was run by the Christian Brothers, a rigorous teaching order. 'They became fascinated by physical punishment. Very harsh. There was sexual sadism involved in it. You were taught and punished in God's name.' The severity of the brotherhood may explain why his formal education had ended by the time he was seventeen. Nevertheless, he does not blame his schooling for any gaps in his knowledge. 'People will tell you that their education put them off poetry for life. It's complete nonsense. The truth is, they had no taste for it and they are ashamed of that, so they blame the teachers.' Case closed. Or he might say: 'The idea that the Irish make good poets is rubbish.' No further explanation required, unless it is to contrast the Irish bards with the Scots, whom he favours: 'The Irish have never produced a MacDiarmid or a Garioch.'

His mother sent him to elocution lessons, and he credits his speech tutor with introducing him to poetry, as well as cultivating what he refers to as his 'la-di-da voice'. 'I was given to learn and recite by heart 'Gunga Din', 'The Lady of Shalott', 'The Walrus and the Carpenter'. I learned the text and the performance of the text at the same time. Poetry and the spoken performance of it were never separated in my mind.' A recently issued box set of seven CDs, *Audiologue*, contains seven hours of Logue reading, much of it devoted to *War Music*. When an early section came out on long-playing disc in the sixties, a reviewer praised Logue's 'clarity and intelligence' as a reader, while pointing out that 'his appetite for the scenes of carnage eventually becomes a trifle ghoulish'.

After school, aged seventeen, and commando training, Logue joined the army, as his grandfather had, and enlisted in the Black Watch. He would have been called up for National Service anyway, but joined as a volunteer. The army was 'a refuge', he says. The posh voice did not impress his fellow soldiers, who called him 'Charlotte'. Several decades later, a comrade wrote to say that he still remembered his 'pompous attitude', but Logue recalls only that he was incapable. In *Prince Charming*, he wrote: 'My webbing was always twisted. On route marches, when my turn came to carry the platoon's 10kg Bren gun someone shouldered it for me. I had never been in a fight. I could not bear to go to the lavatory in public.' Inside the statuette of Napoleon is buried another one – not of 'Charlotte', perhaps, but of someone a little bit helpless.

In 1945, Private Logue was posted to Palestine, where he promptly landed in an army prison for dealing in stolen 'pay books', the equivalent of identity cards. At a court martial, he was sentenced to two years incarceration. In handcuffs and leg-irons, he was taken to a detention camp where he remained for sixteen months. He claims he did not experience any great misery or shame. In prison, he lost most of the sight of one eye, six months after a climbing accident had caused the retina to detach, and began writing poetry. 'He's pretty tough,' says his friend the playwright and novelist Nell Dunn. 'He's a bit of a street child, just doing what he wants to do, and not what someone else wants. He's always been out on a limb. He gets into trouble, but then he makes something out of it.'

Returning to England after his discharge, Logue tried his hand at the literary scene in London, but achieved little more than he had as a soldier. 'There were these university boys all over the place and I had nothing in common with them. A friend and I used to walk up and down the King's Road hoping to meet poets and painters, but we never did. I thought of people like Ezra Pound and T. S. Eliot and Picasso – that was the kind of milieu I wanted to be in. And here was London, after the war, desolate.' In 1951, he went to Paris for five years. 'I didn't know anyone there either, but it was Paris. It was an idea. I could see the Paris of the 1930s, the Paris of the 1880s, the aesthetic capital of the world. That was all much more like it.'

He came under the spell of a charismatic Glaswegian, Alexander Trocchi, later to achieve notoriety as an enthusiastic missionary for heroin use and a more creditable fame as the author of the early postmodern novel *Cain's Book*. Trocchi died in 1984 but is frequently present in Logue's conversation. He was a tall, commanding Lothario, while Logue was just discovering what was to be a long-standing theme in his life: difficulties with girls. 'Alex was very kind to me. He even suggested a threesome with one of his girlfriends. "She quite fancies you," he said. But I wouldn't dare to do it.'

On another occasion, Trocchi rescued him from a suicide attempt, travelling to the South of France for the purpose. 'I used the departure of a girl I was in love with as an excuse to take my own life. It was a pile-up of negativity. There was a great deal of self-indulgence in it, too, of course, as there often is. Trocchi found out where I was and came and rescued me.'

In May 1952, an American named Jane Lougee founded the magazine *Merlin*, with Trocchi as editor and Logue as part of the team. As a spin-off, a book imprint was set up, Collection Merlin, which published two novels by Samuel Beckett, *Watt* and *Molloy*, and also Logue's debut in poetry, *Wand and Quadrant* (1953). Collection Merlin was eventually taken over by the Olympia Press, for which Logue wrote a pornographic novel, *Lust*, under the pseudonym Count Palmiro Vicarion. 'I wasn't very good at it', he says. 'Trocchi was much better at porn than any of us. He wrote several books under various names, and kept the magazine going with the money.'

The Paris adventure displays an essential side of Logue: he senses where the action is and makes a beeline for it. Paris in the fifties was a more fluid place than London. Apart from the Merlin crowd (which included Austryn Wainhouse, whose translations of the Marquis de Sade are now the standard), there were black writers at the Café de Tournon, such as Richard Wright and Chester Himes. On learning of Logue's socialist leanings, Wright, a former Communist who had turned against the party, stabbed a finger into his chest and told him: 'None of your en-ga-jay, please. You've got nothing to fight for, boy – you're just looking for a fight. If you were a black boy, you're so cheeky you'd be dead.'

Logue says: 'When I think now about the Paris of those days it is the black voices that rise up and speak to me. I was very much put in the picture as regards racism, social justice and so on.' Among the most important of his friendships, though of a more deferential kind, was that with Beckett, who was generous to a fault with the magazine and its editors, whom he called 'the Merlin juveniles'.

Logue describes himself as 'very well educated on the Left. I was on the side of the underdog, of the working class.' Asked now what his close-up experience of the working class was up to that time, he replies 'none'. Nevertheless, a residue of the infatuation with Marxism remains. 'I knew nothing. I just knew that Stalin was someone who had saved our lives, by defeating Hitler.' (His first reaction to news of the war in Afghanistan was to think of organizing a march against it.) By the time he returned to London in 1956, the 'moon and man-drake' imagery that dominates his first collection had been exchanged for a more socially conscious poetry: 'By mutual fear / we have come in peace / to the end of the year.'

It was a different city from the one he had left behind. 'You felt there was a change. It took that long for England to emerge from the postwar gloom. There was a reluctance to let go of the war. And it didn't really break until Osborne, with *Look Back In Anger*.' Aged thirty, Logue had no intention of settling down: 'I wasn't interested in family life, marriage, regular employment, that was not the way for me. Also, one had published a book, and so on. I began to get poems into the *TLS* and the *New Statesman*. That was incredibly important.' For the Royal Court he composed the lyrics for a musical, *The Lily-White Boys* (1960), and wrote a version of *Antigone*. He began to give poetry readings, then a rarity.

The jazz singer Annie Ross performed his songs at the Establishment, a cabaret club in Soho, and recorded an album under the title *Loguerhythms*. 'I remember those songs more vividly than the sketches at the Establishment', says Richard Ingrams, who later employed Logue at *Private Eye*. 'They had very clever, satirical lyrics.' The producer of the record, Nat Joseph, remembers 'a pixieish figure who seemed never to stop moving nervously around at some speed'.

In 1957, the disciple of T. S. Eliot entered into an argument with the master in the letters columns of the *TLS*. An article made reference to Eliot's anti-Semitism, to which Eliot replied denying the allegation. Seeing that no one else was willing to contest the matter, Logue wrote: 'Since Mr Eliot wishes to be reminded of his own texts, and since he confesses to a somewhat insecure memory, a third party may be allowed to adduce the evidence...' Eliot responded the following week: 'Mr Logue has supported the accusations with the pieces of evidence which those who share his frame of mind are wont to produce against me.' The row did not alter Logue's opinion of Eliot as the greatest poet of the century.

He frequently reacts with indifference to the mention of other living poets. Logue himself has wilfully avoided the poet's typical neat path, from slim volumes to selected poems with the promise of a collection to crown a career. Each of his books, in the early days, tried not to resemble the one before. *Songs*, for example, prints each poem in a different type. *Logue's ABC* contains twenty-six poems, beginning with successive letters of the alphabet. Another collection consists of a series of cards containing poems and illustrations by the poet.

Poetry in performance has been essential to the Logue corpus. He says he is never nervous before an audience. In 1959, he recorded a set of poems read to jazz accompaniment for the BBC Third Programme. Poetry and jazz was a new thing in Britain, although Lawrence Ferlinghetti and others had been doing something similar in San Francisco. Logue's experiment was called *Red Bird*, with poems adapted from Pablo Neruda. It still sounds good: short numbers, usually under two minutes, combining Logue's excellent la-di-da voice and Neruda's dewy lyricism shot along the surface of the musical arrangements. Seven tracks were released as an EP produced by George Martin and are now re-released as part of *Audiologue*.

August Kleinzahler first heard Logue read at a literary festival in Melbourne in 1986. He says: 'It was one of the most electrifying performances I've ever witnessed: 90 per cent of poetry readings are soporific. What was striking about Christopher's performance is that he is obviously a natural actor. He had a very sure sense of how it needed to come across as a theatrical piece, but without the theatricality that would overburden it with mannerism.' When Nell Dunn asked him to teach her about poetry, he did so by reading aloud. 'He loves to read poetry very loudly. He used to declaim it, like a Roman emperor or something.'

It was in the same year as the recording of *Red Bird* that Logue began the project for which he is currently best known: his 'account' of Homer's *Iliad*; or his '*Iliad* rewritten'; or just 'Logue's Homer'. The uncertainty over how to describe it reflects the originality of the enterprise. There have been three volumes so far – *Kings*, *The Husbands*, *War Music* – and he is at work on a fourth, *All Day Permanent Red*. Since Logue freely admits that he knows no Greek, it cannot be called a translation. It is a rendering of the action of the ancient text, filtered through a modern, at times 'pop' sensibility. Whatever appears to suit his purpose is borrowed and used.

A simple example of how he operates: Logue reads a quotation from a novel by Chester Himes about a fight in a Harlem street: 'One joker slashed the other's arm. A big-lipped wound opened in the tight leather jacket...' Struck by the image, Logue simply lifts it and gives it a different context in *War Music*:

> When all seems lost, there Ido is,
> Grinning among the blades, inflicting big-lipped wounds,
> Keeping his hosts' hearts high...

The ultimate intention is to write 'a dramatic poem in English' dependent on the *Iliad* that will 'revitalize narrative verse'. At first, he admits, he wanted to write an extended poem 'just because I wanted to. I had no theme.' Homer gave him one. The result is a poetry that is dramatic and stately, with extravagant touches: for example, the name 'APOLLO!' in huge letters stretched across two pages, and, in normal print below, 'Who had been patient with you / Struck.' The action and rapid scene-shifting are cinematic:

> Picture the east Aegean Sea by night,
> And on a beach aslant its shimmering
> Upwards of 50,000 men
> Asleep like spoons beside their lethal Fleet.

Logue forces every reader to face the issue of what Homer means now, says the Cambridge classicist Mary Beard: 'It also forces us to look more closely at past translations of Homer. It puts the whole notion of translation from classical languages on the line. Classicists have often approached translation as if it were unproblematic.' She is an admirer of Logue's work but understands why some of her colleagues have been critical. 'To get someone who admits he doesn't know a word of Greek and yet who makes Homer work in a different way for a contemporary world...makes certain people uncomfortable. After all, we are the classicists. There is a sense in which, you know, Logue doesn't know his place.'

On Logue's flow chart, nailed to the wall of his study, a phrase from Pope's translation of the *Iliad* sits next to a quote from a *New Yorker* article about the Gulf War: 'a million footprints, / Empty now'. Gradually, the accretions suggest something worth shaping into verse. 'This is actually in Homer,' Logue will say, next to a reference to Book V, Line 289 (Diomedes prepares to kill Pandarus in battle), 'this I invented'. He is keen to emphasize the shapeliness of his metrics. 'A basic iambic pentameter throughout, from which one may deviate. It's a tremendously versatile line. *The Waste Land* is practically iambic pentameter.'

In the seventies Logue finally seemed to be slowing down. He published little. In his memoirs, he refers to the period as 'years of depression. A decade and more.' Now he relates it to his difficulties with women. 'I was constantly refusing the ordinary human side of life. I didn't want to be committed to anyone – to a very strong degree. I didn't want to get my hands dirty. I didn't want anyone else around – their dirty underwear and all that. If I happened to go to bed with someone, I'd get up in the middle of the night and leave. I never really wanted any children.' He develops the theme. 'Not having a close relation with the world is a common feature of a lot of English poets. It's true of Milton, Pope, Wordsworth. It's not true of Burns, for example. Burns was up to his neck in the world.'

Another factor was post-sixties depression. From the stage of the Royal Court to a cell in Brixton Prison (he was jailed for a second time, for a month in 1961, as part of Bertrand Russell's Anti-Bomb Committee of 100, for refusing to sign a binding-over order), Logue was there wherever the sixties were happening. When the music stopped, he found himself out of place. He became better known for his work at *Private Eye*, where he compiled 'Christopher Logue's True Stories' and selected pretentious prose for 'Pseuds' Corner', than for his poetry. 'He was the right person to do 'Pseuds' Corner' because he has a good eye for pomposity,' says Richard Ingrams. 'One of the things we have in common is an admiration for Dr Johnson, who said: "Clear your mind of cant." Christopher has got that side to him.'

The Homer project, dormant for many years, was revivified in 1984, when Jonathan Cape published all that had been written so far. It was then reissued by Faber, where Craig Raine encouraged him to continue. By the time a second volume appeared in 1991, 'Logue's Homer' was established as an ongoing literary event. 'It is given to few poets to bring Homer crashing into their own time,' the American critic Gary Wills has written. 'In English, only three have done it – Chapman, Pope, and Christopher Logue.'

In 1984, something even more rewarding than critical acclaim occurred: he met Rosemary Hill, who became his wife. 'I first met her in a restaurant. She worked at *Country Life*, where she chose the poems. I sent some and she invited me out to lunch.' At sixty-one, Logue married for the first time. At the slightest excuse, he will sing the praises of his wife, who is somewhat younger than he, and who is writing a biography of the nineteenth-century architect Pugin. Together with Craig Raine – 'a wonderful editor' – Rosemary is given credit for making him 'knuckle down', as he puts it, and get back to work after his fallow decade. Two years ago, a spot of heart trouble seemed to put lead in his boots. He stopped wanting to go out. But lately he has recovered his vigour, and this summer travelled to the West Coast of America for a month, visiting Kleinzahler, Derek Boshier and the poet Gary Snyder in his cabin in the Californian backwoods.

Logue's legacy as a poet will be his Homer. Admirers say that his example lies in his refusal to be boxed in – by cliques, by genres, by forms: he is a walking instruction manual on the art of doing your own thing.

17 November 2001

Life at a glance

CHRISTOPHER LOGUE

Born: 23 November 1926, Southsea, Hampshire.

Education: St John's College, Southsea; Prior Park College, Bath; Portsmouth Grammar School.

Married: Rosemary Hill (1985).

Career: Commando training (1944); Black Watch (1945–8); Berlitz English language teacher, Paris (1951–2); poet, journalist, screenwriter, actor (1951–).

Select bibliography: Poetry: *Wand and Quadrant* (1953); *Devil, Maggot and Son* (1955); *Songs* (1959); *New Numbers* (1969); *Ode to the Dodo* (1981); *War Music* (2001); Anthologies: *The Children's Book of Comic Verse* (1979); *London in Verse* (1982); *Sweet & Sour* (1983); *The Oxford Book of Pseuds* (1983); *The Children's Book of Children's Rhymes* (1986); Memoir: *Prince Charming* (1999); Plays: *The Trial of Cob and Leach* (1959); Recordings: *Audiologue* (2001).

SHENA MACKAY

Bohemian Rhapsodist

Ian Hamilton

Shena Mackay has never been one for trendy self-promotion. Like Lyris, the neglected painter in her novel, *The Artist's Widow*, Mackay would – on balance –
rather be overlooked than vulgarly exposed. 'A publicist's nightmare' is how her
own publicists have now and then described her, and Mackay takes a certain
pride in their exasperation.

Even today, with ten highly-praised books in print (two, *The Artist's Widow*,
and *Dunedin*, are out in Vintage paperback this month), and with a paean from
Julie Burchill to amplify her blurbs (Burchill recently called her 'the best writer
in the world today'), Mackay cannot quite bring herself to bustle on the circuits.

As she told me recently: 'I do think the whole climate for writers these days is
so vulgar. It's all so money-led. I hate going into bookshops and seeing, you
know, the Top Ten Bestsellers, a sort of self-fulfilling prophecy. I just find the
whole thing so vulgar: the books pages, and the way writers are portrayed – snip-
pets in diaries about so-and-so's advance. It all just creates a climate of anxiety for
the majority of writers and gets them into the feeling that it's all a competition.'

A publicist's nightmare, to be sure, and yet Mackay, when she first started out,
seemed quite the opposite. When I first heard of her, in the early sixties, she was
being touted as the youngest and prettiest girl-novelist in town. She was featured in style sections of the tabloids, along with figures like Marianne Faithfull,
and seemed to be heading for a starring role in the about-to-happen
youthquake. She had written her first novel when she was sixteen, we were told,
and by twenty had clocked up quite a few foam-flecked reviews: 'Macabre, zany,
scoffingly droll, sadly beautiful, wildly funny, glitteringly stylish – and quite
brilliant...She stands on her own – an original and a very hot property.' And that
was just the *Daily Mail*.

As for the prettiness – this too was the stuff of dazed hyperbole. A poet friend
of mine, who can't be named, remembers meeting Mackay at a mid-sixties literary festival: 'A vision of blonde, schoolgirl loveliness,' he says, 'but sexy and flir-
tatious too. You should have seen those corduroyed belletrists swoon whenever
she timidly sashayed into the hotel bar. They all wanted to, well, protect her,
advise her, and so on – and in spite of the deadpan wit with which she kept
them all at bay, she did somehow seem to need protecting. Let's just say that she
was the kind of novelist who didn't really need to write another novel.'

Mackay did write other novels, though, and in many of them the lustful male
is skewered with brutal finesse. Her early novels in particular are full of bristly
predators, and we are spared none of the repulsive details: the starings and the
gropings, the bad breath, the drunken bullshit, the love-talk that turns nasty
when our heroine sees through it, and so on.

I asked Mackay the other day if she had ever invented an admirable male character. The question seemed to take her by surprise, and in the end she came up with Stanley in *A Bowl of Cherries*: a wan and ineffectual bedsit loser. 'And what's so terrific about Stanley?' 'Well, he's nice to children,' she replied.

Shena Mackay (nee Mackey) was born in Edinburgh in 1944, on D-Day. Her father was in the army; her mother was training to be a teacher. They had met as students at St Andrews University. He was the son of a headmaster; she the daughter of a Presbyterian minister, and according to Mackay the marriage was a 'genuine love-match'. After the war, the family moved to England, at first to Hampstead (where, for a time, they lived next door to the Saatchis; little Charles, says Mackay, would now and then come crawling through their hedge) and later, via various London locations, to the village of Shoreham in Kent.

Benjamin Mackey, Shena's father, had problems 'settling down' after the war, not least because he seems to have been the victim of a somewhat volatile Scottish temper. He took a succession of short-term jobs, ranging from coal-miner to ship's purser. There were frequent parental absences: not all of these unwelcome to Shena and her two sisters. Nor, maybe, to their mother.

Mrs Mackey was steadfast, intrepid and self-sacrificing. During the family's eight years in Shoreham, the years of Shena's growing-up, it was the mother who kept everything together. Although of an arty disposition, counting as friends many poets and painters of the day, she was also a rigorously conscientious coper. According to Valerie Foster, a childhood friend, the Mackey girls were always 'stylishly turned out', although the family was invariably short of cash.

Certainly, it was from her mother that Mackay picked up several habits and interests that would stay with her later on: her vegetarianism, her interest in modern painting, her passion for wild flowers. 'My mother made us learn the names of all the flowers in Kent,' she says, and there is no book of hers, I think, that does not contain at least one flourish of botanical expertise. Mackay's mother also encouraged her to read. 'Shena was always, always reading', says her sister Frances, and Foster remembers her friend poring over Sherlock Holmes and Billy Bunter.

Mackay herself recalls her mother scolding her, along the lines of 'A big girl of eight and you haven't read *Crime and Punishment*!' But the scolding is remembered with intense affection: 'I adored my mother,' Mackay says today, 'I got all sorts of values from her. She was a trouper, if you like, and lots of fun. But she had very high standards. We were brought up with quite liberal values but with a Presbyterian moral code as well.'

Mrs Mackey made sure that her daughters attended the village church and that they went to Sunday school. Mackay sang in the church choir, and although Foster recalls a few moments of Sunday irreverence, Mackay always remembered the words of all the hymns, and has worked quite a few of them into her books.

These childhood years left a deep imprint, to be sure, and Foster remembers them as an 'enchanted' time. Mackay, she recalls, was always the mischievous tomboy, forever embarking on escapades and getting into scrapes. 'She was always more daring than I was. She liked danger and even then she had a macabre sense of humour.' At Tonbridge Grammar School, the two girls were co-conspirators – mocking the teachers, playing truant and so on – but Mackay (brilliant at English, bad at maths) always came out top of the detentions league. And she had begun writing poems and short stories: dark, horrid stuff, apparently, with lots of gratuitously sudden deaths (which also feature fairly often in her adult work). Even in these early, schoolgirl years, Valerie Foster was in no doubt that her naughty little friend would one day be 'a very well-known writer'.

Mackay's Shoreham childhood features repeatedly in her grown-up writings and is still looked back on with a sense of loss. In some ways, all of her novels and short stories, whatever their actual settings, can seem like attempts to reclaim the sharply circumscribed intensities of village life. She is celebrated now as 'the tenth muse of suburbia', 'the supreme lyricist of daily grot', but her beady-eyed dissections of the London suburb always seem guided by what one might call a villager's sensibility.

She is always on the lookout for oddballs and eccentrics, for tiny gaffes and small-scale self-delusions, and even when she is at her most caustically satirical there is usually an elegiac undertone. She has a wonderfully good ear for bus-stop dialogue ('for reasons best known to themselves'; 'it's the children I feel sorry for') and she always wants to know what's going on behind the counter at the corner shop.

Unglamorous community endeavours – flower shows, amateur dramatics, church socials, and the like – always bring out the mordant best in her writing. She has, on the whole, been happier with close-ups than long-shots. At the same time, the village schoolgirl was, from early on, enticed by the idea of the metropolis. She had observed her mother's arty visitors and friends – the poet W. S. Graham and the painter Glyn Collins seem to have been regulars – and she nurtured adolescent fantasies of the artistic London life.

In 1960, she edged a step closer to metropolitan Bohemia. Her parents moved to Blackheath in southeast London, and the children were switched from Tonbridge Grammar to Kidbrooke Comprehensive, which Mackay hated from the start.

Kidbrooke does seem to have transformed her from a mischievous rural tomboy into a trainee urban disaffiliate. She began to put on beatnik airs, failed most of her O Levels, listened to Radio Luxemburg and got herself an art-student boyfriend, with whom she enjoyed exciting weekend trysts in Soho. On school-days, she and a friend would sometimes bunk off to the big city, encountering predators everywhere.

By this stage, she was reading *Catcher in the Rye* and *On the Road*, classic truant texts, and there were few pop songs that she hadn't learned by heart. Mackay spent one restless year at Kidbrooke before announcing, at sixteen, that she wanted to leave school. She won a £25 prize in a *Daily Mirror* poetry competition – 'Windscattered little bones of birds / Lie on this fallow field' – and began to see herself as thoroughly committed to the writing life.

She applied for jobs in London and eventually landed a quite good one, which, as things transpired, would change her life. 'Girl Wanted for Antiques Shop. Easy Hours. Good Wages.' The antique shop was in London's Chancery Lane and it was one of a pair owned by the parents of the art critic David Sylvester. One of the two shops sold antiques (jewellery, porcelain, etc) and the other specialized in silver. Mackay's job was in the silver shop, which was managed by the soon-to-be famous playwright Frank Marcus (his hit play, *The Killing of Sister George*, is not at all, says Mackay, based on her).

Marcus, now dead, was married to the Sylvesters' daughter, Jackie. In no time at all, it appears, Mackay had the Sylvester household at her feet. Marcus helped her to get moving as a writer, by introducing her to publishers and agents, and David Sylvester began to escort her to art galleries and Soho drinking clubs. Mackay became a Colony Room regular (even the notoriously misanthropic Muriel, the Colony's *grande dame*, seem to have quite liked her), and with a shuddering heart found herself getting introduced to legendary art-world figures like Lucian Freud, Frank Auerbach and Francis Bacon: 'Francis could be vicious, but he never was to me.'

And nor was anybody else, so it would seem. Before long there was scarcely a big-name painter in England with whom Mackay was not on friendly terms: 'David took me to galleries, openings, parties, painters' houses and studios and introduced me to the greatest British and American artists of the day, and to the Australians Sidney Nolan and Brett Whiteley. We visited Henry Moore at Much Hadham and had tea and whisky in bone china cups with David Hockney in Powis Square. I had the great privilege of meeting Giacometti not long before he died. He was gracious and kind, his noble lined face weary beneath his grizzled hair.'

All this was a far cry from Blackheath, where her parents' marriage had gone into terminal decline. Worse still, Mackay's mother had become seriously ill, with rheumatoid arthritis. With both parents out of action, so to speak, the anxious Mackay (who might otherwise have been pressed to sign up at some university or college) was free to immerse herself in the Marcus/Sylvester world of publishers and painters. She took a flat-share in Earl's Court and for a period drank deeply at the well of urban dereliction.

In Earl's Court in the early 1960s, she has said, low life ran parallel to, and sometimes encroached on, backpackers' paradise; corruption coexisted with the conventions. And this, for Mackay, was the perfect mix: Bohemia meets Presbyteria. Her Earl's Court experience coincided with the publication of her first work of fiction – two novellas, published in one volume by André Deutsch in 1964 – and she soon had enough money (just about) to enable her to give up her full-time job at the antique shop.

Music Upstairs (1965) her second book, was a witty and candidly bisexual romp around the sleaze-spots of Earl's Court, and *Old Crow*, two years later, was a murky and staccato rendering of rustic angst: surreal lyricism combined with a high body-count is how she now describes it. In these early books, Mackay's gift for the killing simile and the surprising, spot-on image was splendidly in evidence. The plotting was half-hearted and oblique and some of the characters were caricatures, but line by line, the writing had a studied and altogether individual brilliance.

Quite clearly, hers was an authentic talent. At the age of twenty-two, she was a presence to be reckoned with. 'People often remark,' she says, 'that it must have been exciting to be published so young, and it was, but it was also terrifying. I was both blasé and shy, and I was entering an entirely new world, with holes in my shoes, and, as often as not, a dog in tow.'

In the early 1960s, she recalls, all books by young persons were treated in the papers as dispatches from front-line Swinging London. She was regularly interrogated on matters youthful by magazines and TV shows. Her opinion, she says, was sought on everything from the Beatles to reasons why a pretty girl should waste her time writing novels. And she was certainly not getting rich. In spite of a small subsidy from André Deutsch, she still had to look for part-time jobs. 'I was a model for classes taught by gruff, white-bearded Chelsea artists, and a shop assistant for a morning at Chic of Hampstead – I fled at lunchtime because I could not fold cashmere sweaters – and I worked at a greetings-card warehouse where we had the perfect line-up for a sitcom along the lines of *Are You Being Served?'*

In 1964, Mackay got married, to a boyfriend she had left behind in Blackheath. Robin Brown was an engineering student and not in the least literary; indeed, that kind of people made him nervous. 'But I married him for love, and we had many happy times together.'

Three daughters followed, and one further novel, *An Advent Calendar*, published in 1971. Then came what critics have described as Mackay's doldrum years, from 1971 until 1983, the year of her next publication. Doldrum they may have been for admirers of her work, but for the author herself these were the years of young motherhood and marriage, and pretty busy years at that. 'Maybe I was exhausted,' she suggests, 'I didn't have much time. I was running a big house. My mother was unwell. We took in lodgers. And there were three children to bring up.'

As a mother, Mackay is extolled by her friends as wonderfully conscientious. 'She always made sure they had their name tags sewed on,' was just one of many accolades. In 1972, she and Robin moved the family from East Finchley to Brockham, a village in Surrey where Mackay perhaps hoped to give her daughters a taste of her own enchanted childhood, and thence to Reigate, scene of several of her subsequent suburban tales.

During the 1970s, though, her marriage began to falter. David Sylvester had reappeared (indeed, he is the father of her youngest daughter, Cecily Brown, now a highly thought-of artist who recently sold a painting to the Tate Gallery). Why didn't she go off with Sylvester? 'When it came to the point neither of us could do it. I couldn't do it to my children and he couldn't do it to his. We would probably have driven each other mad very quickly.'

During the so-called 'doldrum years', Mackay continued writing – several of her most incisive and merciless short stories belong to this period – but found it hard to get to grips with anything large-scale. One novel, *The Firefly Motel*, was completed, then abandoned, although some of it was salvaged for *A Bowl of Cherries*, her next full-length work, which was submitted to Jonathan Cape, with whom she had a contract.

Cape turned it down. Approaching her forties, Mackay found herself without a publisher, a dispiriting situation considering her early triumphs, and all the more galling, maybe, because with this new book she had made a conscious effort to move beyond the disjointed lyricism of her first three novels. She wanted, she says, more narrative straightforwardness, more explanation.

It was around this time that she met Brigid Brophy, then a highly prominent figure on the literary scene. Over the ensuing years, Brophy would become one of Mackay's closest friends. In 1982, her help was crucial. She read *A Bowl of Cherries* in manuscript, liked it a lot (she had already admiringly reviewed some of Mackay's early work) and passed it on to Iris Murdoch, who in turn recommended it to a small publisher, the Harvester Press.

Harvester published the book in 1984, to excellent reviews. Shena Mackay's barren years – 'barren, indeed' she says – were over. In 1984, she turned forty, her children were getting ready to leave home, she was finally divorced (in

1982), and she was enjoying a second wave of recognition. Her life had become simpler in some ways but, as she points out, it was not quite a bowl of cherries. She had to support herself with part-time work at Reigate Library, her mother was still seriously ill and needed much attention (she would die in 1993) and Brigid Brophy was also in poor health (she died in 1995), and there were other turbulences too, some of them to do with drink.

On this topic, Mackay is undeniably reluctant to hold forth, but she does admit to having suffered from a 'genetic predisposition to use drink as an anaesthetic against anxiety and depression. To deny it would be to deny the wonderful people who have helped me...I wouldn't be the artist I am if I didn't know about the dark side of life and the dark night of the soul.'

Nowadays, Mackay doesn't touch a drop, but it has not been easy. It obviously pains Shena Mackay to talk about such matters, just as it pains her to be quizzed about her sometimes close relationships with other women. She loathes the word 'bisexual' and visibly winces when the subject is touched on. 'If you love someone,' she says, 'it doesn't matter what sex they are. I go along with Keats in being certain of nothing but the holiness of the heart's affections and the truth of the imagination.' And it would be a vulgar inquisitor, indeed, who could insist on pressing for more details.

For a shy person, Diet Coke is not a great loosener of tongues. For her, though, the correct place for eloquence is on the page, and over the last decade, she has been eloquent indeed. Since 1984, there have been four novels and three volumes of short stories. There has also been some progress in the marketplace: her 1996 novel *The Orchard on Fire*, was short-listed for the Booker prize and paperback sales are heading for six figures.

Mackay despises book-hype, but on the other hand, she has no wish to be marked down as merely 'quirky' or 'stylishly off-beat'. Her mother used to warn her, in jest: 'Please don't end up like Jean Rhys' – by which she meant 'neglected and admired'. Perhaps Mackay's fictions are still more likely to be valued for their brilliant detail than for their narrative excitements. When I asked a few of her admirers to nominate the features of her writing that they most admired, nearly all of them remembered similes, plane trees in the sunshine looking like giraffes, the flames of a gas fire like lupins, a collapsed umbrella like an injured fruitbat, and so on. Or they mentioned her sly, semi-private jokes.

For myself, I always chuckle when I recall one of her characters attempting to quote Yeats: 'The falcon cannot bear the falconer,' he says. 'That's not a misprint, is it?' I once asked her: 'What do you think?' she replied. (The 'bear', in case you don't know, should be 'hear'.)

It is not common for compulsively 'visual' writers to be good at telling stories; they are always dawdling so that they can take a closer look. But with recent novels like *Dunedin* and *The Orchard on Fire*, Mackay does seem to have been trying for a new structural surefootedness. And she is nicer to her characters these days, although, it must be said, she's still not very nice to them. As one of her admirers pointed out to me the other day: 'Mackay simply does not know that she is being cruel to people in her books. She says that she means them to be sympathetic. And this does seem to be the case. When I put it to Mackay that the pervert Greenidge in *The Orchard on Fire* is a triumph in sheer loathsomeness, she looked seriously troubled. Apparently, we are meant to feel sorry for this child-seducing wretch.

But then feeling sorry for people – and feeling sorry for flowers, animals, insects and sometimes the whole planet – seems to be ingrained in Mackay's nature. 'I can't see a distressed pigeon in the street without wanting to look after it,' she says. 'And if I come across a snail on a pavement, I have to move it to a safer place, where it won't be trodden on.' Does all this make her better than the rest of us? 'Oh no, not at all. I wish I didn't feel like this. It's sometimes a real nuisance, an affliction.'

A new Mackay novel will be finished by the end of the year, she tells me, but that's all she wants to tell. Her life now is industrious and calm. She has a circle of devoted and protective friends, not all of them literary, and she has what she calls 'a huge extended family', including two grandchildren, on whom she evidently dotes. She sits on committees (she is a Booker prize judge this year), supports environmental causes, is indignant about Nato and her favourite politician is Tony Benn.

'You can say that I live quietly in south London with my cats,' she says. But what about the old days? Has the Bohemian been altogether vanquished by the Presbyterian? She smiles what I take to be an enigmatic smile. 'There's a wonderful play by Rodney Ackland,' she says. 'It's called *The Pink Room* [later renamed *Absolute Hell*] and it's set in a club rather like the old Colony Room. The production I saw a few years ago ended with Judi Dench, who played the club owner, alone on the stage. The club is closing down. It has to, for some reason. And Judi Dench's last despairing cry is: "Where are the pink lights? For God's sake let's have the pink lights on!" There's still part of me that wants the pink lights, the *vie en rose*, the artifice, the tawdry glamour. Outside is the cruel daylight and all that. But most of me doesn't want that. Most of me wants to live in the country, really.'

10 July 1999

Life at a glance

SHENA MACKAY

Born: 6 June 1944.

Education: Tonbridge Girls' Grammar School; Kidbrooke Comprehensive.

Married: Robin Brown (1964), divorced; three daughters: Sarah Frances, Rebecca Mary, Cecily Rose.

Select bibliography: *Dust Falls on Eugene Schlumberger* (1964); *Toddler on the Run* (1964); *Music Upstairs* (1965); *Old Crow* (1967); *An Advent Calendar* (1971); *Babies In Rhinestones* (1983); *A Bowl of Cherries* (1984); *Redhill Rococo* (1986); *Dreams of Dead Women's Handbags* (1987); *Dunedin* (1992); *The Laughing Academy* (1993); *Such Devoted Sisters* (editor, 1993); *Collected Stories* (1994); *The Orchard on Fire* (1996); *Friendship* (editor, 1997); *The Artist's Widow* (1998); *The World's Smallest Unicorn* (1999).

Awards: Fawcett prize (1987).

CZESLAW MILOSZ

A century's witness

Nicholas Wroe

In December 1980, a monument was unveiled at the Gdansk shipyard in Poland, birthplace of the Solidarity trade union, in memory of ship workers killed by the security forces during riots a decade earlier. Inscribed on the base was a line from Psalm 29:11, translated into Polish by the poet Czeslaw Milosz: 'The Lord will give strength unto His people.' The following year Milosz returned to Poland after thirty years' exile in the West. When he went to view the Gdansk monument, members of Solidarity unfurled a huge banner bearing the message: 'The People Will Give Strength Unto Their Poet.'

In the immediate postwar years, Milosz actually worked for the People's Republic of Poland as a cultural attaché in America, but by 1951, he had broken with the regime and gone into exile in Paris, and his writing had been banned in Poland. However, his work was widely circulated in samizdat editions and he went on to become an almost mythical figure among the dissident community. His 1953 study of totalitarian ideology, *The Captive Mind*, had dared to face up to both its subtle attractions as well as its mechanisms of enslavement. In his poetry, particularly his autobiographical works, his depictions of an idealized and peaceful homeland provided solace to a nation living in an uncertain world under foreign domination. He was awarded the Nobel prize for literature in October 1980, and following a highly symbolic meeting with Lech Walesa at the Catholic University of Lublin in 1981, his status as national bard was confirmed.

Also engraved on the Gdansk monument is the defiant penultimate stanza of Milosz's poem 'You Who Wronged': 'Do not feel safe. The poet remembers. / You can kill one, but another is born. / The words are written down, the deed, the date.'

Milosz wrote these lines in 1950 when working in the Polish diplomatic embassy in Washington, and for some sections of the Polish opposition, particularly the more nationalist tendencies whose chauvinism he had attacked during the interwar years, his time working for the government made him an unsuitable choice as a moral and cultural conscience. But for most Poles, his lack of ideological purity made him more representative of the complex national experience.

The final, bitter stanza of 'You Who Wronged' – 'And you'd have done better with a winter dawn, / A rope, and a branch bowed beneath your weight' – leaves little doubt as to his profound and angry disillusionment with what had become Stalinism, even though it was not a poem written for publication. 'I was following the situation in Poland and I was quite desperate,' he now says. 'But it was written for myself, for my drawer. It had to wait thirty years for its moment.'

Milosz is now aged ninety and throughout his life and career he has often had to wait for his moment. Even his triumphant 1981 return to Poland turned out to be something of a false dawn. Within days of his visit, the first official Polish publication of his poetry sold 150,000 copies, only to be once again banned and forced underground when martial law was imposed shortly afterwards, as part of a government attempt to crush the Solidarity movement.

But Milosz's game has always been a long one, and it is hard now to comprehend the extraordinary times he has lived through. He was brought up a Pole, in Lithuania, under Russian tsarist rule, and as a child witnessed the October Revolution and the First World War. As an adult, he lived through the wartime Nazi occupation of Warsaw and then the Soviet domination of Poland. In exile, he navigated the choppy intellectual waters of 1950s Paris as an impoverished writer, and then the counter-cultural revolution of 1960s California as a professor at Berkeley.

Fellow Nobel prize-winning poet Seamus Heaney described Milosz as 'among those members of humankind who have had the ambiguous privilege of knowing and standing more reality than the rest of us'. Another Nobel winner, Joseph Brodsky, said: 'I have no hesitation whatsoever in stating that Czeslaw Milosz is one of the greatest poets of our time, perhaps the greatest.'

This month sees the publication in Britain of his *Collected Poems*. It contains work written from 1931 right up to earlier this year. Jerzy Jarniewicz, a poet and professor of English at the University of Lodz, says his impact on twentieth-century Polish and world literature has been immense. 'Milosz's poetry of the thirties foreshadowed the cataclysm of the war. Then, in 1943, after the Warsaw ghetto uprising, he was unique as a Polish poet who witnessed, responded to and articulated something that had been silent for decades in Poland: the relationship between Poland and Jews, and the feeling of moral guilt for what was going on. After the war, he helped open up Polish poetry to many European and American poets. It was Milosz who made the first translation of *The Waste Land*, for example.'

The British poet laureate Andrew Motion says that Milosz's influence extended to the West. 'You cannot understand where Ted Hughes's poem 'Crow' is coming from, formally, unless you understand its deep roots in Middle-European writing. Milosz was a part of that. Everyone said when 'Crow' came out that it was new, but, of course, it wasn't. It is idiomatically – and, in terms of its symbolic life, extremely – influenced by Middle-European poetry, which has a different way of advertising its existence as symbolic writing or allegory.'

But Motion also acknowledges that Milosz's use of Polish history and literature as subject matter can be difficult for the uninitiated reader. 'I very much enjoy his work, but I recently read a volume of his poetry and I spent a lot of time thinking, "I don't get this". It was having an interesting effect on me, but I realized that I was missing so many of the references.'

Robert Hass, the former poet laureate of the United States, has been the primary translator of Milosz's poetry from Polish into English. He agrees that the details of Polish artistic and cultural life sometimes found in the poetry can seem 'almost like a soap opera you'll never understand the whole plot of. But also, when Czeslaw deals with the details of his world, it is, emotionally, some of his most powerful writing. Working with Czeslaw is like reliving the whole of the twentieth century through this prism of great specificity. It has been very important to him to remember exactly how, say, wine was stored in 1930s working-class Paris, or the precise details of the elaborate hairdo of his piano teacher in Vilno in 1921.'

Czeslaw Milosz was born in June 1911 in the Lithuanian village of Szetejnie. The family belonged to the Polish gentry, but while Milosz was bequeathed their culture, little was left of their wealth by the time he was born. His father was an engineer for the tsarist army during the First World War and his work took him, and his family, all over Russia, repairing bridges and highways. Milosz has one younger brother, Andrzej, who now lives in Warsaw. 'He is eighty-six and he doesn't know how to walk because he runs so much,' laughs Milosz. 'He was a journalist and made film documentaries, but he had a very difficult time in Poland in the fifties because I left the country. I was very sorry about that.'

Milosz has been an American citizen since 1970, but was granted honorary Lithuanian citizenship when he returned to the newly independent country in 1992, after more than half a century away. The barn at his childhood home has been converted into a literary and cultural conference centre under the name The Czeslaw Milosz Birthplace Foundation. As he shows photographs of the newly renovated building, he points out the large, open plain in the background. 'There used to be three villages there, all with orchards,' he explains. 'Now it is known locally as Kazakhstan because that is where the population was forced to move to. The villages and everything there were destroyed.'

All this happened after Milosz had left Szetejnie, and he remembers his childhood there, returning after the chaos of war and the 1917 revolution, as an idyllic period. It is one he has returned to time and again in both his poetry and his prose, most notably in his charming 1955 novel *Issa Valley*, and his very guarded 1958 autobiography, *Native Realm*.

Milosz attended both school and university in Wilno (now Vilnius), and remembers watching Charlie Chaplin and Mary Pickford films. Although he started out studying literature, he graduated in law in 1934. 'There were so many girls studying literature it was called the marriage department. So I switched to law and I reluctantly passed my studies. But I never planned a legal career.'

Ignacy Swieckicki, an engineer now living in Pennsylvania, is a friend from his schooldays and remembers Milosz as 'always very busy with poetry and literature. He was not interested in sports, although he was in the boy scouts, but he was a boy who displayed many talents and many people expected a great future for him. His difficulty has been that he was trying to combine his faith and tradition with ideas which were rather contrary to the surroundings in which he was brought up.'

Milosz received a strict Catholic education, but wrote as a young man that 'in a Roman Catholic country intellectual freedom always goes hand in hand with atheism'. He later returned to the Church, and learned Hebrew in order to translate the Psalms into Polish, but has said that while he is a Catholic, he is not a Catholic writer. 'Because if you are branded as a Catholic, you are supposed to testify with every work of yours to following the line of the Church, which is not necessarily my case.'

Milosz's first published poems appeared in the Wilno University journal, and in 1931, he co-founded a literary group called Zagary, whose bleak political outlook and symbolism saw them dubbed the school of 'catastrophists'. During the same year he made his first trip to Paris, where he came under the influence of a distant cousin, Oscar Milosz, a French-Lithuanian writer who had been a representative of independent Lithuania at the League of Nations. 'Oscar Milosz was a very important influence on my poetic life, particularly in the religious dimension,' he says. Czeslaw returned to Paris for a year in 1934 when he won a scholarship to study at the Alliance Française.

Robert Hass says that in Milosz's own hierarchy of his readership, Parisian opinion remains important. 'Polish readership comes first and then an international readership of other writers that matter to him. But for many Poles of his generation, the ultimate source of judgment was Paris and my impression is that he is still very aware of the French response to his work.'

After returning to Wilno, Milosz worked for Polish Radio there, but was transferred to Warsaw in 1937 because of his leftist sympathies in general, and his willingness to allow Jews to broadcast in particular. When Germany invaded Poland in 1939, he was briefly sent to the frontline as a radio reporter before making his way back to Wilno. Following the Soviet invasion of Lithuania the following year, he made a dangerous journey across Soviet lines and returned to Nazi-occupied Warsaw where he found a job as a janitor at the university, making ends meet with some black-market trading. Throughout this period, he wrote and edited for underground publications, and even underground theatre, using his grandmother's maiden name, Jan Syruc.

'It was a very strange time to translate *The Waste Land*, in the middle of the German occupation,' he now acknowledges, 'but it was all part of me gradually acquiring self-awareness of how my road would be different to before the war.' The poems he wrote directly confronting the horror of what was going on around him – 'Campo dei Fiori' and 'A Poor Christian Looks at the Ghetto' – have become some of his most famous and influential works. But Milosz points to another poem written in the wake of the failed Warsaw uprising of 1943, 'The World', which was published in 1945, as equally important to him and his move away from the catastrophism of his youth to a more philosophical and transcendent faith in the future.

While he has directly engaged with enormous historical and intellectual horrors, Milosz has done so not as a politician, but more as a theologian, philosopher or mystic meditating on the nature of humanity and culture. 'I lived through the horror of the extermination of the Jewish population in Warsaw,' he says, 'and I wrote about that. But in the same year I wrote "The World", which has nothing to do with the horror of the war but instead gives an image of the world as it should be – a counterbalance and a restoring of dignity to the world as it was. I didn't know at the time that I was repeating the procedure of Blake, who had written *Songs of Experience* and *Songs of Innocence*. It was very difficult to liberate myself from pre-war patterns and tastes and styles, but I knew when I wrote these poems that it was a turning point in my poetry.'

During the Warsaw occupation, Milosz married Janina Dluska. They had met in the late thirties when they both worked for the radio station. They had two sons who both still live in California: Antoni, who was born in 1947 and is a computer programmer; and Piotr, born 1951, who is an anthropologist. Milosz has one grandchild, Erin, who is in her third year of a joint medical school PhD in New York City. Janina died in 1986 after suffering from Alzheimer's disease for ten years. In 1992, Milosz married Carol Thigpen, who was associate dean of the College of Arts and Sciences at Emory University in Atlanta, Georgia. They have a home in Berkeley, but over the past few years have spent most of their time in Krakow. Seeing Milosz in the city is to glimpse his place in Polish life. People spontaneously come up to him to say hello and take his photograph. The image of the dourly forbidding sage – he often looks darkly brooding in photographs – regularly dissolves into a huge, red-cheeked smile and rich chuckling.

Milosz first came to Krakow in 1944 after the failed Warsaw uprising. When the war ended, he became a government attaché. 'I have never been a Communist, but I did have leftist inclinations before the war, largely because I was against the kind of alliance that existed between the Catholic Church and the nationalists,' he says. 'But after the war, I had a very ambiguous attitude towards the changes that were underway. On the one hand, the country was completely dependent on Moscow and it was obvious that it was a new occupation. But on the other hand, there were some radical reforms and that was good. For a time, I had a hope that things would develop as I wanted, but in fact, for countries such as Poland and Hungary, that initial period was just an introductory period of Stalinization.'

In 1946, Milosz began working at the Polish embassy in America, and says that while he always had political doubts about the regime, they weren't crystallized until he returned home in 1949 and saw first-hand the direction the regime was taking. He attended a lavish evening function attended by most of Poland's ruling elite. On his way home, at about four in the morning, he has said that he came across some jeeps carrying newly arrested prisoners. 'The soldiers guarding them were wearing sheepskin coats, but the prisoners were in suit jackets with the collars turned up, shivering from the cold. It was then that I realized what I was part of.'

As his increasing doubts became known, so he fell under official suspicion, and when he made another trip home from Washington in December 1950, his passport was confiscated. However, only eight weeks later, he was allowed to travel to Paris, where he sought political asylum. Official connivance has long been suspected in his escape, but for many years, Milosz has been reluctant to discuss the details. 'But now it is the remote past, so it can be told,' he says. 'The wife of the Polish foreign minister was a Russian woman. She helped me, but she said: "In my opinion a poet should stay with his country, but the decision belongs to you. But if you decide otherwise, remember that you have a duty to fight him [Stalin], the executioner of Russia." It's a very romantic story, yes?'

Has he ever thought that she was right and he should have stayed? 'Many times I wondered what would have happened. I have no answer, because one doesn't know oneself enough to know how one would behave in different circumstances. Maybe I would have made a fool of myself, like the friend I describe in *The Captive Mind*, by writing what the party desired.' In *The Captive Mind*, Milosz wrote that ultimately his decision came, 'not from the functioning of the reasoning mind, but from a revolt of the stomach. A man may persuade himself, by the most logical reasoning, that he will greatly benefit his health by swallowing live frogs; and, thus rationally convinced, he may swallow a first frog, then the second; but at the third his stomach will revolt. In the same way, the growing influence of the doctrine on my way of thinking came up against the resistance of my whole nature.'

Milosz says that he doesn't like the word 'defect' and prefers to say that he broke with the regime. Regardless, his move to Paris was physically, politically and artistically dangerous. Parisian intellectual life was overwhelmingly pro-communist and many of Milosz's Parisian friends were party members. 'It is very difficult to restore today the aura and climate of politics at that time,' he says. 'Today, the division seems completely mythical. But among intellectuals then, there was great admiration for life in the East. They were very dissatisfied by me, and I was considered, at best, a madman. I had left the world of the future for the world of the past. That made my life in Paris very difficult.'

Among the few intellectuals to assist him was Albert Camus, but most of his old friends shunned him, including Pablo Neruda, who went on to become the 1971 Nobel literature laureate. He and Milosz had translated each other's work, but Neruda denounced Milosz in an article entitled 'The Man Who Ran Away' in the Communist Party newspaper. Things were made even more difficult by the fact that his family had remained in America, and he was denied a US visa to join them because of his association with the Polish Communist government.

However, despite this, his early years in Paris were productive, and he published *The Seizure of Power*, the first of his two novels; *Treatise on Poetry*, a vast, poetic overview of twentieth-century Polish poetry, only recently translated into English; and *The Captive Mind*, in which he attempted to explore 'the vulnerability of the twentieth-century mind to seduction by socio-political doctrines and its readiness to accept totalitarian terror for the sake of a hypothetical future'.

Madeline Levine, professor of Slavic literatures at the University of North Carolina, has been translating Milosz's prose since the late eighties and says that, starting with *The Captive Mind*, there is a remarkable coherence to his vast prose output. She adds that he once claimed that the twentieth-century novel would have to be capacious and include all the intellectual trends of the century, and contends that Milosz's subsequent prose work, in a fragmentary way, has, in effect, been this novel as a work-in-progress. 'In his writing, there are so many people who almost become fictional characters,' she says. 'It's not that they are fictionalized, but they are as vivid as characters in a novel. He has measured the intellectual engagements of these people against all the trends of the twentieth century. In some ways, it has been hermetic in making the passions of Polish culture and literary life come alive, but it has also been engaged with wider intellectual currents. It is about the attractions of communism and socialism, and so is often about people much like himself, people whose attraction to communism came from a principled rejection of capitalism at its worst.'

The Captive Mind was the first of Milosz's works to make a significant impact on the West, but it threw up two obstacles to his future career. 'It was considered by anti-communists as suspect because I didn't attack strongly enough the communists,' he recalls. 'I tried to understand the processes and they didn't like that. And it also created the idea, particularly in the West, that I was a political writer. This was a misunderstanding, because my poetry was unknown. I have never been a political writer, and I worked hard to destroy this image of myself. I didn't try to get a teaching position in political science. I went to America as a lecturer of literature.'

Milosz started teaching at Berkeley in 1960 and was granted tenure a year later as professor of Slavic languages and literature. He retired in 1984. At the time of the Berkeley campus revolution in 1968, when the students began to assess their professors, he was proud to receive excellent grades. That said, he found much of the sixties student radicalism depressingly shortsighted and familiar. 'I was rather sad to see every stupidity I had experienced before being re-enacted.'

He says that the years at Berkeley were a time of solitude that was good for his work but left him feeling lonely. Friends say he can have periods of melancholy, but is generally a highly gregarious companion who is enthusiastic about food, drink and conversation.

'Living in Krakow, I have plenty of friends, but in Berkeley, while I talked to colleagues and students, I had very few friends. I was in constant correspondence with good friends in Paris, as my friendships were based upon my poetry.' Milosz has always written in Polish, and it was not until 1973 that a volume of his selected poetry was translated into English. Robert Hass has said that during this time, Milosz was living in 'intolerable obscurity and loneliness. He had to invent the idea that there was still somebody to read his poems.'

The sign that his reputation had changed from political essayist to poet was the award of the Neustadt International literary prize in 1978 – described as the introduction to the Nobel because so many laureates have won it first. Two years later he received a 3 a.m. phone call at his Berkeley home from a journalist in Stockholm, telling him he had won the Nobel prize. 'The next morning, all hell broke loose. I tried very hard not to change my habits and I went to my class not to break the routine. I tried to save myself from too much turmoil, but it was very hard. I am a private person and have resisted being made a public one.'

Milosz seems to have been content to occupy this public role in Poland, but Jerzy Jarniewicz says that he may be the last in a line of Polish poets who have acted as a spokesperson for their society. While he fulfilled an important moral duty to bear witness, more recently younger poets have rebelled against this idea. 'Poets who published their first books in the late eighties and nineties have largely rejected both the official culture and the underground ethos,' explains Jarniewicz. 'Theirs is a poetry of enormous scepticism and distrust. It goes in fear of anything that is pretentious and prophetic, and so they have replaced communal experience – which is a key idea in Milosz, and in Polish poetry generally – and instead focused on what is unique and individual and personal. As one younger poet said: "There is nothing about me in the constitution."'

When Milosz's poem about the siege of Sarajevo was published on the front page of the biggest-selling Polish newspaper, it was also attacked for attempting to deal with a contemporary issue in a diction that had become anachronistic. He has also been criticized for what is seen as an over-romantic defence of Polish and European culture. 'He has criticized Western Europe for its secularization and loss of metaphysical feeling,' says Jarniewicz. 'This is counterpointed by his equally strong belief that the metaphysical is still alive in certain parts of Eastern Europe. Many younger poets look with great suspicion on this, but for Milosz it is something that is very much alive.'

Milosz says he is uneasy about trying to assess contemporary Poland – 'such a big subject' – but acknowledges that the country has changed in ways he finds difficult to recognize. 'I ask myself about the country and I can't explain it. For instance, isn't it paradoxical that a country where most people go to church on Sunday should vote for the post-Communists? But although the last election to the parliament had an anti-intelligentsia tinge, I have never been a pessimist. For instance, the book market is extremely lively in Poland and there is a lively cultural life. There are many papers and periodicals, and I collaborate with a weekly Catholic magazine here in Krakow.'

He also takes an indulgent delight in his work still being read by a young readership. His long 1956 poem, *Treatise on Poetry*, has recently been translated into English for the first time. 'It has been a great pleasure to see my poem apparently not getting old,' he smiles. 'It is really a history of Polish poetry in the twentieth century, in connection to history and the problems of so-called historical necessity. And I am proud of having written a poem that deals with historical, political and aesthetic issues even though, of course, I know that for students, the parts of the poem where I deal with Hegelian philosophy and Marxism are, for them, completely exotic. They have such short memories.'

10 November 2001

Life at a glance

CZESLAW MILOSZ

Born: 30 June 1911, Szetejnie, Lithuania.

Education: Zygmunt August High School, Wilno; Stefan Batory University, Wilno.

Married: Janina Dluska (1943, died 1986; two sons); Carol Thigpen (1992).

Career: Polish National Radio (1935–9); Polish cultural attaché in America (1946–51); freelance writer (1951–60); lecturer then professor, University of California, Berkeley (1960–84).

Select bibliography: Poetry: *Poem of the Frozen Time* (1933); *Rescue* (1945); *Light of Day* (1953); *City Without a Name* (1969); *From the Rising of the Sun* (1974); *Facing the River* (1995); *Collected Poems* (2001); Non-fiction: *The Captive Mind* (1953); *Native Realm* (1958); Fiction: *The Seizure of Power* 1953).

Awards: Neustadt International literary prize (1978); Nobel prize for literature (1980).

JAN MORRIS
The long voyage home

Nicholas Wroe

On the Sunday after the attack on the World Trade Center, the *New York Times* published a special supplement of essays about the city. While the articles were mostly written by New Yorkers, the introductory essay was by a product of the British Empire who is now a Welsh nationalist. A few lines from Jan Morris's 1987 book *Manhattan '45* were placed below an apocalyptic picture of the newly shattered cityscape: 'The Manhattan skyline shimmered in the imaginations of all the nations, and people everywhere cherished the ambition, however unattainable, of landing one day upon that legendary foreshore.' Morris says she was 'deeply touched' to see her writing used to help capture the catastrophe that had overwhelmed a city she loves.

But the conjoining of her words to important world events is nothing new. It was Morris who broke the news that a British-led expedition had conquered Mount Everest the day before the Queen's coronation in 1953. Then working as a young reporter on the *Times*, Morris describes the assignment in the Himalayas as 'an exercise in splendidly old-fashioned journalism'. Final preparations included packing a new ribbon for the typewriter and collecting a pair of corduroy trousers from the cleaners. But allied to physical courage in getting down the mountain and a dogged resourcefulness in getting the news home, Morris scooped the world and was launched on one of the most remarkable literary careers in the second half of the twentieth century.

As a foreign correspondent in the fifties, Morris chronicled the rolling back of the British Empire from North Africa and the Middle East. It was Morris as star reporter who delivered set-piece reportage from Adolf Eichmann's 1962 Jerusalem war-crimes trial. The early travel books about America, Oman and South Africa were all well received before the publication of a cultural and historical study of Venice in 1960 elevated Morris to the first rank of writers. The book has become a classic, never out of print. Equally acclaimed studies of Spain and Oxford followed, as did the *Pax Britannica* trilogy, encompassing the rise and fall of the British Empire from Victoria's accession in 1837 to Churchill's death in 1965. Later still came a Booker short-listed novel, a fiercely patriotic series of articles and books about Wales and a continuing stream of journalism and criticism.

Alistair Cooke dubbed Morris 'the Flaubert of the Jet Age' and Rebecca West hailed 'perhaps the best descriptive writer of our time'. But what makes this body of work unique is the story contained in an autobiography, *Conundrum*, published in 1974. As one reviewer pointed out: 'No writer of such intelligence, humour and sensitivity has ever undergone a complete sex-change and written about it so well.' James Morris, as she was until then, was not only an extremely famous writer, but was also married and had fathered five children. The publication of *Conundrum* was a source of intense public interest, as well as one of the major cultural events of the seventies.

Nearly thirty years on, Morris declares herself 'bored to death' with her sex change, but she did speculate in 1978 – reluctantly, one suspects – that in its aftermath she became a writer of 'changed sensibilities, of a softer prose style'. One critic notes that while James's early books convey exotic parts of the world almost through adventure stories, 'Jan hasn't really written that type of book. Hers are more leisurely strolls.' The writer Simon Winchester, a long-standing friend, says the 'brilliant foreign correspondent, reporter and raconteur rather left her reporting roots behind. She began to get much more imaginative both in her writing and thinking.'

These developments have not been to everyone's taste. Rebecca West cuttingly claimed that 'he was a better writer than she', and others have complained about a flowery prose style and tendency to feyness. The criticism of Jan's increasingly personal approach to her subject matter reached a peak two years ago with historian Andrew Roberts's review of Morris's biography of Abraham Lincoln. 'The sixteenth president gets only an occasional look-in, and readers will discover more that is factual about him from a Ladybird book than from this fantastically self-indulgent concoction of suppositions,' wrote Roberts. 'Jan Morris, who has some fine works of serious, evidence-driven history to her name, should have known better.'

Morris, who has been known to write aggrieved letters to hostile reviewers, was not only taken aback by the comments, she also tended to agree with them. The upshot is that she says her latest book, about Trieste, which is out this month to coincide with her seventy-fifth birthday, will be the last she publishes. 'But I have decided to end with a bang and make it the most self-indulgent of the lot,' she laughs. And indeed, the part-history, part-memoir of the 'ethnically ambivalent, historically confused' Adriatic seaport is typically full of personal flourishes.

As a soldier, Morris was posted to Trieste just after the war and has returned regularly ever since. Her leisurely and apparently freewheeling approach to the subject captures its strangely shifting geographical and cultural significance. But underlying the book is a strain of melancholy, and at one point Morris compares the city to a 'specialist in retirement', no longer reading the journals because they make him feel out of date, pottering about the house trying to keep himself busy, while all the time knowing that 'the fascination of his calling that has driven him with so much satisfaction for so many years, is never going to be resumed'. It begs the question about her withdrawal from publishing.

'I will be writing other things, but that review of *Lincoln* did hit home,' she says. 'It does seem that almost everything I write comes back to me. When I write about a city, I'm writing about my response to the city, my invention of the city in a way. There are a few exceptions – I think the Empire books were more detached – but many of the others have been concerned with myself and I'm getting a bit tired of that. But having said that, and you must forgive me for this, all this is because if you look at it, my life has been interesting.'

James Humphrey Morris was born in Somerset in 1926. His Welsh father was an engineer and his English mother a pianist who had studied in Leipzig and went on to give recitals for the fledgling BBC. Morris has two brothers who were also musical; one became head of music publishing at the Oxford University Press and the other, a flautist, also had a role in the family's contribution to the Coronation by playing at the Westminster Abbey ceremony.

Although Morris won't talk about her childhood beyond saying that it 'was entirely happy', it is said that some members of her immediate family took many years to accept her change of gender. But she says she knew from the very beginning that she had been born the wrong sex. When aged three or four, Morris remembers sitting under the piano as his mother played Sibelius, thinking he should really be a girl. By the time he was five, this notion was 'profoundly ingrained'.

At nine, he was sent to Oxford to be a chorister at Christ Church. Five years later, he began boarding at Lancing College, West Sussex, where she recalls in *Conundrum*, in one of the rare passages she has written about sex, that it was 'fun to be pursued and gratifying to be admired' by older boys. But he never felt homosexual, always regarding himself as 'wrongly equipped'. Even as an adult, she says, his 'libidinous fancies' were always far vaguer than his contemporaries', being 'more concerned with caress than copulation'.

His first job in journalism came when he was seventeen, with a six-month unpaid stint for the *Western Daily Press* in Bristol, where early career coups included interviews with James Cagney and Cary Grant. Despite claiming to have been 'frightened' by the strictly hierarchical disciplinary regime at Lancing, Morris then enrolled at Sandhurst before joining the 9th Queen's Royal Lancers, where he served as an intelligence officer in Italy and then Palestine. Surprisingly, he had a wonderful time.

'I was rotten military material,' she now recalls. 'I arrived in the Po Valley, fresh from Sandhurst all weedy and hopeless, at one of the best and grandest regiments in the British army. I walked into the commanding officer's tent and to my astonishment this war-worn, very distinguished colonel rose to his feet to greet me. And from that moment of courtesy, I knew life in the army was going to be OK. At last, in the army of all places, I felt I was free.' After demob in 1949, he took a course in Arabic back in England then returned to Cairo to work as a reporter for an Arab news agency before returning to Oxford, where he read English and edited the student magazine, *Cherwell*. 'I loved Oxford but didn't much like academic life,' she now says. 'Really, I just read books, which is what I would have done anyway.'

By this time Morris had married Elizabeth Tuckniss, the daughter of a Sri Lankan tea planter. Tuckniss had been in the Women's Royal Naval Service, and they met in London while Morris was on his Arabic course. They went on to have five children, born between the early fifties and early sixties, one of whom, Virginia, died aged only two months. Of the others, Mark, who edited an encyclopedia of twentieth-century composers, lives in Canada, Henry is a musician and teacher living in Devon, Susan is a mature student at the University of Wales reading Celtic studies, and Twm, an acclaimed poet in Welsh, also makes television programmes.

There has been much speculation as to how the children responded to their father's sex change. Morris has written about how supportive the family have been, and indeed, Mark provided the artwork for *Conundrum*'s cover. Twm, now a close neighbour, was also quoted a few years ago as saying: 'The effect on me has not been unhappy. On the contrary. It is fascinating. For Jan it has been a kind of journey, which few people, except in myths, have undertaken.' Two of the children have adopted the Welsh spelling of their name, Morys, and Jan says she'd have done it if she were a bit younger. She began to learn Welsh in 1960 and says she can read it adequately, but speaks only pidgin-Welsh.

Jan and Elizabeth divorced, but today they still live together, sharing a converted stables with a cat called Ibsen in the small north Wales village of Llanystumdwy, just up the road from Lloyd George's old home. Their relationship is, of course, by any standard remarkable. Elizabeth knew of Jan's belief that she was a woman from the outset and observers claimed that, if anything, Elizabeth accepted the inevitability of the sex change before Jan did. Watching them now when they are together, preparing lunch or prompting each other with old stories, they are a touching mixture of old friends, sisters and, still, husband and wife.

Trieste, like many of Morris's other books, is dedicated to Elizabeth, and Morris has already taken possession of the headstone that will go on their joint grave on a small island on the River Dwyfor behind the house. The inscription will read, in Welsh and English: 'Here are two friends, at the end of one life.' 'It was a marriage that had no right to work,' claimed Morris in *Conundrum*, 'yet it worked like a dream, living testimony, one might say, to the power of mind over matter – or of love in its purest sense over everything else.'

But even without the sex change, Morris's extensive travelling meant the marriage was never a clichéd suburban arrangement. Elizabeth would be left holding the baby, literally, so their son Henry was born when James was on Everest. Sir Edmund Hillary is his godfather. Morris had gone to the *Times* straight from Oxford, and within two years was being vetted by Everest expedition leader John Hunt for his suitability to make the trip. 'Hunt had been Montgomery's staff officer,' Morris explains, 'and he had the same attitude. Instead of "this fellow Rommel is a nuisance", it was "this mountain Everest is a nuisance, let's fix it."' Morris says he would have done anything to get the story. 'I was a sucker for the romance of newspapers, especially for a huge story like that. If someone had turned up with a radio, I would have happily smashed it up if they were going to get the story before me.'

Morris's first book came in 1956, when he published *Coast to Coast*, about a journey across America. It was ecstatically reviewed, particularly in America where her reputation has been, if anything, greater than at home. His journalism was in huge demand and one friend recalls Morris buying a car on the proceeds of one article. She has subsequently spent more time in America than any other country outside the UK.

The book of the Himalayas expedition, *Coronation Everest*, was not published until 1958, by which time Morris had left the *Times* because the paper would not allow its journalists to write books. His family moved to a home in the French Alps, from where he intended to be a full-time writer, and in the next two years he published *Sultan in Oman*; *The Market of Seleukia*, a political *tour d'horizon* of the Middle East; a book of reportage about apartheid called *South African Winter*; and a history of the Hashemite Kings. But he was again working as a journalist, this time for the *Guardian*, which had lured him back to cover the Suez crisis, offering him the chance to work six months of the year for the paper and six months on his books. This arrangement lasted five years, but Morris says he was never really comfortable, complaining: 'The paper had its roots in Northern non-conformism, not a faith that appealed to me.'

A proposed move to the *Observer* was abandoned after a disastrous interview with then editor David Astor. Morris had just covered the British withdrawal from Iraq and Jordan for the *Guardian* and Astor asked him his opinion. 'I said I think the British Empire, although in retreat, is on the whole a force for good in the world, and therefore I think that fighting a rearguard action is the right and honourable thing to do,' recalls Morris. 'Of course, this was the exact opposite of what the *Observer* thought, so I didn't join the paper.'

The journalist and television presenter Alan Whicker, then a fellow war correspondent, first met Morris when they shared a flat in Egypt. Morris was already a star because of Everest, and Whicker says: 'He was easy to admire as a colleague. He was quite quiet, very neat and rather a prim young man, although also laconic and funny. She is patently very nice now and he was too, although he was a little waspish at times, and I think she has retained just enough acerbity to avoid boredom.'

Morris's period of dissatisfaction with his newspaper career ended in 1960 with the success of *Venice*, which enabled him to write full-time. The book was written while the family were living in the city during six months away from the *Guardian*. 'It didn't seem like a key moment at the time,' Morris says now, 'but it was. It was better than anything I'd written before, and some would say better than I've written since.' She says it was less a case of finding a voice and more the voice finding something that was right for it. By the mid-sixties it had been followed by studies of Spain and then Oxford, which cemented his reputation.

Paul Clements, who has written an insightful, critical study of Morris, says the strength of these books, all still in print, is that 'James Morris's writing is almost impervious to time. *Venice*, *Oxford*, and *Spain* are timeless books. Even if the buildings change, the way he describes, for instance, the sound of a place, makes it still fresh.'

Simon Winchester also commends Morris's use of the narrative periphery. 'She is great with the little charming and tangential footnote. She can tell a ripping story, but then attaches to the main core so many little asides and adornments that you feel constantly rewarded by her writing.'

Morris says that *Pax Britannica* 'is the best thing I've done. I'd been reading Gibbon and I thought how wonderful it would be if some Roman centurion in the last days of the Empire had written not only a description of the Empire, but also something about his own feelings as well. Then I thought: "Here I am, on the collapsing frontiers of the British Empire, why don't I do it?" I hope that's how it is read in a hundred years, as being by someone who was actually there.'

The three parts of the trilogy were published in 1968, 1973 and 1978. All were initially published under the name James Morris, although subsequent reprints have used Jan. Morris's physical transformation from man to woman had begun in the early sixties, when he began taking female hormones, and was concluded with an operation in a Casablanca clinic in 1972. Morris will publish a new edition of *Conundrum* next year, thirty years after she became a woman. 'Some of it now reads as very dated,' she says, 'particularly passages about the attitudes of men to women, but I've decided to leave it – it's such a period piece.'

Morris has endured constant physical scrutiny ever since. People comment that she drives her sporty cars like a man and that she whistles, apparently a male trait. The writer Paul Theroux, who says he doesn't 'think there is a writer alive who had Jan Morris's serenity or strength', ended an account of a visit to her home with a reference to *Tootsie*, the 1982 film in which Dustin Hoffman plays an actor who pretends to be an actress. Whicker speaks for many when he says how uneasy he was about their first meeting after the operation. 'I was staggered to learn that he had gone to Morocco, and was nervous about meeting her afterwards. Do I shake her hand or kiss her cheek? Do I buy her a beer or a plate of cucumber sandwiches? A few years later I was in Hong Kong, and out of the street maelstrom I heard someone shouting my name. Jan came over to me all smiles and said I hadn't changed a bit. I couldn't say the same for her...'

Robin Day, an Oxford contemporary of Morris, claimed the most embarrassment he ever felt on television was when asking Morris about her sex life. 'I was reduced to a gibbering, incompetent mess,' he recalled. 'I said: "Do you...? Can you tell us how often? Can you live a f-f-full life?" Of course, she knew exactly what I was getting at. She pulled herself up and said it was the most disgracefully intrusive question and that she would be complaining to the director-general.'

Sir Patrick Nairne, a former senior civil servant, first met Morris as a neighbour in London nearly fifty years ago. He praises her bravery in every aspect of her life. 'The descent down Everest was exceptionally dangerous; it was just one example of the courageous commitment to exploration which, I have sometimes thought, led Jan Morris to face the dangers of fulfilling what she had always felt – that she was really a woman, and then to go through with it alone in North Africa.'

Morris acknowledges that 'I do like a bit of danger and I don't get much now,' and says she mostly enjoyed the social dangers of the sex change. 'There was a spice to it as there is in any undercover work. For a time I was a member of two clubs in London, one as a man and one as a woman, and I would sometimes, literally, change my identity in a taxi between the two. Anyone would be entertained by that.' Nairne says that a couple of Morris's own lines about one of her heroes, Admiral of the Fleet Jackie Fisher, who was First Sea Lord at the outbreak of the First World War, could equally apply to her. 'She wrote that the '"greatest of his gifts was an ageless genius for delight",' recalls Nairne, and that "he played life as an artist might play it". I think that is also true of Jan.'

Morris has said that her first ambition was to be a novelist, but that she was ruined by journalism. 'I thought journalism was the route in because I'd read people like Hemingway and Steinbeck, but I don't think I was right.' However, *Last Letters from Hav*, her debut novel published in 1985, made the Booker short list, although Morris was dismayed that her notes from the imaginary city of

Hav were assumed to be an orthodox travel book: 'The map room of the Royal Geographical Society asked for a copy.' A second novel, *Our First Leader*, was published last year. It is a satirical account of an independent Welsh state being established by a victorious Adolf Hitler following the Second World War.

Morris claims that the idea of Wales was there from childhood, although it played little part in her upbringing. 'I knew it was my dead father's country, and so properly mine too.' The distinguished Welsh writer Emyr Humphreys praises Morris for making 'a considerable contribution to Welsh cultural and literary life. She has always backed the language in a very positive way and she lives in a sort of a Welsh Shangri-la centred round Portmeirion, where there's quite a circle of people who write and are interested in the arts.'

She was awarded a CBE in 1998, but calls her 1992 election to the Gorsedd of bards – the assembly of poets, musicians and other representatives of Welsh culture – her proudest honour. She is a member of Plaid Cymru, although currently out of sorts with a leadership she regards as seeking votes in the English-speaking south Wales valleys at the expense of its traditional Welsh-speaking supporters in the north. One observer says 'a lot of English-speaking Wales would look a little askance at her. They would see her as a romantic nationalist who has come from the outside with a selective and distorted view of Wales, based on a too-passionate identification with a small, marginal and reactionary part of it.'

Simon Winchester says: 'I was reading *Decline and Fall* the other day and there is a paragraph in that from the hero, who loathes the Welsh. I realized I couldn't even bring myself to read it to Jan because she'd be so furious.' A hint of how mainstream her views are in the culture in which she lives is that, in what some would see as a socially conservative region, she has never lost a friend because of the sex change.

Professor M. Wynn Thomas, director of the centre for research into English literature and language in Wales at the University of Wales, Swansea, says: 'You could say she has gone native, but a kinder, and more accurate description, is that she is an elective Welsh person, in a distinguished tradition of writers who have chosen Welshness. These people imaginatively reconstruct Wales as much as they discover it.'

Morris goes out of her way to draw a careful distinction between nationalism, 'with its implications of chauvinism and aggression, and a patriotism that respects language and tradition and national traits'. She has been a long-standing and idealistic supporter of a European Union project that is not a melting pot, but a framework for coexistence between independent and distinctive cultures. At its most benign, this could also be a description of the old British Empire, but the attack on America has shaken her hopes and beliefs.

'Last summer I travelled round the world sort of looking for the new *Zeitgeist*,' she explains. 'I always thought one of the most hopeful things about my century – the last century – was that people and cultures were coming together. But travelling around, even before New York, it seemed to me that this really wasn't working. Everywhere I went people were either fed up with being bullied by other cultures, or of other cultures coming in.

'I was in Sydney when the Afghans were on that freighter. And even in the

Australians, whom we thought had at last come to terms with the Aboriginals, all the racism that was instinctive and intuitive came out again. You can see it here as well, with the response to asylum seekers and the religious or race riots in Bradford. I was going around thinking about the *Zeitgeist* and getting pretty gloomy, and then on the day I got home there was the World Trade Center. The *Zeitgeist* had declared itself.'

6 October 2001

Life at a glance

JAN MORRIS

Born: James Humphrey Morris, 2 October 1926, Clevedon, Somerset.
Education: Chorister at Oxford University; Lancing College; Sandhurst; Christ Church, Oxford.
Married: Elizabeth Tuckniss (1949; five children).
Career: British Army (1945–9); staff reporter, the *Times* (1951–6); staff reporter, the *Guardian* (1957–62).
Select bibliography as James Morris: *Coast to Coast* (1956); *Sultan in Oman* (1957); *The Market of Seleukia* (1957); *Coronation Everest* (1958); *Venice* (1960); *The Presence of Spain* (1964); *Oxford* (1965); *Pax Britannica* trilogy (*The Climax of Empire*, 1968; *Heaven's Command*, 1973; *Farewell the Trumpets*, 1978).
Select bibliography as Jan Morris: *Conundrum* (1974); *The Matter of Wales* (1984); *Last Letters from Hav* (1985); *Manhattan '45* (1987); *Hong Kong* (1988); *Pleasures of a Tangled Life* (1989); *A Machynlleth Triad* (1994); *Fifty Years of Europe* (1997); *Lincoln* (1999); *Our First Leader* (2000); *Trieste* (2001).

V. S. NAIPAUL
A singular writer

Maya Jaggi

One of the literary world's more bizarre vendettas was resumed recently when Paul Theroux laid waste in the *Guardian* to V. S. Naipaul's first novel in seven years, *Half a Life*, as 'clumsy, unbelievable, badly written, wilful and weird'. Theroux's book *Sir Vidia's Shadow* (1998) portrayed his one-time friend and mentor as snobbish, miserly, unforgiving and blunt to the point of brutality. While many of Naipaul's supporters discount Theroux's critique as that of a jaundiced former disciple, it stokes a wider reassessment of Naipaul's oeuvre that has been smouldering for more than a decade.

Naipaul's reputation, as a novelist and travel writer, has always been split. For John Thieme, editor of the *Journal of Commonwealth Literature*, he is a 'remarkable forerunner of displacement and migrancy as the late twentieth-century predicament'. Resident in Britain since 1950, he has won all the major literary prizes – including the Booker in 1971 – and was knighted in 1990. He scooped the first David Cohen British literature prize for a lifetime's achievement in 1993, beating such contenders as William Golding, Ted Hughes and Iris Murdoch. Only the Nobel has eluded him.

With twenty-six books over a forty-five-year career, Naipaul has become the foremost literary interpreter of the Third World for a British and American readership. Yet his pronouncements such as 'Nothing was made in Trinidad' or 'Africa has no future' have brought much hostility. The 1992 Nobel laureate, St Lucian poet Derek Walcott, who called him 'V. S. Nightfall' in a poem, described him as 'our finest writer of the English sentence', whose beautiful prose was 'scarred by scrofula', by his 'repulsion towards Negroes' and the 'self-disfiguring sneer that is praised for its probity'.

Edward Said, professor of English and comparative literature at Columbia University, says that while Naipaul, in the West, is 'considered a master novelist and an important witness to the disintegration and hypocrisy of the Third World, in the postcolonial world he's a marked man as a purveyor of stereotypes and disgust for the world that produced him – though that doesn't exclude people thinking he's a gifted writer.'

Increasingly, Naipaul's public attacks have been on targets closer to home. He likened Tony Blair to a pirate whose 'socialist revolution' had imposed a 'plebeian culture'. He has said Dickens 'died from self-parody' and E. M. Forster knew nothing of India but 'the garden boys whom he wished to seduce', and states that he does not have the time to read Salman Rushdie.

Naipaul, whose humour is often facetious, has of late been seen as a worthy heir to Evelyn Waugh – a good writer and a reactionary – whose son, Auberon, was a close friend. On stage at the National Theatre in 1990, Naipaul described Ayatollah Khomeini's 1989 fatwa against Rushdie as an 'extreme form of literary criticism', then threw his head back and laughed. A decade earlier, asked by Elizabeth Hardwick what the dot on a Hindu woman's forehead meant, he replied, 'It means: "My head is empty."'

Naipaul is never short of champions of what is described as his fearless veracity. Jason Cowley, in the *Observer* last month, said he was a 'cold, clear-eyed prophet, a scourge of sentimentality, irrationality and lazy, left-liberal prejudices'.

Naipaul, sixty-nine, has always sought to position himself as a lone, stateless observer, devoid of ideology or affiliation, peers or rivals – a truth-teller without illusion. As Said says: 'He's thought of as a witness against the postcolonial world because he's one of "them"; that there's an intimacy with which he can tell the truth about their pretensions, lies, delusions, ideologies, follies.' Yet how convincing are these claims? And how far does the writer's vision transcend the prejudices of the man?

Alastair Niven, a judge of the David Cohen prize, sees Naipaul as a 'man of great fastidiousness, who finds life quite painful and distasteful, and of great charm when he wishes to display it'. Yet he is also given to contemptuous rage. '"Creolized"? That comes from France. It has no meaning, like so many things that come from France...If ever you wish to meet intellectual frauds in quantity, go to Paris.' A sense of beleaguerment tips into bitterness, even malice. Claiming that a new book by his friend Farrukh Dhondy on the Trinidadian intellectual C. L. R. James misrepresents his relations with James, Naipaul says: 'All the time, it's false attribution, like Farrukh Dhondy on me sparring with James in 1950s London – it's a fantasy...Please speak about these absurd things that are attributed to me. This comes of too many interviews. You know, the monkey goes away and gets it all wrong, and no one corrects monkey.'

His second wife, Nadira Khannum Alvi, is on hand as spin doctor ('He has this image of being irascible but that really isn't true') and nurse ('Calm down, Vidia, drink some water'). Naipaul maintains that he has not read Theroux's book, which blamed Lady Naipaul for the breakdown of the writers' friendship. It was at her instigation, *Sir Vidia's Shadow* alleged, that Naipaul sold off the copies of Theroux's books that Theroux had inscribed to him in friendship; Theroux had chanced on them in a bookseller's catalogue ('the new spouse is a bridge-burner', he said). Naipaul will not speak about his former friend.

Half a Life, Naipaul's twelfth novel, is set in 1930s India, 1950s London and a Portuguese colony in Africa resembling Mozambique around independence in the mid-1970s. Its publisher, Picador, is also set to republish his entire backlist. His fiction has become increasingly sparse, and he was believed to have turned his back on it. 'I've never abandoned the novel,' he says. 'It's just disconcerting that when people talk about intellectual life they always talk about the novel, as though it were the highest form; it's a hangover from Bloomsbury. Great writing can be done in biography, history, art.'

He also denies claims that his later fiction has been increasingly autobiographical. 'I've used an autobiographical frame. I try to make my fiction as close to life as possible, leading the reader through deception into my narrative. It's an illusion.' The sexual development of his latest novel's Indian hero, Willie Somerset Chandran, closely recalls Naipaul's own sexual history, as revealed in 1994 to the *New Yorker* magazine.

Naipaul was married for forty-one years to Patricia Hale. Though she was always his first reader, he later described their marriage as 'incomplete'. During it, he confessed, he was a 'prostitute man...the most unsatisfying form of sex', then in the early 1970s formed a passionate relationship with an Anglo-Argentine woman, Margaret, which lasted until his second marriage. His mistress often travelled with him while his wife remained in their Wiltshire home – in the grounds of an Edwardian manor house. He now lives in a cottage in the Avon Valley, and also has 'two places' in the Gloucester Road area of London. Naipaul has never had children, whom he has said 'would have come between me and the work'. He has also said: 'I love privacy. I couldn't bear the idea of having children. I don't want a crowd,' a view which he once ascribed to having grown up in the claustrophobia of an extended family.

In his new novel, the hitherto sexually inadequate Willie thinks of his mistress: 'How terrible it would have been if...I had died without this deep satisfaction.' 'Please don't think that this is only about Willie,' says Naipaul. 'It's about really everyone I know. I know very few people who are totally fulfilled sexually, who are complete, not nagged by some feeling of "might have been", or "if only". That's where we get into trouble: we start thinking, "Everybody else is complete, fulfilled, and I'm not". It's not like that at all. Everyone's just like us...The theme of sexuality [in the book] represents something of my own, but not my life; it's not a copy.'

Vidiadhar Surajprasad Naipaul was born in 1932 in Chaguanas, Trinidad, a market town where his father, Seepersad, was a correspondent for the *Trinidad Guardian*. The island's sugar-cane fields were worked by impoverished Indians who had crossed the British Empire as indentured labourers. Although Naipaul's Brahmin grandparents had 'lost caste' as they crossed the waters in the 1880s, his mother Droapatie's family were landowners and pundits who bestowed 'a caste certainty, a high sense of the self' in 'our island India', as Naipaul wrote in *Finding the Centre* (1984), his 'prologue to an autobiography'. He adds: 'We were brought up aware of this ancestry but there were other things around one – the African world, the American base, the British-style school.'

When he was six, the family moved to Trinidad's capital, Port of Spain, the setting for his first novel, *Miguel Street* (published in 1959). It was a 'migration: from the Hindu and Indian countryside to the White-Negro-mulatto town', where the family held itself apart. 'In a ritualized society,' says Naipaul, 'their world is enclosed by ritual; they hardly know where they are. They're not like other people who wish to adapt.'

Naipaul's father transmitted his unfulfilled writing ambitions to his son, a 'fantasy of nobility' along with a 'hysteria', a 'fear of extinction...a panic about failing to be what I should be', as Naipaul wrote in his essay 'Reading and Writing' (2000). Seepersad had a nervous breakdown, and was often dependent on his wife's family. His failures helped make Naipaul aware that Trinidad could not support a literary career. As he wrote in a foreword to his father's book, *The Adventures of Gurudeva* (1976), talent was not enough 'in a society as deformed as ours'. Naipaul later wrote of Trinidad as 'unimportant, uncreative, cynical…a dot on the map', a place he was determined to leave.

He won an exhibition to Queen's Royal College in Port of Spain, and, in 1948, a Trinidad government scholarship to read English at University College, Oxford, which he took up in 1950. It was a time of loneliness and penury, covered in *Letters between a Father and his Son* (1999). (Seepersad died of a heart attack in 1953.) V. S. Naipaul himself had a nervous breakdown that lasted eighteen months, and made a suicide attempt – thwarted when the gas meter ran out. Yet he now professes to have experienced 'intense boredom… intellectually, Oxford was a disappointment to me. There were a lot of working-class people who'd been given special grants… They were not all fine. Some were; most were not. But they've disappeared. Most people who go to Oxford disappear – dross.' His tutor, Peter Bayley, reportedly said years later that Naipaul had 'not quite forgiven us for giving him a second-class degree'.

In 1955 he married Patricia Hale, whom he had met at Oxford. While editing a weekly radio programme for the BBC Caribbean Service, he wrote *Miguel Street*, his third published novel. It was followed by *The Mystic Masseur* (1957), *The Suffrage of Elvira* (1958) and what many still believe to be his masterpiece, *A House for Mr Biswas* (1961), based on his father's life, and with a character, Anand, who resembles the young Vidia. All these novels were set in the Caribbean, where he found his material in 'the city street from whose mixed life we had held aloof, and the country life before that, with the ways and manners of a remembered India'.

Naipaul says of his early works: 'I adore them. They're very original. *Miguel Street* remains rather wise. I'm slightly amazed.' Caryl Phillips, who wrote the screenplay for a Merchant-Ivory film of *The Mystic Masseur* to be released this autumn, admires in them 'the humour of Caribbean patois, captured in funny, accurate dialogue'.

Yet Naipaul's vision darkened. Twenty years after *A House for Mr Biswas* was published, the author heard it abridged on the radio and was in tears. 'It affected me,' he says, 'the emotions of the work itself, of discovering one's talent, the two or three years of great excitement writing the book – because life wasn't so easy afterwards; it was full of ups and downs.' Those early books won prizes, yet he insists they had 'no critical success – that's a myth'. Proud to have had only brief non-literary jobs (one as a copywriter for a cement company), Naipaul says he lived by journalism and reviewing. 'I made no money from the books. They were hard to place in paperback. That's important to know. There's an idea that people were falling on them, but no, no. One always had to just pick oneself up and begin again, always. That's become my nature. To be a writer one has to be extraordinarily tough.'

Other writers of the receding British Empire were beginning to be published in London in the fifties and sixties, including the West Indians Sam Selvon, George Lamming and Edgar Mittelholzer, the Nigerian Chinua Achebe and the Indians R. K. Narayan and Raja Rao. But of contacts with West Indian contemporaries, Naipaul says: 'My relationship was as a [radio] editor. There wasn't more.'

'People reinvent themselves,' says Phillips. 'In the 1950s, Naipaul was one of a group of writers from the Caribbean, India, Africa, with the emergence of what became Commonwealth literature – though he's always pretended this was not the case. Those writers were engaged not only in pursuit of their own careers but in building a national literature, hand in hand with a people finding a voice. Naipaul decided to reinvent himself as separate.'

His next novel, *Mr Stone and the Knights Companion* (1963), contained only English characters. He also began his travel-writing career when the Trinidadian prime minister Eric Williams commissioned what became an account of the Caribbean, *The Middle Passage* (1962). Its often perceptive criticisms were couched in the tone of aloof disdain that became his hallmark, from its first sentence – 'There was such a crowd of immigrant-type West Indians on the boat-train platform at Waterloo that I was glad I was travelling first class to the West Indies' – to his admission that 'the steel band used to be regarded as a high manifestation of West Indian Culture, and it was a sound I detested'. He returned to Trinidadian history in *The Loss of El Dorado* (1969).

'I didn't know how to travel when I began,' says Naipaul. 'I loved the idea of being on the road, with money in my pocket and introductions, going to people's houses and having dinner. But the problem is how you make a narrative out of that...It's important to remember that to be a colonial writing about colonial societies was new. There'd been no one doing it before.'

An Area of Darkness (1964) was more difficult. 'Again, that was a new kind of book: no one of Indian ancestry had written a book like that about India, trying to look at the whole country.' Naipaul's childhood faith in the 'wholeness of India' was dispelled by his first visit. He hated Westerners who found spiritual succour where he found only dirt and disease. In *India: A Wounded Civilization* (1977) he described a Hindu land injured by both the British Raj and the preceding Islamic conquest, India's 'dark ages'.

Travel, wrote Naipaul, 'broadened my world-view...and took me out of my colonial shell'. Argentina in 1972 was a 'breakthrough: far from being a colonial traveller, I was becoming an inquirer'. He took his experience of 'half-made societies' – 'Argentina, Congo, places created by the colonial system' – into his fiction. *The Mimic Men* (1967) and the Booker-winning *In a Free State* (1971), dwelt on 'mimic men' absurdly imitating their former colonial masters, and on the anxiety of displaced individuals.

Naipaul was writer in residence at Makerere University in Uganda in 1966, and began using his trips as inspiration for both fiction and essays. His novel *Guerrillas* (1975) fictionalized Caribbean black-power leaders of the 1970s, while *The Killings in Trinidad* (1980) was based on the real Michael X. A return visit to Zaire in 1975 grew into the novel *A Bend in the River* (1979) as well as the non-fiction *A Congo Diary* (1980).

In Thieme's view, the hand of Dickens gave way in these novels to Conrad's. *A Bend in the River* saw *Heart of Darkness*'s Mr Kurtz reincarnated as a despotic Mobutu figure, the 'Big Man'. The Turkish writer Orhan Pamuk admires Naipaul's 'representing Third-World people not with sugary magic realism but with their demons, their misdeeds and horrors – which made them less victims and more human'. But Chinua Achebe dismissed *A Bend in the River* as 'pompous rubbish', sensing that 'although Naipaul was writing about Africa, he was not writing for Africans'.

Naipaul has often been accused of pessimism. 'I don't know what it means,' he says. 'I don't know if it means they adored Mobutu. Maybe it means just that, that in Argentina they adored Peron and his successors, who looted the country to its bankrupt state. I didn't make the world; I tried to record it accurately and without prejudice. To have a political view is to be prejudiced. I don't have a political view.' However, Naipaul is a 'profoundly political writer' according to Said, who adds: 'He takes a dim view of decolonization, and thinks modern nationalism is a disaster.'

With his 1970s fiction, Naipaul overtook his contemporaries in praise. Phillips believes his career 'cast a big shadow over that generation of writers because, with his dyspeptic, apocalyptic vision of the Third World, he was anointed as the one authentic voice'.

After the deaths of his sister, Sati, in 1984, and younger brother Shiva – also a writer – in 1985, Naipaul entered perhaps his third, 'autumnal' phase. *The Enigma of Arrival* (1987) and *A Way in the World* (1994) combine autobiographical elements with wider histories – of postwar migration and the new world. The first is an elegiac novel, set largely in rural Wiltshire and overshadowed by death. While Walcott called it a 'melodious whine – Trinidad injured me; England saved me', Rushdie found a total absence of love. Phillips says that 'for the last twenty years, Naipaul's subject has been himself'.

'I don't know why people think it's autobiographical,' says Naipaul. 'I was writing about myself as a writer. It has nothing about my wife, my girlfriends – all that's left out. The aim was to write about looking for subjects, being deceived by what you think you should write about, missing the real subjects – the writer coming to a boarding house in London full of displaced persons in Europe, a kind of flotsam after the war. That was a big subject, if only the boy of eighteen could have seen it. Then the great irony of coming to rest in this manor house with imperial associations, which is itself in a state of decay. It's about England, a kind of country life, but not as others write about it. It sets ideas about country life on their head.'

With *India: A Million Mutinies Now* (1990), Naipaul returned to his area of darkness. He analysed the shame and 'neurosis' with which he first visited the country as a 'fearful traveller', and chided himself for having seen 'only the surface of things'. This time he found evidence of intellectual regeneration, and appeared to allow his subjects to speak for themselves. 'Now, at the end, I feel that when you travel in a country, you, the traveller, are not the most important person; the important ones are the people you're travelling among,' he says. Yet he was accused of substituting for bitter negativity a sanguine faith, not least about phenomena such as Hindu fundamentalism that others found alarming.

Naipaul reacts with sarcasm to the charge of wilful optimism. 'That assumes; "Here is India being the same old India, and it's the writer who has changed. India itself has gone along on its own messy way, in sloth and ignorance, and the writer now adores sloth and ignorance..." It's not like that. The world changes.'

The charge was different for his book on Islamic fundamentalism, *Among the Believers* (1981), and its follow-up, *Beyond Belief* (1998), travels though non-Arab, 'converted' Islamic countries. Edward Hoagland in the *New York Times* thought

Among the Believers a 'vitriolic tour [that] evinces an inherent antipathy to the religion of Islam so naked and severe that a book taking a comparable view of Christianity or Judaism would have been hard put to find a publisher in the United States'. Said describes *Beyond Belief* as an 'intellectual catastrophe. He thinks Islam is the worst disaster that ever happened to India, and the book reveals a pathology. It's hard to believe any rational person would attack an entire culture on that scale.'

In *Half a Life* there are traces of the early humour that most agree is absent from his later books, though he insists: 'In all my work there's humour, all of it, even the darkest.' It reprises a doom-laden vision of Africa, as civil war, fuelled by a neighbour resembling apartheid South Africa, hangs over the former colony. 'The history of the Portuguese colonies in Africa is an appalling history; it's not over,' Naipaul says. 'To think that one can arrive at some serene view of Africa is foolish.' Yet while he is contemptuous of Westerners who cheer revolutions with a return air ticket in their back pocket, despair may also be a luxury of the visitor, the option of flight to the West a prerogative of the few.

The novel sees mixed-race, 'half-and-half', 'second-rank' people – including the half-Brahmin, half-low-caste Willie – as lost. It is the 'pure' Africans who are happy. Though a product of several cultures, Naipaul's work betrays a dread of miscegenation, a hankering for racial, even cultural, separation. According to Thieme, 'in *The Mimic Men*, he almost looks to an Aryan purity...He sees the pre-colonial period as Edenic, which is troubling.'

Naipaul's first wife died in 1996, and that year he married Alvi, a divorced Pakistani journalist who is twenty-five years his junior. Among the guests at their wedding dinner in London were Harold Pinter and Lady Antonia Fraser, the writer Francis Wyndham and the former editor of the *London Review of Books*, Karl Miller. 'I trust Nadira, I lean on her,' he says. Owing to failing health he travels far less, but of death he says with grim satisfaction: 'I'm looking forward to it.' After his wife remonstrates ('he goes to the gym three times a week'), he resumes: 'As long as one is alive, one has to be OK, so one's committed to the gym...But I'm actually looking forward to death. It's going to be hard, if you've been writing all your life, to imagine a time – which is not far away – when one will no longer be writing. I don't know how I'll cope with it. It'll be very painful.'

He has given thought to posterity. 'Nearly everything written in the last century will crumble away to dust – all the novels,' he says. 'In every novel written now, there's an element of mimicry...People will still want to read the originals, the masters.' Among these, he counts early Dickens, Balzac, Flaubert and Maupassant. 'No one in his right mind wants to read Hemingway for pleasure, or Galsworthy or Snow.'

He seems to take most pride in his travel books – which are arguably, even for many admirers, his weakest. 'The work I was doing on Islam, that kind of human narrative, was profounder and truer to our time than any novel of imitation,' he says. 'The travel books have all been original; there was nothing like them before. It would be easy for them to have copies.'

For Naipaul, Britain remains 'somebody else's landscape'. While Niven believes he has been absorbed into a British literary tradition, Naipaul demurs.

'I'm completely outside it; I have no part in it. I'm my own writer. My material means I'm entirely separate.'

In Phillips's view, Naipaul has 'allowed himself to be accepted by an English tradition but not absorbed. He'll accept garlands and applause, but he won't position himself at the centre publicly. His own tradition is being separate, different, apart.'

'One's done an immense amount of work,' says Naipaul. 'Every book is an effort; every book extends vision. I'm not a detective-story writer. I'm not Agatha Christie, who ends as she begins, in the same limited view of the world. Nor Graham Greene, or P. G. Wodehouse – their world doesn't change. I'm quite different: my world changes as I write.'

How far Naipaul's world changes remains open to dispute. But there is no doubt that his vision reveals as much about the man as about the world.

8 September 2001

Life at a glance

VIDIADHAR SURAJPRASAD NAIPAUL

Born: 17 August 1932, Chaguanas, Trinidad.

Education: Queen's Royal College, Port of Spain; University College, Oxford.

Married: Patricia Hale (1955–96); Nadira Khannum Alvi (1996).

Select bibliography: *The Mystic Masseur* (1957); *Miguel Street* (1959); *A House for Mr Biswas* (1961); *An Area of Darkness* (1964); *The Mimic Men* (1967); *In a Free State* (1971); *India: A Wounded Civilization* (1977); *A Bend in the River* (1979); *Among the Believers* (1981); *Finding the Centre* (1984); *The Enigma of Arrival* (1987); *India: A Million Mutinies Now* (1990); *A Way in the World* (1994); *Beyond Belief* (1998); *Half a Life* (2001).

Awards: John Llewellyn Rhys memorial prize (1958); Somerset Maugham award (1961); W. H. Smith award (1968); Booker prize *In a Free State* (1971); T. S. Eliot award for creative writing (1986); knighthood (1990); David Cohen British literature prize (1993); Nobel prize for literature (2001).

EDNA O'BRIEN
Country matters

Nicholas Wroe

On 15 June this year, the eve of Bloomsday, a party was held in Dublin to launch Edna O'Brien's book about James Joyce. The Irish Taoiseach, Bertie Ahern, made a neat joke about Joyce and Guinness deserving equal credit for the proliferation of Irish pubs all over the world, before pointing out the connection between Joyce and O'Brien, who, he said, had both been critical of conventional pieties.

The Irish nation, he declared, 'owes it to them both that we are more realistic about our country'. Ahern then noted that the very fact of his congratulating O'Brien on her achievements was in itself a remarkable event. 'I'm sure that the Taoiseach of forty years ago would hardly have agreed to launch her first novel.'

How true. In 1960, the Irish censor was so appalled by *The Country Girls*, O'Brien's account of sexual awakening in a repressed Ireland, that he banned it, and her next six novels as well. Her parents, who were themselves deeply ashamed of the book, were vilified by their neighbours and O'Brien became a national hate figure. Somehow four copies of the book turned up in a shop in Limerick. One allegedly induced a seizure in a woman reader, but the other three were bought by the O'Brien family's parish priest, who secreted them back home to the village of Tuamgraney in County Clare, where they were publicly burned.

It all seems a long time ago now to O'Brien, who has lived in England since just before publication of *The Country Girls*. She has gone on to hobnob with presidents, prime ministers and film stars while continuing a prolific career as a writer of stories, screenplays, journalism, plays and novels. Her latest novel, *Wild Decembers*, is published this week, and November sees her new play, *Our Father*, staged at the Almeida theatre in Islington.

But if O'Brien has come a long way since those fraught days, Ahern's comments show that Ireland has come even further. Nearly four decades on, her story about Kate and Baba and their adventures in life and love has been officially rehabilitated from 'a smear on Irish womanhood' to a brave early-warning signal of the birth of the new Ireland.

The Nobel prize-winning poet Seamus Heaney agrees. 'Edna is actually very important in the history of this country. And those early books weren't popular just because of their subject matter and because they broke taboos. They are actually very good books.' Earlier this year, O'Brien was awarded a doctorate by Queen's University in Belfast. It was conferred by that honorary Ulsterman, former US senator George Mitchell, and the citation read that O'Brien's early novels had 'changed the fate of Irish womanhood'. A recent study placed *The Country Girls* in the top twenty best-selling Irish books of the century, alongside Joyce, Beckett, Wilde and Synge.

So is it the familiar story; the *enfant terrible* transformed by the powers of time and fashion into the *éminence grise*? Not quite. Nothing is ever that straightforward in O'Brien's life. While her personal and critical reputation has been clawed out of the mire in Ireland, on this side of the Irish Sea she has faced increasingly hostile criticism.

In this paper's review of her book about Joyce, the critic – albeit an Irishman – concluded: 'All Edna O'Brien's effort proves is that lightweight novelists should stick to what they do best.' Her recent novels – *Wild Decembers* is the final part of a trilogy dealing with three key issues in modern Irish life; the IRA, abortion and land – have seen her castigated as out of touch with modern Ireland, and her heightened prose style as out of touch with modern readers.

'It can be so hurtful,' she says, 'and I'm incapable of growing a thick skin. The "slings and arrows" actually cut more as time goes on because you know what you are attempting to do. I can take up a book that has been praised and it may not be for me, but I still give it its place in the horse race. Some don't do that. It's just bile and demolition.'

And O'Brien is not entirely without heavyweight support. Harold Pinter has known her for thirty-five years. 'Edna does expose herself and her characters in a very courageous way,' he says, 'and I admire that. People usually tend to automatically hide, and she, instinctively, doesn't hide. Such absolute honesty is a very unusual position to sustain these days. And her Joyce book was in fact a very singular achievement. She really got under the skin of Joyce. It was as if she was sitting in a café with him, but that is the nature of her. She has a very keen sensibility and a very acute perception into other people's lives.'

The writer and critic Francis Wyndham reinforces the point. 'She says she is not thick-skinned, but her skin does have another quality to it: resilience. She doesn't go off after a bad review and write a different type of thing; she carries on. She is completely serious about her writing and maybe some critics are embarrassed by this, or think it ridiculous. She does attract some sort of animosity among some reviewers because maybe they think she was too successful. All writers go on television and radio now, but she did that sort of thing a little bit earlier than other literary writers and she was very much in the public eye. Although I must say that she was always there for being a writer, rather than just as a Liz Hurley-type celebrity.'

O'Brien's lifestyle, as it wasn't then called in the sixties, has long been a source of fascination. It seemed she knew everyone, drank champagne with most of them and, if even half the rumours are to be believed, slept with a quite a few. She is well aware of the impact her own myth has had on her life and career. For instance, after her second novel was filmed as *Girl with Green Eyes* – a quintessential piece of sixties British realism starring Rita Tushingham – 'my eyes were deemed green,' she says, 'but they are really bluey-grey. It's like I never read about Richard Harris or Peter O'Toole without coming upon the word "tearaway". Some people are always happier to rush to assumptions about me without ever reading a line.'

Her agent, David Godwin, acknowledges the point. After detailing her continued success in America and her substantial sales in Europe, he sees a 'sort of Puritanism' in some of the responses to her work. 'She is exceptionally acute and a far better writer than, say, Doris Lessing. But because Edna is a more glamorous woman sometimes people don't take her so seriously.'

For all this complaint about the life getting in the way of the art, there is no escaping the contrast between where O'Brien came from and where she is now. Sitting in a brown velvet Jasper Conran dress in her rented Kensington house, with its louchely lived-in French furniture and blood-red drawing room walls, the woman may be the same, but the way she lives could not be more different to her early life on a pre-war farm in County Clare. A bottle of extremely good white Burgundy sits in the fridge and she has a stylishly abundant town garden. While posing for photographs outside, a rotten fig fell from a tree and landed with a loud splash on the path. 'So it is the garden of earthly delights,' O'Brien laughed, before adding in her still seductively soft Irish voice – and staying just on the right side of self-parody – 'but I don't think this is the time to start smearing our naked bodies with figs.'

There had been money in the O'Brien family but her father dissipated it, 'in a way that is not uncustomary in Irish mythology'. The fortune he drank and gambled away was made by priests who patented a cure-all elixir called Father John's Medicine. Its contents are not known – 'I think it was mainly cod liver oil with something else,' says O'Brien – but it paid for a large family house in Tuamgraney called Drewsboro. Before she was born, 'during that all-embracing word, the Troubles', the Black and Tans were due to billet the house, so her father and four other men set fire to it. The O'Briens moved to another house close by and she grew up within sight of the ruins. 'There was a corner of a coral wall with kitchen gongs still attached – silent, rusted – and thorn trees were growing in the rubble.'

It was not a happy home. O'Brien talks of 'fear and ructions'. The family were named in the same debtors' magazine as the Joyces had been. 'Once, after reciting some poetry to a couple of old local shopkeepers, I was given a silver threepence which I had to gave straight back to them to take off my parents' account. But while I saw the shame of debt, I haven't really learned from it because I am a bit extravagant myself.'

The only books in the house were prayer books, cookery books and bloodstock reports – 'my mother honestly believed in the sinfulness of literature even though she never read any' – and convent school didn't suit Edna. 'One of the teachers had a real set on me, as we call it. I was very bright and she resented it. Envy is sixth in the seven deadly sins, but it deserves higher billing, I think.' But she outlasted the teacher when, in a scene straight out of one of her books, the hated woman was removed to a lunatic asylum in the middle of a lesson.

While O'Brien's English was always 'too exuberant' to get top marks, she did well at mathematics and science, which led her to being enrolled in pharmaceutical college. She was then forced by the family to work in a chemist shop. 'I suffer from obedience,' she explains.

O'Brien was, however, from the very outset never more than a semi-detached member of her community. The youngest of four siblings by six years, she always felt like an only child and although she has 'beautiful, adoring and adored children and a few terrific friends', she says 'I do feel a bit lonely and I always have done. Some people seem to understand the game of life, but I never grasped it.'

Her cousin, Jack Keane, recalls her as an engaging but unusual child. 'She was very graceful and slim and made even the most little event seem very important. She was the sort of girl who had a name for all the cows in the field, and one time, when she was about three or four, and we were going to mass in the jaunting car [a horse-drawn carriage with seats that folded up like a bird's wing] Edna asked: "Is the bird going to take us to see God?" Which was childish, but also true in a sort of a way.'

O'Brien was never destined to stay long in the pharmacy but her escape was none the less dramatic. She eloped with the Irish-Czech writer Ernest Gebler to County Wicklow. They married a few years later, just before their son Carlo, now a writer himself, was born. Another son, Sasha, now an architect, was born a year later.

Her elopement confirmed her break with the Catholic Church, although it came not because of any intellectual rejection on her part, more her acceptance that she had indeed 'broken their precepts and become a sinner. As Marcel Proust glowingly shows us, the imagery of childhood stays with us for ever. It is thrilling and ghostly. Yeats described this when writing about Shelley: "how there is for the lucky man some one picture that is the image of his secret life". For me it is the vision of Christ: sallow-faced, dark-eyed, a gravity.'

These days she prays 'increasingly' but complains about modern liturgical practice. 'There are some things I have an intellectual rigour about, but not God or eternity. These are mysteries. I was so religious as a child. I imbibed every word of the gospels – which were perfect prose. I wish to God there was more writing like that around now. I absolutely believed in the hellfire. But the sermons are too secular now. Although the sermons in Ireland were hair-raising, they did bring God and Satan into it. Now it's public relations.'

The couple moved to London with their children in 1960. 'Ernest Gebler said' – she always uses both his names – 'that we moved because of my career, but I had no career. I was a mother.' Although she had been contributing short nature pieces to Irish newspapers, she had not written any fiction until 'two things changed my life'.

'First I bought a book on James Joyce with an introduction by T. S. Eliot for fourpence, although I didn't know who T. S. Eliot was. I couldn't approach *Ulysses* but I knew that *Portrait of the Artist* was an autobiographical work and I knew then that the old family cauldron was the place to go for the stories. The second thing was that I got to read novels for Hutchinson. Iain Hamilton, who was the boss, read some of my reader's reports and he, along with Blanche Knopf in America, commissioned me to write a novel. They paid £25 each, and me, being the obedient wife, spent the money on a sewing machine, which of course I never used.' She takes this opportunity to deny, unprompted, that she had an affair with Hamilton. 'I had no affair with anyone while I was married.'

O'Brien, who throughout her life has been surrounded by rumours of relationships with married men, was deeply upset by the way revelations about Ted Hughes's infidelity recently emerged. 'I'd never do that. Never.' Hughes was a friend and she proudly displays a note sent to her while she was writing *Wild Decembers*, in which he enquires how she is getting on with her 'kindershriek'.

Having been given her break by Hamilton, she wrote *The Country Girls* in a three-week spasm and can still recite the opening paragraph word-perfectly. 'It wrote itself,' she says. 'I was crying a lot because I had left Ireland, although I was not driven out. I was a voluntary exile. And yet the landscape here was alien. I arrived on Remembrance Sunday and had no idea even why all the wreaths were out. Plus I was bidding goodbye to a former world and childhood. Life is a series of goodbyes until the final one.'

The book's immediate success and notoriety quickly propelled her into a new world. After publication, Blanche Knopf asked her to tea at her suite in Claridge's. 'It was a summer's day but she was still asking for a fire to be lit in her room,' laughs O'Brien. 'She was very remote and very patrician and asked me did I have the same nightmare as her and the writer Elizabeth Bowen – you're staying in a very grand country house and nobody brings you breakfast in the morning? "My fear is that I'll never be invited to such a house," I said.'

O'Brien then heard that author Elizabeth Bowen had described her as talented, but completely mad. 'And I remember thinking even then that madness is no drawback to a writer. Obviously, if, like Virginia Woolf or Gogol, you cross the frontier then that is fatal. The hope is to come "back from the Azores", as Joyce said of himself.' Her own occasional visits to the Azores have been mercifully brief, but she has been in analysis as well as having a 'rough ride' with LSD while under psychiatrist R. D. Laing in the sixties – 'a pioneer, but not a healer'.

When her marriage to Gebler eventually foundered after thirteen years, the break-up was highly acrimonious. 'I had a Jane Eyre-type marriage...I took the Brontës a little too seriously. It was never a marriage of equals, it was always master and pupil. Now, of course, I admonish myself for being such a fool.' Having walked out with the boys, she agreed to Gebler's request that his sons should come to stay with him. 'So I dropped them off and they ran inside, and he said: "Thank you. Legally, you have just deserted your children." And that was true in those days, so I had to fight to get them back.'

To her great surprise, O'Brien eventually won custody. 'A considerable tonnage of bile was brought into the courtroom. I was called a nymphomaniac and a lesbian and it was said I took drugs. In fact I didn't even smoke.'

Gebler died a few years ago in a Dublin nursing home after suffering from Alzheimer's disease.

O'Brien says now that it was easier to be a mother and a writer than a wife and a writer, though she acknowledges it was hard on her children. 'But the boys were little warriors. I think it's wounded Carlo more, but then he's a writer, so he has to explore the wounds.'

This was all taking place in the late sixties when O'Brien was a major celebrity. She had completed *The Country Girls* trilogy and a sexy, soft-focus photo of her adorned the paperback version. She gave grand parties at which only Dom Pérignon was served – 'I was mad about this brilliant theatre designer, Sean Kenny, so I really gave the parties for him, but he was blind to my entreaties' – and regularly appeared on television. Then – as now – she knew her worth. Julian Barnes tells how, as a young journalist, he interviewed her, and as they proceeded, 'it became clear that I hadn't come to do the Big Interview on the grown-up pages, but the quick snooty para at the back of the mag. A certain unease established itself.'

The hard work and success meant there was enough money for both Carlo and Sasha to be sent to Bedales School. A fellow pupil recalls the glamour attached to the boys, who cut languorously elegant figures as they consumed the contents of their mother's lavish hampers on the school tennis courts.

'I suppose I am a bit bohemian,' says O'Brien, 'but I've always regarded being bohemian not as being scruffy, but having a bit of style. But writing is essentially a monastic activity. There are the odd moments; parties, public readings, but that's just the dew drop. There is the plant with the roots underneath it and that is much more eternal. I want life. But I know that for a writer to become famous like a rock star or film star is destructive. We all want a bit of money, but fame thwarts the creative juices.'

The other thing that thwarted O'Brien's creative juices was a long-term affair with an (unnamed) politician in the eighties, during which she stopped writing novels. She now says she would never give up her work for anyone again, but equally that 'I have been in love and I've known love given back to me and it is the most wonderful, tremulous, sublime state to be in. Don't knock it. And maybe you need to have that sort of a death sometimes, to plumb the depths before you can rise again and write.'

Her renaissance in the nineties has produced her latest trilogy. *House of Splendid Isolation* concerned the relationship between an old woman and an IRA fugitive based on Dominic 'Mad Dog' McGlinchey, whom O'Brien visited in prison. The second novel was prompted by the 'X Case', in which a fourteen-year-old Irish girl was refused an abortion. '*Down by the River* was disgracefully neglected,' says Francis Wyndham. 'It is a powerful and beautiful book.'

Wild Decembers centres on a protracted land dispute between two farmers. 'But it's not just about land,' she explains. 'The craving for possession is fundamental; it's also about a man and a woman; the whole caboodle.'

O'Brien says that the *Country Girls* trilogy was not as painful to write as this latest work. 'Things get more complex, more searing. The early books were more personal, accessible. Now the subjects are about the country of Ireland and it entails more rummaging around. I drove people mad looking at tractors with this one.'

Her intense relationship with Ireland is under permanent review 'My own part is imprinted in me for ever. And while that's a bonus, it also exacts a price. I don't want to sound too occult but places talk back up to you. The place I come from in Ireland isn't beautiful like, say, the lakes of Killarney, but it has a magic. I definitely have an ancestral memory of that place and it was a place where I could feed my own fantasies.' But, she says, she is divided. 'I am thankful for the stuff that Ireland gave me, but there is plenty of animosity in it as well.'

Her parents are both now dead, but a rough equilibrium had long been in place between them and their rebellious daughter. 'My mother was very ashamed but, for want of a better word, she forgave me. There was obviously a tension, but there wasn't a rift. There was more of a question mark, which is true for the families of many writers who expose what they see as skeletons.' She says she wrote home every week and visited them regularly. 'I was dutiful. Part of me always loved them and part of me didn't. I have all my mother's letters and they break one's heart. Every single one ends with the hope that we shall be buried together, but I want my own grave. My son Sasha says it's the only piece of property I'll ever own.'

O'Brien lives alone, as she has done since the end of her marriage. 'It's thin on jocularity, but good for the soul,' she smiles. 'Ordinary life bypassed me, but I also bypassed it. It couldn't have been any other way. Conventional life and conventional people are not for me – and I could lose a lot of readers saying this – because it's a barrenness, a shrivelled life,' she sighs.

'Writing is very hard. Keeping faith in it is very hard. I know people who have a surplus of self-congratulation. Even after I finish a book or a play, I can't draw breath. Look at me now, scrambling up a hill trying to write another. In some ways, I suppose a lot of the material of my life has been ripe for literature, but a bit of a handicap for what is laughingly called everyday life. But that's the bargain. Mephistopheles didn't come, you know. He was already there.'

2 October 1999

Life at a glance

EDNA O'BRIEN

Born: 1932, Tuamgraney, County Clare.

Education: Scariff National School; Convent of Mercy, Loughreu; Pharmaceutical College, Dublin.

Married: Ernest Gebler (1954, divorced 1967); two sons, Carlo and Sasha. Four grandchildren.

Select bibliography: Plays: *A Pagan Place* (1970); *Virginia* (1979); *Flesh and Blood* (1987); *Madame Bovary* (1987); *Our Father* (1999); Stories: *Night* (1972); *Mrs Reinhardt and other stories* (1978); *A Fanatic Heart* (1985); *Lantern Slides* (1990); Novels: *The Country Girls* (1960); *The Lonely Girl* (1962), (filmed as *Girl with Green Eyes*, 1963); *Girls in their Married Bliss* (1963); *August is a Wicked Month* (1964); *Casualties of Peace* (1966); *The High Road* (1988); *Time and Tide* (1990); *House of Splendid Isolation* (1994); *Down by the River* (1996); *Wild Decembers* (1999).

HAROLD PINTER
Under the volcano

Stephen Moss

A woman once wrote to Harold Pinter to ask him to explain *The Birthday Party*. 'These are the points I do not understand: 1. Who are the two men? 2. Where did Stanley come from? 3. Were they all supposed to be normal? You will appreciate that without the answers to these questions I cannot fully understand your play.' Pinter replied: 'These are the points I do not understand: 1. Who are you? 2. Where do you come from? 3. Are you supposed to be normal? You will appreciate that without the answers to these questions, I cannot fully understand your letter.'

Alan Ayckbourn, then a callow twenty-year-old playing Stanley in an early production of the play in Scarborough, also had the temerity to ask Pinter for some biographical details of the mysterious concert pianist. 'Mind your own fucking business,' he was told. 'Just say the lines.'

Undeterred, Ayckbourn pursued him to a pub – most Pinter stories involve pubs – where he intended to press the point, but before he could, a man rushed in claiming to have killed his mother-in-law by ramming her up a chimney. Pinter had to hear the man's story, and Ayckbourn never did discover where Stanley came from or where he was going. Nor do we know what happened to the man, or his mother-in-law.

Stories and batty characters tend to cling to Pinter. The one about the rehearsal in which he stopped an actor in mid-flow and told him he was playing two dots rather than the three that were written; the time he had a BBC journalist who was eating at the River Café thrown out because he thought he was there to spy on him; the fallings-out with Peter Hall, Alan Coren, Simon Gray. All good knockabout stuff and the makings of a legend – irascible, menacing, self-important, egoistical. But is it true? Who is this man? Where did he come from? Is he normal?

The media think not: they – we – portray him as an impatient, aggressive control freak. How does he plead? 'I don't believe I'm particularly egoistical. To be egoistical is to be ambitious and also indifferent to the views of others. I am neither. I'm not in the least ambitious, never have been, and I don't tread on people. To a great extent, my public image is one that's been cultivated by the press. That's the Harold Pinter they choose to create.

'I'm perfectly prepared to admit that there have been times in the past when I have exploded, sometimes justifiably, sometimes stupidly. But most of these incidents are at least ten years ago. I don't do that kind of thing any more – or very rarely anyway. When the press write about me, they are digging up references in the cuttings to things that happened a very long time ago at some damn dinner party.'

If there's one thing that makes Pinter really angry, it's being characterized as someone who is permanently enraged. It is, he believes, a way of marginalizing him. 'According to the press I rage about everything. If I said casually, for example, that Flintoff should bat at number three for England, there'd be a headline the next day saying: "Pinter rages against England selectors". The thrust of it seems to be: "This man is deranged." I tend to believe that it's a calculated act, though who is doing the calculating I can't say.'

Certainly, the effect is to undermine his arguments, to allow them to be discounted in advance. Pinter, a good conspiracy theorist, sees it as organized denigration, but he reckons without media laziness. We love to categorize: Amis is the money-grubbing bloke who needed a big advance to fix his dodgy teeth; Stoppard is that clever fellow with a neat line in cod Shakespeare; Pinter is the chap who goes puce, tells journalists to fuck off, and is forever banging on about Iraq or the Kurds or the iniquities of US imperialism. We prefer *idées fixes* to ideas.

One of the myths about Pinter is that he doesn't talk to journalists. Interviews with him are invariably labelled 'rare', which is odd because he makes himself far more available than, say, Stoppard. He is naturally gregarious and enjoys conversation, though he will not attempt to explain his work. 'Everything to do with the play is in the play,' he wrote in 1958, echoing Eliot. 'Meaning which is resolved, parcelled, labelled and ready for export is dead, impertinent – and meaningless.' In that, he has not wavered, but he will talk in general terms about his life and career, is generous with his time, is far from the menacing caricature of media myth.

This week sees the publication, in paperback, of a collection of occasional writings by Pinter called *Various Voices* – memoirs, reflections, letters, speeches, poems, polemics, shreds of a long, remarkably productive life. The anniversary is entirely coincidental, but this year also marks his fiftieth in professional theatre; he will be seventy next year. It may be a moment for remembering and for celebrating, two acts at the heart of his life and art.

The man who greets you at the door of the squat house in Holland Park that serves as his office is dark, tough, fit, intensely physical. As an actor in rep in the fifties, Pinter was always cast as the saturnine heavy, the man who could turn nasty at any moment, and he retains that aura, a still energy, a volcano that might just blow.

His book-lined study is peaceful, ordered. He has scrapbooks filled with notices of his plays, from his first, *The Room*, performed by Bristol University's drama department in 1957. (He recently went back to Bristol to collect an honorary degree and was taken to the cramped room where it was originally performed; the room is now used for storage.) He may be suspicious of critics, but he catalogues their verdicts. The scrapbooks also seem to log his life. He has every Wisden (the first ten in facsimile only) neatly arranged – the entire history of first-class cricket, its collective meaning and memory, at his disposal. He once enumerated his family, the theatre and cricket as his principal pleasures, adding sex and drink as an afterthought.

It is a cliché but you can't enter a room with Pinter without thinking of his plays, of other rooms, of characters vying for territorial and psychological advantage. He will answer frankly, often effusively, talks affectionately of his childhood and his early days as a struggling actor, but also protects his private space, says little in reply to questions that threaten – his divorce from his first wife, Vivien Merchant, his estrangement from his son, Daniel. That is his business, he will imply politely; the life and the art are separate; have another glass of wine.

The cover of *Various Voices* is a portrait of Pinter by Justin Mortimer, which is in the National Portrait Gallery (Pinter the political firebrand is also Pinter the Establishment man, though he did turn down John Major's offer of a knighthood). The portrait captures much of Pinter: his intelligence, inquisitiveness, wariness, physicality. He looks strong, and yet there is a hint of self-consciousness and insecurity; his sharp eyes look down; he has seen something that intrigues him; one day he will use it.

Pinter was an only child in a large, noisy, extended Jewish family in London's East End. He was born in 1930 and evacuated during the war, experiencing the pain of separation and the fear of an uncertain future. If you wanted to be mechanistic about it – he would hate this – you could trace much of what follows from that: impersonal forces that destroy our security; the oppressive effect of religious (and by extension political) orthodoxies; his celebration of life; his lament for loss. 'I saw Hutton in his prime; another time, another time,' as his couplet about his cricketing hero, Sir Leonard Hutton, has it. Such beauty, elegance and strength; now gone. Cricket is a game that mixes ordered violence with sentimentality and a longing for a lost world. A cricket team is a surrogate family. Cricketers are simultaneously deeply selfish and interdependent. Discuss with reference to the works of Harold Pinter.

In his admirable (and admiring) biography of Pinter, Michael Billington presents memory – the way he remembers – as the key to unlocking Pinter's work and world. Billington cites Peter Hall, the director most closely associated with Pinter. 'There is,' says Hall, 'an almost mystic quality about things and people from his past.' Billington goes on to show how specific incidents inspired many of the, for want of a better word, character plays – *The Birthday Party*, *The Caretaker*, *The Homecoming*, *Betrayal*, *Moonlight*. *No Man's Land*, too, since Pinter has said it began when he was sitting in a taxi and saw (and, oddly, heard) a man in a room offering another a drink. 'You have to follow the clue of what you're given, but the crucial thing is to get a clue in the first place, to have a *donnée*, a given fact. If I don't have that, I'm in the desert.'

His childhood gave him many *données*. Moreover, he had the artistic advantages of the only child – the parental attention, the ready-made audience, the need to invent childhood friends. Billington latched on to a remark by Joan Bakewell, who had a seven-year affair with Pinter in the sixties and remains close to him: 'He's immaculate about the significance of his life. Which is why he doesn't need to do much more than walk to the Tube – that is full of significance for him.' He has the only child's sense of his own importance.

'I was very close to my parents, especially my mother,' says Pinter. 'My father was a pretty volatile, abrasive fellow, but warm-hearted too. He was a tailor and worked nearly twelve hours a day, so I couldn't blame him for being a bit short-tempered. I was part of a very big family. Although I was an only child, I had lots of cousins and aunts and uncles. We were Jewish, but I had a very odd relationship with being Jewish. I felt both Jewish and not Jewish, which in a way remains the case. After my bar mitzvah when I was thirteen, I hardly ever set foot in a synagogue again.'

Evacuation was a key formative experience. 'Separation made a great impact on me. I was evacuated three times. I came back right into the Blitz, went away and came back to the V1s, then went away again and came back as the V2s were being dropped. The condition of being bombed has never left me.'

Did the fear and dislocation influence his writing? 'I can't subject myself to that kind of analysis. It's very difficult to be objective about one's self, although I do try. I suspect that when I started to write plays, people like Goldberg and McCann in *The Birthday Party* did reflect forces that I had appreciated in the world. But I didn't write *The Birthday Party* with a conscious awareness of those issues.'

But the sense of arbitrariness, the fact of being removed suddenly from a warm, loving family – that must have had an influence? 'Oh yes, ungovernable forces, things you couldn't control, things that were totally out of your control. I do indeed see that. I think that is now a common experience. It doesn't simply apply to one's childhood under those conditions; it seems to apply generally for most people – that forces are operating which are outside your control. Power certainly doesn't rest with Joe Dokes and you and me; it rests with others, and one is less and less able to define them.'

The connection between life and work is easy to draw, but Pinter prefers not to draw it. He has an almost mystical view of the act of artistic creation, a life-long aversion to attempts to reduce the irreducible. The first words in *Various Voices*, written in 1950, would be just as applicable to his view of art today: 'The mistake they make, most of them, is to attempt to determine and calculate, with the finest instruments, the source of the wound.' He is writing in praise of Shakespeare – his many-sidedness, mystery, inexhaustibility – but he is also, at a tender twenty, recognizing that great art, like life, resists analysis.

Pinter writes quickly. His *donnée* prompts him to pick up his pen, he reaches for the yellow pads on which he always writes, and something happens. He trusts the initial inspiration, prefers not endlessly to revise it. 'It's very easy to fuck up a play,' he once said. Last month he took his yellow pads on his annual family holiday to Dorset and something came – a play called *Celebration*, 'a kind of farce', which he reckons will run to forty minutes on the stage. He only finished it this week, and he is elated. 'It surprised me. I began it four months ago, then stopped. It stuck. Then, while I was in Dorset, it clicked – the sea burst, the waters broke. It made me laugh; I am very high on it.' Pinter has said that when he isn't writing he feels 'banished from myself'; he has known bleak periods when he could not write; in the fifth decade of his writing life, his joy at creation is still palpable.

His refusal to explain, to seek the roots of his inspiration, can be frustrating for audiences. He doesn't care. 'Will the audience absorb the implications or not?' he once wrote to a bemused director. 'Ask the barber.' He was even more explicit in an interview in 1993. 'As a director I give the actors one note at the very end of the other notes, one note: fuck the audience. And every actor knows what I'm talking about. If you want the audience to love you, you're finished.

When an audience is a good and intelligent audience, I like them as much as anybody does. But you've got to take a strong view, saying you're going to get what we're giving you, you're not going to get what you want. There has to be someone in charge of a theatrical enterprise, and it has to be the work itself.'

Pinter sometimes implies that he is not writing the work; the work is writing him. That also helps to explain the long periods between plays in the past twenty years and the increasing difficulty of writing as his career has progressed. He has to wait for the *donnée*, for the image that sparks the thought, for the stream of consciousness to flow. Many of those *données* were drawn from his childhood, from what he remembers as a glorious adolescence with a band of highly literate mates at Hackney Downs School immediately after the war, from his impoverished years in rep in the fifties, and from his marriage to Vivien Merchant, from whom he separated when he met Antonia Fraser in 1975. Later, the stream became more irregular; as he lived the life of the writer, he found it harder to write.

It wasn't just the content of his work that was influenced by his rumbustious early days, it was the style too – the music of his writing, the joyous playing with words. 'In the East End of London, where I grew up, it was a very lively, active kind of world – a lot of people who talked a lot and very fast,' he told New York drama critic Mel Gussow in 1993, in one of a series of conversations between the two that punctuate Pinter's career. 'There was a kind of vitality in the world I grew up in.'

That vitality is brilliantly caught in the early plays: even at their most desperate, they are filled with life, energy, comedy and, central to that comedy, a love of language. Pinter adores poetry, would perhaps have preferred his poetry to have taken precedence over his plays, and his prose often has the compression and musicality of poetry, what he calls the 'question of rhythm'. 'Why don't you just say the line, rather than thinking and thinking,' he once said to an actor rehearsing one of his plays. 'It will come and you'll feel OK, really.'

His great influence at Hackney Downs was a teacher called Joseph Brearley, who taught him to love language, introduced him to the plays of John Webster (another lifelong passion), and cast him in Shakespeare. When Brearley died in 1977, Pinter marked his death with a poem which ended: 'You're gone, I'm at your side, / Walking with you from Clapton Pond to Finsbury Park, / And on, and on.' The emotion, the affection and the specificity of the memories are typical of Pinter, who is a dedicated memorialist for whom the past, while lost, is recoverable. There is a brilliant memoir in *Various Voices* of Anew McMaster, the charismatic actor-manager with whom Pinter toured Ireland for two years in the early fifties; in four thousand words Pinter captures the man, the place, the times, a vanished touring tradition, the glories of Shakespeare.

The poem about Brearley, the memoir of Mac, the loyalty to his friends from Hackney Downs (he is still, fifty years on, in regular touch with three of them, even though two live in Canada and the other in Australia), the Wisdens and scrapbooks and numerous postcards in his study are all redolent of a man for whom the past is ever present. He adores Proust, and in 1972 spent a year adapting *A la recherche du temps perdu* for the screen; the movie has yet to be made, but the effect of living with Proust was profound.

For Pinter, past, present and future at times become one. He told Billington a story. 'I have a son, Daniel, who is now a grown-up man, but when he was very, very young indeed I woke up one night – this is forty years ago, but I can't forget it – and I found myself in tears. My first wife said to me: "What in heaven's name is the matter?" Daniel, who was about six months old, was in a cot in the room. I didn't know what was the matter or how to explain what was happening to me. But I realized what was happening after half an hour or so. It was simply that I couldn't bear the life that was in front of him. I thought: "Here he is, having a good time, quietly asleep at this moment" – but I actually looked ahead and thought: "My God, what is in store for this infant?"'

How poignant that story is now, knowing what we know. That Pinter and Vivien Merchant were to divorce; that she was to die in 1982, an embittered alcoholic; that his son was to suffer a breakdown and become a recluse – father and son now have no direct contact. It is inconceivable that so emotional a man as Pinter would not be moved by these traumas. He will say little about his first marriage, but his comments on the separation from Daniel are heavy with regret. 'We haven't spoken for about six years,' he tells me. 'It was by mutual agreement – we decided to have a break. I miss him because I was very close to him when he was young, very close. He lives alone and we don't have any contact. I think that's the way he now wants it. He's an extremely gifted writer and musician, but I've lost track of him and that's the way it sometimes goes, you know. And you have to accept it. I respect his decision to be alone.'

In 1993, talking about the broke but buoyant early years of his marriage to Merchant, he hinted at why the marriage fell apart: 'When you're right up against the wire, you share a lot. We both in fact fought our way out of it. She was pretty indomitable in those days. She was acting with a three-month-old baby in the dressing room. She used to feed him in the intervals...I think in a way Vivien probably enjoyed acting in rep more than anything else. There was less pressure, naturally...But gradually, as the big world started to roll up, I think it proved rather destructive...Vivien was a hell of an actress and a woman of undoubted independence of mind, but having said that, she was also very dependent.'

When Merchant met Pinter, he was using the stage name David Baron, and she always called him David. But when David Baron, the struggling actor, had been transformed into Harold Pinter, the acclaimed playwright, the marriage was on the skids. A partnership of equals had become desperately one-sided. Pinter was travelling, he began his long affair with Joan Bakewell, he and Merchant started to resent each other; yet the decade of pain and deceit was highly productive in terms of work: not just the plays, but his most highly regarded screenplays, *The Servant*, *Accident* and *The Go-Between*. That is not to denigrate (as many of his critics do) the value of what has been produced in the past twenty years – *Moonlight*, *Ashes to Ashes*, the shorter, political plays – but domestic accord, a powerful personal partnership with Antonia Fraser, a growing public role, an increasing dissatisfaction with character plays and stage mechanics have all contributed to a diminution in the volume of new work.

In 1971, he said an extraordinary thing: 'I think I am in a trap, always. I sometimes wish desperately that I could write like someone else, be someone else...I often feel that about waking up with myself in the morning. You're trapped with yourself all your damned life.' This at a time when he was successful in every sphere. Four years later came *No Man's Land* and the portrait of Hirst – a rich, successful but creatively (spiritually?) bankrupt writer; surely, as Billington suggests, a fleshing out of Pinter's fears of what he might become.

In 1975, as *No Man's Land* opened at the Old Vic, Pinter was beginning the remaking of himself that he had so fervently desired. He left Merchant, began living with Fraser, and they married in 1980. 'My life has undergone a considerable transformation,' he says now. 'Antonia and I have been together for nearly twenty-five years. I have six step-children for whom I feel great affection, and we have thirteen grandchildren, who are a delight.'

He has also become increasingly absorbed with politics. Some attribute this to Fraser's influence, but his public role began before the start of their relationship, with his opposition to the US-backed coup against the Allende government in Chile in 1973. He became increasingly vocal during the Reagan-Thatcher hegemony of the eighties, and in 1988, he and Fraser launched a left-leaning discussion group that was mocked in the media; he took it as confirmation that no one cared about the damage being caused by Thatcherism. (Ironically, Pinter had voted for Thatcher in 1979, as a protest against a strike at the National Theatre that was dogging a production he was directing. He now calls that vote 'the most shameful act of my life'.)

There are those who lament Pinter's growing engagement with politics, and who would swap all the proselytizing for one more big, broad-canvas play. Political pundits are many, great writers few – shouldn't the passion he devotes to politics be devoted exclusively to his work? 'I don't believe that at all,' he insists to me. 'The only obligations I have as a writer are to the work I write. I don't see it as a public obligation. I've no obligation to society to write anything. Just because people say I am a writer doesn't mean I have to write. If I feel like it I will, but I write only for myself. If that strikes a chord with anybody else in any terms, either political or non-political, that's fine. But I have a responsibility as a citizen which I take seriously.'

Certainly, he has nothing left to prove. Bristol University may not have turned the room in which *The Room* was first performed into a museum, but posterity is likely to be kinder. The media, hooked on its caricature, may not realize it, but Pinter is a writer of worldwide renown.

In receiving the David Cohen literature prize for lifetime achievement in 1995, he spoke of the sheer pleasure that writing gave him: 'I'm well aware that I have been described in some quarters as being "enigmatic, taciturn, terse, prickly, explosive and forbidding". Well, I do have my moods like anyone else, I won't deny it. But my writing life…has been informed by quite a different set of characteristics that have nothing whatsoever to do with those descriptions. Quite simply, my writing life has been one of relish, challenge, excitement.' That speech, needless to say, didn't get many column inches; relish is so much less marketable than rage.

4 September 1999

Life at a glance

HAROLD PINTER

Born: 10 October 1930, London.

Education: Hackney Downs Grammar School, East London.

Married: Vivien Merchant (1956, divorced 1980; one son); Lady Antonia Fraser (1980).

Stage career: Actor (1949–60); director (1962–), theatres including Aldwych (*The Birthday Party*, 1964, etc); National (*Blithe Spirit*, 1977, etc); Royal Court (*Oleanna*, 1993).

Select plays: *The Birthday Party* (1957); *The Dumb Waiter* (1957); *The Caretaker* (1959); *The Homecoming* (1964); *Old Times* (1970); *No Man's Land* (1975); *Betrayal* (1978); *A Kind of Alaska* (1982); *Mountain Language* (1988); *Party Time* (1991); *Moonlight* (1993); *Ashes to Ashes* (1996); *Celebration* (1999).

Select screenplays: *The Servant* (1962); *Accident* (1967); *The Go-Between* (1969); *The French Lieutenant's Woman* (1981); *The Comfort of Strangers* (1990).

PETER PORTER

Triumph of the downside

Ian Hamilton

Last Tuesday at Australia House, they were throwing a beaut wingding. The Australian High Commissioner invited everyone who's anyone in London literary circles to celebrate the seventieth birthday and the *Collected Poems* of Peter Porter: a poet now accepted, it would seem, as a national treasure to be truly treasured. This celebration came not long after Porter received an 'Emeritus' award: an A$30,000 prize given to Australian artists who have brought great honour to their country's name. In other words, Peter Porter is now – without argument – fair dinkum.

It was not always thus. Thirty years ago, if you had told Porter that such would be the crown to set upon his lifetime's efforts, he would almost certainly have laughed. He has lived and worked in London now for nearly half a century and throughout the first two or three decades his back-home compatriots routinely sniped at him as a Pom-lover or, worse still, as an Aussie who liked being loved by Poms. And those who didn't snipe at him ignored him.

I remember visiting the Adelaide Festival in the mid-1970s and discovering, with some astonishment, that Porter scarcely figured in any of the indigenous anthologies. To the local literati, he was a renegade, a sort of traitor. Other expatriate Australians – Clive James, Germaine Greer, Barry Humphries and the like – were similarly viewed, I found, but with a lot less vehemence. They had achieved real fame in foreign fields and, at the very least, had proved that not all Australians were as grotesque as Humphries made them seem.

But Porter, I would try to say, was also quite well known. His fame, though, was not thought to be an asset. It was poetry-fame, obscure fame that was known about only by other poets. And few career groupings are more poisonous than 'other poets'. In Adelaide and elsewhere in Australia back then, the Porter story was the same. OK, he was building a reputation in Britain as one of Australia's best poets. But why wasn't he building it in Sydney? That was long ago. Nowadays, Porter is accepted in London and Sydney as one of the most important Australian poets, and everyone is happy. Hence the party at the High Commission, part-hosted by the Oxford University Press (Porter's *Collected Poems* could well be the Press's final flourish as a publisher of current verse). But it was chiefly an Australian affair. Peter Porter, it declared, you're one of us, even though you happen also to be one of them.

How does Porter himself feel about this late acceptance? 'Well, pleased of course,' he says, 'but cautiously so. If anything, I am probably now enjoying a higher status in Australia as a poet than I am here. In England, I'm not part of the main scene any more. But then Australia, you've got to realize, is trying to establish a national pantheon. It clutches at whatever it can find.'

His fellow countrymen may be prepared to love him now, at this late hour, but Porter will probably have to think twice before he loves them back. For him, this half-century has been a long, and sometimes painful haul. He now visits his homeland fairly often and is grateful for the gongs, annuities and university appointments that have begun to come his way, but he does not always find it easy to forget why, in the first place, he decided to clear off.

Australia, after all, was where – in Philip Larkin's phrase – his childhood was unspent. Or rather, in Porter's case, endured. He was born in 1929, in suburban Brisbane, and his growing-up was wholly shaped, or wholly wrecked, as he would say, by the early death of his mother. Marion Porter was forty-eight when she died and Peter, an only child, was nine. For him, the loss was catastrophic: a banishing, as he has often said, from Paradise.

His mother had been the family's source of energy and fun. His father was timid, hesitant and ineffectual. Suddenly widowed (and, an extra twist, about to lose his job), he couldn't cope. Little Peter was sent off to a boarding school which he would later describe as 'not very far from Auschwitz. In fact, I'm sure some people did not survive it. They are probably buried in the grounds.' And thirty years later, he put it into verse:

> I am a castaway in a world
> Ruled by Matron
> She is the right hand
> That makes my world left-handed
> I dredge
> My hate of her to understand her.
> Her brain is sick with health, mine with fear...
> Let me dream about
> My Mother and the Airedale as I used to.
> I have only this black orphanage
> And the map of the world with all its red
> To make me real.

Thus, from the age of nine, Porter's boyhood, he has said, became 'a sort of pilgrimage. I had to get away from Australia – it was the cause of my fall and my unhappiness.' He left school at eighteen, failed to go to university (his father could not afford the fees), and for a year or two marked time in Philistine Brisbane. He already saw himself as an artistic loner. He listened to good music and wrote plays. He took a job with a local newspaper and got himself dismissed for lack of worldliness. And all the time he was plotting his escape. By getting to Europe, he 'could let the print of the past slowly work through the new, uprooted personality I had invented for myself'.

In January 1951, he set sail for England. The voyage lasted fifty days. After two weeks of fidgety deck-pacing, he encountered the novelist-to-be Jill Neville. She too was a fugitive, in search of a new personality. The couple clicked. Years later, Neville described their meeting and subsequent affair, in a novel called *Fall-Girl*, in which Porter is portrayed as Seth, a gawkily neurotic poet-figure much given to 'cracking his knuckles and glancing nervously from left to right'. Neville's heroine had hoped that she'd run into a 'living, breathing poet' but Seth was not quite the broody, romantic type she'd had in mind. On the contrary, he was voluble, outgoing, down-to-earth: more friend than fling.

In England, Neville would soon enough move on to darker friendships. For Porter, though, this first romance cut deep and when it began to falter he cracked up. Friends of the time recall his black despairs, his rage attacks and suicide attempts. And England did not help. For two years, throughout his sufferings with Neville, Porter moved from crummy job to crummy job, from clerking with International Paints to boat-cleaning on the Thames.

And his poetry was sodden with self-pity. 'To Jill Neville, Cold as Night,' he wrote. 'Unwind me / Out of the springs that stiffen me / Out of the love of winter binding.' And so on. In *Fall-Girl*, there is a scene in which Seth gets talking to an Australian waiter in a Lyons Corner House. The waiter has been in London for ten years, and doesn't like it. Seth says to his girlfriend: 'That's what we'll be like after ten years in this bloody dump of a town. All the life beaten out of us. You'll have gone off and married one of these smart young men in charcoal grey suits, and I'll still be a clerk.' By 1954, Porter had had enough, and set off back to Brisbane. But within ten months he was back in London, this time determined to shape up. He took a room in Notting Hill – 'as large as a coffin on its side' – and taught himself to refocus his frustrations. The tormented lover began to reshape himself into the acrid social satirist we now think of as 'the early Porter'. He also began to make connections with the London literary scene, and in particular, with a set of young ex-Cambridge poets who called themselves the Group.

These Groupees were headed by the poet-critic Philip Hobsbaum, and they used to hold weekly get-togethers at which they would read and criticize each other's work. The new, determinedly prolific Porter became one of their most conscientious members. For the first time, he felt part of what seemed to be an authentic literary movement. 'They accepted me as one of them overnight, just like that: no question of them saying you're a colonial, or uneducated, or who are you, or anything like that.' The Group was an inclusive, largely social phenomenon, but before long, critics began identifying it as a new power bloc in the poetry world. It was said to have affinities with the anti-bardic, anti-Romantic New Lines movement – which included Philip Larkin, Kingsley Amis and John Wain – of the 1950s. At the same time, it was held to be more susceptible to florid diction and disorganized technique – 'more Hughes than Larkin' was the general drift. (Ted Hughes, indeed, attended one or two meetings.) It also had a journalistic edge.

Members were expected to be sardonically alert to headline issues of the day and to direct their firepower at the currently emerging consumerist culture.

All of this fitted well with Porter's lofty eighteenth-century-satirist disposition, and he was soon being talked of as a key figure in the new satire-for-the-sixties boom. Even then it was clear that he was the Group's most gifted, and perhaps its defining presence. So Groupee Margaret Owen remembers that 'no one else had Porter's note of pain and indignation. But he also had a kind of gracelessness which was potent and surely Australian.' This so-called gracelessness took many forms. For instance, Porter and some of the bigger, noisier Group members used to enjoy gate-crashing polite literary soirees: C. S. Fraser's poetry evenings in Beaufort Street would be from time to time disrupted by small deputations of Group poets, with Porter to the fore.

And Anthony Thwaite (now, like Alan Brownjohn, one of Porter's closest friends) has spoken of Porter showing up at Fraser's evenings with Group buddies Martin Bell and Peter Redgrove as 'a kind of troika or trinity or three-headed monster – quietly chortling, vaguely truculent and conspiratorial'. There has been talk of fights and vomitings, of stubbings-out of cigarettes on first editions, and other confrontations, most of them no doubt misremembered, or hyperbolized.

Some of this, however, did get into Porter's poems. He liked to use shock words like 'piss', 'semen' and 'vagina' in his early verse, and was drawn to fixing punch-ups between the vernacular and the arcane. Posh dictionary words were made to jostle with Queensland demotic, and sometimes the mismatch was compelling. Porter was ever anxious to refute any suspicion that he had turned into a Pommy aesthete; at the same time, he couldn't stop himself exhibiting his bookish eloquence.

His Group co-members were staggered by his erudition. As Alan Brownjohn now recalls: 'Peter seemed to know everything, not just about literature but also about music and painting. He was a bit like Henry James and T. S. Eliot: he knew more about Europe than the Europeans. We thought we knew things that we didn't, and talking to Peter was a quick way of finding out how ignorant we really were.'

Porter's association with the Group got him started as a published poet: his first volume, *Once Bitten, Twice Bitten* appeared in 1961. The Group also fixed him a new job, as an advertising copywriter. He signed up with an agency called Motleys and worked there for the next decade, a career move that made sense. For one thing, he needed the money: in 1961, he married Jannice Henry (a former nurse whom he had met at Bumpus Books), and two daughters followed, in 1962 and 1965. But Porter also liked the company at Motleys: his co-admen included William Trevor, Gavin Ewart, Edwin Brock and Peter Redgrove.

As to the work itself: 'I was never any good at clever copy,' Porter says, 'I never went to work on an egg.' He toiled as best he could, though, and actually completed a commissioned book on Queen Alexandra's Royal Army Nursing Corps – a rare item, surely, of Porteriana. He also wrote army recruitment ads and knocked off a few plugs for Guinness: 'I invented a little-known opera by Donizetti called *Arturo di Guinness*, but they told me: you must never knock the product!' In 1968, Porter quit advertising and set up as a freelance writer and, with one or two small interruptions (term-long teaching stints at several universities), he has been freelance ever since. Indeed, he is one of the very few poets I can think of who doesn't have a 'proper job', a rich wife or a private income. For someone with his special gifts, the freelance life will always be tough going: he knows about Auden and Stravinsky, but when it comes to mass culture, the best he can come up with is a tune by Manfred Mann.

Luckily, though, he does know how to talk. He is, as everyone who knows him testifies, a fountain of allusive, epigram-packed eloquence, and he can keep it up for hours. This talent has guaranteed him regular employment on the radio, a medium in which by 1968 he was well known, thanks to a Third Programme reading of one of his early poems. 'Your Attention Please' was written as a spoof warning of an imminent nuclear attack and was read in a BBC news announcer's voice. Some panic in the streets ensued, à la Orson Welles, and Porter enjoyed a day or two of front-page notoriety.

In addition to his radio work, he wrote columns for the *New Statesman* and the *TLS*, and was in demand for poetry readings, book reviews, prize panels and all the other modestly fee-paying chores that poets do to pay the rent. Porter's own running costs have never been excessive: that's to say, he doesn't get dressed up or drive a car or draw the line at eating out at two-star pizzerias. All the same, the financial going has now and then been tough. But the freelance life suited him in many ways, not least because it allowed him to spend more hours in the National Gallery or at home listening to music. At forty, he wrote gratefully: 'Much have I travelled in the realms of gold / For which I thank the Paddington and Westminster Public Library, / And I have never said sir / To anyone since I was seventeen years old.'

Porter's British reputation in the early to mid-1970s was maybe at its peak. At this stage, certainly, he felt himself to be more English than Australian. Indeed in 1970, he said so, in a note to his collection called *The Last of England*: 'I have made a decision,' he wrote, 'to change myself from an Australian into a modern Englishman…I am saying farewell to my past and the country my family went to in the middle of the last century.' Porter had an English wife, two children growing up in English schools, a circle of close English friends, an English reputation, and it was now almost twenty years since he had left Australia. Why not, finally, declare himself to be a Pom? And it so happened that his poetry, around this time, was more steadily self-confident than it had ever been. This was the period, he says (late 1960s–early 1970s), 'when I was most seriously trying to make an effort to be a fine poet'.

In 1972, which he nominates as his 'best year', he published two new books: *Preaching to the Converted* and *After Martial*, which he now thinks of as his favourites: 'I think to some extent I write rather better now than I used to, but I shy away from very difficult things in a way I didn't then. In 1972, I had a go, as Archie Rice would say. Maybe I was trying to do the big American thing – trying to be an innovator. That didn't come naturally to me.' As a newly self-appointed Englishman, Porter began making regular trips to Europe to view some of the great art works he had read about. In *Preaching to the Converted*, the poet is, perhaps for the first time, disposed to measure his own gifts against those of the great artists of the past.

The experience is both humbling and inspiring. It was not in Porter's nature to entertain grandiose ideas about his own poetic talents. But, on the other hand, why not? 'There are certain ambitions that your inner personality can't accept, but which the thrust of your creative desire will have a go for. You can become more experimental and daring than you ever seem to be in your own vision of yourself.' *Preaching to the Converted* does not now seem all that experimental, but it does evince a new spaciousness and calm. There is an air of purposeful, unrushed contentment, despite routine bouts of cosmic gloom. This contentment, though, was soon to be appallingly subverted. In 1974, his wife Jannice killed herself. She was found dead in the nursery of her parents' home in Marlow: her own nursery, that is. And Porter's world would never be quite the same again.

Jannice Porter died in December. Several months earlier, he had revisited Australia, on his own, for the first time in two decades. It was a visit that had rattled him in many ways, and cheered him too. He had begun to feel that, in spite of all his English ties, he might yet forge some reconnections with his past. And then came his wife's suicide.

'I believe that in marriages, husbands become fonder of their wives and wives become less fond of their husbands. In a way, the alienation Jannice felt at the end of her life was not just an alienation from me, but an alienation from existence. And it had been there all along.' Porter says this now, but at the time, he took his wife's death as a kind of reckoning. He felt that his poetry, or at any rate his all-out commitment to the idea of writing poetry, had been definitively called into question. 'I saw pretty sharply the appalling natural selfishness of, on the one hand, the actual literary career and, on the other hand, the literary impulse and ambition. I did feel very strongly that she paid a high price. If I had my time over again, I'd tell her: don't mix with this man. You can find someone better. Not because I am so bad but because of my obsessional personality – this obsessional vision. It's quite inhuman sometimes.'

With Jannice's death, which he mourned with an oblique but powerful eloquence in his book *The Cost of Seriousness*, Porter began to think that he might go back to Australia. Perhaps a new life could be made there, the old pioneering dream. At the same time, though, he had two distressed daughters to bring up. 'We wanted to stay together and we did.' He recalls the ten years or so after his wife's death as almost the worst years of his life and they were made all the more difficult because Jannice's sudden death felt like a re-enactment of his childhood loss. 'The girls stabilized me,' he says now. 'If I hadn't had them, the skids would have been under me. Jane, the younger girl, had a terrible time. And Katherine did too. She had to be a mother to her sister. And neither of them wanted to go back to Australia. And they didn't want me to go. They had lost their mother. They weren't going to lose their father too.' In the end, the family decided to stay put. Porter, it was agreed, would make regular trips back to the homeland that, for the first time since 1951, he had begun to miss. He took a creative-writing appointment at Melbourne University and threw himself into the work there. As an old friend, Evan Jones, recalls: 'They were coming from fifty miles away to show him their poems. He was buried in manuscripts. He was so dutiful.' This was followed by almost annual visits through the 1980s.

With each one, Porter began to feel a deepening allegiance to the place: both as an Australian and as a poet. And the Australians responded, with both praise and money. He has continued, though, to live in London, which he still thinks of as his home.

In 1991, he married Christine Berg, and this marriage he describes warmly as 'an equal partnership'. Over this last decade, he has been startlingly prolific, even by his standards. There are some five hundred poems in his two-volume *Collected Poems*, about half composed since 1984. Will he eventually go back to Australia? He thinks not. And yet, 'until the day I die I will be torn, I suppose. But I don't feel torn. I feel I can ride two horses, even though they are so far away from each other.' Porter's poems, since the death of Jannice, have, he would agree, been subjected to tests that he would have preferred them to avoid. His most popular book, he acknowledges, is *The Cost of Seriousness*, which is dominated by thoughts of his wife's death. Poems like 'An Angel in Blythburgh Church' can readily be cited now as evidence that Porter Impersonal does have a gift for heartfelt self-expressiveness.

For him, though, such praise is thoroughly unwelcome. He likes to present himself as a rough-edged poetic Everyman, discursive, worldly, unpretentious, who makes no special claims on behalf of his own personal travails. 'Confessional' poetry stands pretty high on his hit list when he is writing as a critic, and he is altogether suspicious of any inspiration-based aesthetic. Poetry for him can be like chatty prose. What matters is that the chatterer has brains and wit and an ingenious command of language.

'Perhaps it's the Australian in me that makes me suspicious of poets who think they're special human beings. I find the public, the generalized, the proverbial, as moving as the personal. The poems of mine that people find moving are not really very personal, even the poems about Jannice. I like fiction in poetry and I like phrase-making. I can invent phrases. Whether I can invent whole poems, or whether the phrases just sit in them like raisins, I don't know.' Porter's distrust of the personal clearly seems rooted in his distrust of affectation, of the putting-on of airs. For his friends, when you consult them, the first trait of his to be insisted on is his self-deprecation, his near-compulsive need to play down any triumphs and disasters that have come his way. With Porter, nothing is ever quite as bad, or quite as good, as it may seem – especially, he might add, never quite as good.

Bad things can be endured but good things can never be enjoyed, not altogether: for Porter, something better is always happening to someone else, somewhere. His friend Clive James once translated Enobarbus's speech in *Antony and Cleopatra* into vintage Porterese, and started with the line: 'There goes the barge, without me...' Julian Barnes, an amused and affectionate observer of the Porter psyche, told me of a British Council tour on which Porter reported to his London friends: 'The reception was held in a magnificent fifteenth-century palazzo. Of course, I didn't stay there. They put me in some ghastly modern annexe.' Porter cheerfully acknowledges this tendency he has to seek out the downside. It's just another way of making sure he doesn't get above himself. And in this, he says, his children have been very useful, as when in 1983 a book of his won the Duff Cooper prize. 'I've won the Duff Cooper prize,' he told one of his daughters. 'How much?' she replied. ' £250.' 'Oh, Daddy, that's just like you. Why couldn't you have won the Cooper prize?'

His self-deprecation leaves a mark on almost everything he writes: in his most characteristic work, there is a deep impulse towards anonymity. Early on, he tended to mythologize himself in verse, but mockingly; he was a comic character in his own fictions. Nowadays he is more likely to disappear behind a screen of high-cultural allusiveness.

But there is little of the show-off in all this. On the contrary: his culture-vulturism (which he happily confesses to) quite often comes across as yet another aspect of his generally low self-esteem. 'I may call myself an artist, but I can't compete with this' is how it reads.

And this, I think, has let him into a perhaps too eager down on his own art form. For him, poetry cannot finally compete with music, which he thinks of as the greatest of the arts. He has a library-sized record collection and he listens to two hours of classical music every night before he goes to bed.

Although he can rhapsodize impressively about the genius of Pope and Byron, you should hear him on, say, Mozart. Has this passion perhaps damaged his own writing in some way? Has it caused him to think of what he writes as necessarily, generically, belonging to the 'second best'? I put this line to him the other day and he replied: 'I plead absolutely guilty', as he often does whenever he picks up the merest hint of a reproach.

But this time he went on: '*Mea culpa, mea maxima culpa*. If I had the intensity of belief in poetry that, say Geoffrey Hill has, or Les Murray has, or even Seamus Heaney has, I would write a different sort of poem. But poetry doesn't quite claim my love as music does, although I am very serious about the things I write.

'What I have written I have written, and I do the best I can. But I don't think of poetry as an exalted calling, as some poets do. I love music so much that, in poetry, I'm always looking for an authority in language that is not wholly dependent on meaning. I want meaning to be elsewhere. But that authority, of course, cannot be found.'

20 February 1999

Life at a glance

PETER NEVILLE FREDERICK PORTER

Born: 16 February 1929, Brisbane, Australia.

Education: Church of England Grammar School; Brisbane Toowoomba Grammar School.

Married: Jannice Henry (1961; died 1974), two daughters; Christine Berg (1991).

Career: Journalist (Brisbane); came to England 1951, then clerk, bookseller, advertising copywriter; full-time poet, journalist, reviewer and broadcaster since 1968.

Select bibliography: *Once Bitten, Twice Bitten* (1961); *Penguin Modern Poets No. 2* (1962); *A Porter Folio* (1969); *The Last of England* (1970); *Preaching to the Converted* (1972); *After Martial* (translation) (1972); *The Cost of Seriousness* (1978); *Collected Poems* (1983); *The Automatic Oracle* (1987); *The Chair of Babel* (1992); *Dragons in their Pleasant Places* (1997); *Collected Poems 1: 1961–81* and *Collected Poems 2: 1984–98* (1999).

Awards: Duff Cooper prize (1983); Whitbread Poetry award (1988); The Gold Medal of Australian Literature Society (1990); The age of Poetry prize (1997); The Emeritus Award of the Australian Council (1998).

NAWAL EL SAADAWI
Lone star of the Nile

Raekha Prasad

Nawal El Saadawi liked school. Her favourite lessons were art and literature. History bored her. It made heroes out of corrupt rulers and told her nothing about the British invasion of her country. She wanted to become a writer, but her father said there was no future for writers in Egypt. They live and die in poverty, he said.

Her parents had pinned their hopes on her older brother, but he failed at school time after time, while she soared. She grew tall, too, and when she hit her teens she trained herself to sleep curled up like an embryo and walk with a stoop to counter what she had read was 'manliness'. For her parents, the image of their daughter's future – wearing a traditional wedding dress – was slowly replaced by that of a tall, slender woman enveloped in a lawyer's robe, or a doctor's white coat.

Her parents may have treated her brother preferentially but the favouritism could have been much worse, she says. Her family was educated and her father, a teacher, was broadminded. And yet she felt her brother could move freely while she had to sit politely. Her grandmother would counter her protestations by telling her to control her 'long tongue'.

But what was not said was written. One day her Arabic teacher asked the class to write an imaginative story. She handed in the novel she had secretly written. It tracked a twelve-year-old girl's doubts about religious ritual and parental rules. ('The child is myself,' El Saadawi says now.) She was fourteen. Her teacher gave her a zero and scrawled on her story 'strange distorted ideas which should never occur to a girl of your age'.

The zero was to be the first of many rebuffs that El Saadawi has received for her writing. But there have been many accolades too. Since 1957, when her first novel was published, she has written thirty-two books, including articles, short stories, plays, memoirs, polemics and novels covering Arab women, colonialism, fundamentalism and globalization – red flags to many bulls. She writes in Arabic and almost all her books have been translated, into more than thirty languages; twenty-seven into English and fourteen into Japanese.

The novelist and activist, who trained as a doctor, has survived censorship, incarceration and, most recently, exile, for putting pen to paper. Despite the efforts of her teacher, El Saadawi is the leading voice of her generation on the status of Arab women. She compares a pen to a scalpel. 'Words should not seek to please,' she writes in *A Daughter of Isis*, the first part of her autobiography, adding that words 'should not hide the wounds in our bodies, the shameful moments in our lives.' When she was six, she underwent a clitorectomy at the hands of a daya (midwife), who said it was the will of God. Nawal called for her mother to rescue her, only to find that she had been present all along.

She later wrote a letter to God saying: 'I'm not ready to believe in you if you're not just.' Everywhere she looked she saw 'double standards, contradictions and injustices. That's why I don't agree with religion,' she says. 'All religion is political. It's full of war and peace, economics and sexuality.' Her father made his children pray, but told them not to believe in God unless they were convinced of his existence. This played a major role in the young El Saadawi's development. 'I never feared discussing whether God existed or not,' she says.

Her first lessons in philosophy, religion and politics were learnt, she says in Kafr Tahla, her father's obscure village on the Nile. Her paternal grandmother, an illiterate peasant, would say to the village headman: 'We are not slaves, and Allah is justice.' Her mother was from an upper-middle-class family. Her maternal grandfather's house in Cairo, a villa with a garden was 'like a palace' compared to the village home where the family slept on mats laid on the dust floor. Levels of education, 'the way they talked' also contrasted. 'I was brought up between two classes,' El Saadawi says. 'Peasant and bourgeois.' Physically, she moved between the two houses, but it was the village that she thought of as home.

El Saadawi was the second child of nine. Her mother's loving care made her childhood very happy. Her father was a just and kind man who never raised his voice. He was 'atypical. I wasn't brought up by a masculine man. That's why I had such problems with men,' she says. When he came home from work, he laid the table, prepared food, washed the pots and pans and sewed his own clothes. When Nawal was four, the family moved to Alexandria. Her mother became more distant and Nawal became closer to her father. He had marched against the British in the 1919 revolution and was active in anti-colonial struggle. 'Because of my father I lived politics every day.'

In 1938, when she was seven, the government transferred him to the small town of Menouf in the middle of the Nile delta – punishment for his participation in student demonstrations against the acceptance of British rule by the Egyptian king and his government. She loved to listen to her revolutionary father, but his words were always addressed to her brother. Her job was to take care of her younger siblings. 'A boy's childhood is much longer,' she says. Her brothers and sisters were never friends. 'Their way of thinking is totally different. They conform.' Her sisters cover their heads. Her brothers are very religious. 'They never challenged. Maybe they never faced the obstacles I did.'

She didn't want to be a doctor, but a girl with good grades had to do something respectable. She won a scholarship and went to medical school 'to satisfy my parents' and dreamed of being an artist, a singer, a musician, a painter. 'I hated doctors, death and disease.' Her graduation from Cairo University's medical school in 1955 left her 'more ignorant than when I entered'. It began her slow-burning disillusionment with the idea that illnesses could be cured by medicine alone.

She had joined other students on the streets in demonstrations against the British occupation of Egypt and began to write articles for Egyptian newspapers about the links she had seen between poverty and disease. Her reading widened to sociology, philosophy, religion and literature. 'To see the human body as a whole, to see society and knowledge as a whole,' has been her life's work, she says. 'To break down and analyse, only to build up and synthesize. This was my progression from the particular to the general, from the personal to the political, from one woman to all women, from the individual to the collective.'

El Saadawi, now sixty-eight, is acknowledged as a uniquely powerful voice in the international women's movement. 'She's an amazing gift to the movement,' says Beatrix Campbell, the writer and broadcaster, who met her in the mid-eighties at a rally in Hyde Park in support of the miners' strike. 'She was a woman who in that period of British feminism was a remarkable presence. She was one of the first to initiate the engagement between black and white feminists.'

Women And Sex, her first work of non-fiction, slashed at the mythology surrounding sex, virginity and marriage. Until then, she had written novels as well as newspaper articles drawn from her observations as a rural doctor in the 1950s. *Women and Sex*, published in 1971, when she was Egypt's director general of public health, went much further. El Saadawi became the first Arab woman to write against female circumcision, arguing that it stems from the ancient practice of monogamy for women and polygamy for men.

Because of the ensuing controversy, she lost her job, as well as her seat on the board of the government medical syndicate in 1972. Her writing was banned. The magazine she edited about social influences on health was closed down. 'I think women can be easily attacked,' she says. 'They said I was promiscuous. Oh yes, they said everything.'

El Saadawi's own writing is often a form of attack, delivered behind a shield of scholarly authority. She relates the history of Arab women's liberation to the anti-colonial struggle. Her novels veer towards reportage: clear and precise accounts of stories previously untold. 'I have my utmost pleasure when I'm writing my novels,' she says. 'It's the present tense, the here and now, that I enjoy. It's my constitution. I love novels more than anything because they help us to understand.'

She was cooped up in Cairo writing from home following her censorship in 1972. While her work was sent to Beirut to be published, she felt isolated. In 1978, she took up a post with the United Nations as an adviser on women's development. The job took her all over the Middle East and Africa. In retrospect, she says, it was way of seeing for herself 'that the UN was not seriously interested in either development or women'.

In 1981, a year after she returned to Cairo, Sadat put her in jail along with more than a thousand others for 'crimes against the state'. She hid her pen and notes written on toilet paper in a camouflaged hole in her cell. These notes were to become *Memoirs from the Women's Prison*, an account of the 'terrible' months she spent in a jail bursting with prisoners.

She shared a cell with twelve others, some imprisoned for their fundamentalism, others for their Marxism, but all facing the grim daily reality of bread and beans with worms, the floor or plank of wood for a bed, the fleas and the bugs. Obedience, El Saadawi says, was the only way to avoid being beaten.

Imprisonment accentuated life, she says. 'I remember anger and extreme happiness,' she says. Simple things such as the smell of tea made her ecstatic. Her release after three months was thanks to Sadat's assassination and the succession of the present Egyptian president, Hosni Mubarak.

'Hers was a project of social realism: to speak of all those things that had never been said,' says the writer and poet Michèle Roberts, who met El Saadawi in London in the early eighties. 'Many British women read her books. We shared the ideology of novel writing. We believed in telling the truth and that novels could testify and affect social reality.'

In 1993, with Muslim fundamentalism growing in Egypt, her name was put on a death-list. Government security guards surrounded her home and a body-guard trailed her. She believed the government was largely to blame for religious extremism and was suspicious of the guards. With her husband, she boarded a plane for North Carolina in the United States. She watched Egypt from a dis-tance and taught a course at Duke University about the experience – 'Dissidence and Creativity'. Exile made her feel 'like a fish outside the sea'. She was home-sick. 'Life became very dear,' she says. 'I felt death was over my head like a big black cloud. So I wanted to write my life. I became very sensual. I loved food. I loved sex. That's how we survive.'

In the eighties she had become involved with British political campaigns: the miners' strike, Greenham Common, sit-ins against NHS cuts, demonstrations against the National Front, CND. Her position as an Eastern intellectual embraced by the West has led her work to be used in the West to justify objec-tions to Islam, while in the East there are hopes that her writing will serve as an antidote to Western misconceptions about Arab women as supine, veiled crea-tures in need of rescuing.

'She had a knowledge and critique of British feminism while British feminism didn't have a confident engagement with African or Middle Eastern feminism,' says Beatrix Campbell. 'Here was a woman sustained by feminism and in an argument with it. And while defending her own society in an argument with it and ours.'

The arguments, when first expressed, were revelatory. It is not Islam, she argued, that oppressed women in the Arab Islamic countries, but the inability of Arab people to take control of their economic potential and resources. 'I have never separated women's liberation from the liberation of my country,' she says. Economics, she argues shapes the standards and values of all religions. She rails against the prevalent conception of women's liberation as a Western invention that has trickled to women in the East.

Lives have been changed by El Saadawi. Marlyn Tadros first met her in 1988 at a book fair in Cairo. At the time Tadros was twenty-eight and had worked as an air hostess, but her husband had confiscated her passport. She had just read *The Hidden Face of Eve*, El Saadawi's 1980 work on the status of women in Arab coun-tries. 'It was only Nawal who said how I felt was unnatural,' she says. 'When you live in a mainstream that tells you "this is natural", it's extremely empowering to find someone out there who thinks differently.' Tadros, now the senior director of programmes for a human rights organization, after a stint as a visiting fellow at Harvard, cites this meeting as the beginning of her own activism.

El Saadawi writes in *The Hidden Face of Eve*: 'There are still so many thinkers...who wish to separate the arduous struggles of women for self-eman-cipation from the revolt of the people everywhere.' She is interested in what we share, rather than what separates us. She tells a story about how, when giving a lecture in the States, a woman in the audience asked: 'How do you explain why some Muslim women want to wear the veil?' She relishes her reply: 'In the same way that I'd explain why you choose to wear make-up. Like make-up, it hides the face of women. They both show conformity to a culture's idea of what is feminine.'

Her analysis is a series of cultural and political dot-to-dots. 'I think clitorec-tomy is done to all women,' she says. 'Be it physical, psychological, educational.

When Freud said the clitoris is a male organ in a female body and clitoral orgasm is related to childhood, he cut the clitoris psychologically because he abolished its function.'

Unusually for an Egyptian woman, El Saadawi has married three times; the first time, aged twenty-four, to a fellow student two years her senior at medical school. Like her father, he was active in the anti-colonial struggle: a guerrilla fighter against the British military occupation of the Suez Canal. Nationalist sentiment and the humiliation of the Egyptian armed forces during the war against the newly independent state of Israel precipitated a coup, led by Mohammed Neguib in July 1952, in which the ruling King Farouk was deposed. When Neguib's political rival Gamal Abdel Nasser assumed power two years later, El Saadawi's first husband came out of hiding and returned to her. But he had become embittered and disturbed by his enforced self-exile and fled to Upper Egypt, racked with depression.

'The depression added to his patriarchal tendencies,' she says. 'I was a successful doctor. He tried to dominate me.' The couple had a daughter, Mona, now forty-four, a writer and essayist living in Cairo. When El Saadawi's salary could no longer stretch to supporting her husband and their daughter, she turned to her father. He helped her get a divorce and she lived with her parents in Giza, a district of Cairo, until they died a couple of years later. Her second husband, a lawyer, hated being married to a woman who ruffled so many feathers, and they divorced within a year. 'I didn't love him very much, but he said he'd accept my conditions. I needed a partner. A secret love affair would have ruined my career. The social pressure to be married was great.'

In 1964, she married Sherif Hetata, a doctor, writer and activist. They have a son, Araf, now thirty-nine, a film director, who lives in Cairo. Hetata is her English translator and companion. They are a beautiful, entertaining double act: 'I wanted to be with a political man,' she says. 'That's not what you told me,' he interrupts. 'You said you wanted to marry a man who'd been in prison.' They met at the Ministry of Health, where he was setting up a rural health programme. He had just been released from a fourteen-year prison sentence for membership of a communist party that had criticized Nasser's regime. Hetata 'was sure of himself, thoughtful, calm and serious,' she says. 'I felt I could trust him.'

El Saadawi has never belonged to a political party. 'I was never a Marxist, never a Communist. Why should I belong to Marx, or Nasser or Sadat and abolish my name? Marx is a man who created a theory. We can all be philosophers. I was always just myself.'

It is an attitude that over the years has made her enemies and brought her criticism. Marlyn Tadros says El Saadawi is a pioneer, 'but she's a very, very difficult person and I don't want to stay around her. She has to have everything her way. There's often only a semblance of democracy. Her self-confidence goes against her.' Recognition for pioneering work, Tadros says, is particularly hard to come by in Egypt and the Middle East, and so El Saadawi 'has to act up for it. She has been isolated by the women's movement in Egypt – other feminists have not included her in projects.'

Beatrix Campbell says British feminism 'deified' El Saadawi. 'There's always a risk that black women are rarefied, exoticized and isolated. It's easier for the white world if there's only one different voice. It doesn't have to deal with the clamouring; all those things that different people have to say. El Saadawi moved very easily in a white woman's world. She was received as a lone star.'

It is a position that makes Yasmin Alibhai Brown, a commentator on race affairs, uncomfortable. 'There was something alarming about the way one woman's life was grabbed and used to simplify all Arab women's lives. She's from that final wave of colonialism where being a member of the international Westernized elite was desirable. There are new kinds of writers now.'

El Saadawi's friend of twenty years, Haleh Afshar, professor of politics and women's studies at York University, says that El Saadawi has been bashed both ways. 'In the States she is often seen as an Eastern intellectual exotic on the sidelines. She is no longer a prophet in her own land, and she wasn't one in the States.'

At the beginning of this year, after six years' exile in the United States, El Saadawi returned to Egypt to finish the third and final part of her autobiography. Mubarak's government, itself threatened by the extremist Islamic groups that wanted her dead, is now beginning to tackle them, she says. She feels safer. Part one of her memoir, covering the first twenty-four years of her life, is a sensuous recollection: the smell of her mother's skin, the pain in her growing bones.

Back home in Egypt, other women have been slogging away to change the nitty-gritty details of areas such as the law, health and education to improve women's lives. They are not starry-eyed over El Saadawi. Hala Shukrallah, a member of the New Women Research Centre in Cairo, which campaigns, offers legal support and community-based projects for women's rights, is unequivocal about how El Saadawi's absence from grassroots activism in Egypt has diminished her significance there. 'She was important in the seventies but I don't think she's had an influence in the nineties,' she says. 'She's not here. When you're not here and not struggling on the same level, you're out of it. She's been shaped by her audience and has directed her work to the West when she's there. That's natural.'

El Saadawi compares herself to a horse jumping over obstacles. 'When I clear one jump, the next is higher.' She has set herself some tough hurdles. She was among a delegation of nine women to Baghdad a month before the expiry of the UN deadline and the outbreak of the Gulf War in 1991. She met the UN secretary-general in New York and toured the US for two weeks to rally support for peace and an Arab solution to the war. The initiative grew out of the Arab Women's Solidarity Association, the first pan-Arab organization to be accorded international status at the UN, which El Saadawi founded to counter the 'isolation' of writing. The government closed the Egyptian branch of the association later that year.

She appeared at the 1985 United Nations women's conference in Nairobi, but did not attend the international debate in Beijing a decade later. Why not? 'I received an invitation,' she says. 'But after the UN's intervention and collaboration with Western powers in the Gulf War, it became the United Nations of America for me: a tool in the hands of global capitalist powers. I'm wasting my time going. Women will never be liberated if the UN is involved.'

The world has not turned out in the way that El Saadawi once hoped. 'Those countries with global power bring barriers between countries so capital can flow more easily. They speak about diversity, freedom, multiculturalism, and divide people by religion and race in the name of postmodernism. We should be undoing the differences between us.'

Haleh Afshar detects a lament for lost opportunities in El Saadawi's autobiography. 'It's full of bitterness and sadness,' she says. 'Nawal started in an era where modernity and progress meant that a young woman from a village could, as she did, become a government minister. You can't do that in Egypt today. There is less social mobility. She had a vision that didn't come good. It's so different from the exuberant, lively person she is.'

El Saadawi's journey between Cairo and the village is all the travelling she wants to do for now. She and Hetata have built a small house in his family village just north of hers in the middle of the delta. They go there two or three times a year to write and relax, she says. The village is 'typical – just fields, animals everywhere, small streets and children running around'. Every other year she will spend a month teaching at Florida Atlantic University. Dissidence and creativity will still be her subject.

Next month she must submit the third and final part of her autobiography to her Egyptian publishers. More meetings are planned to discuss setting up an Egyptian women's union. El Saadawi hopes as always that links will form between the fragments. She's trying to find 'a charismatic woman' to lead it. She's very busy with her writing these days. The movement needs someone less controversial, she says. Someone with a clean slate. 'I'm arguing,' she says, 'that it may be better for the union to have a young woman leading it.'

Will she miss America? 'I miss teaching. It allows me to speak my mind but I was always going to be an alien there. I needed to be near my children, my village, my friends. I told Sherif that it's better to die here. But wherever I am, I'm criticizing the government. Now I feel at home in every country. I feel as if I belong to the world,' she smiles. 'I don't belong to a certain place.'

17 June 2000

Life at a glance

NAWAL EL SAADAWI

Born: 1931, Kafr Tahla, Egypt.

Education: Helwan School, Cairo; Cairo University (1949–55), doctor of medicine; Columbia University, New York (1966), Masters in public health.

Married: Ahmed Elmy (1955–7; one daughter); [name withheld] (1960–61); Sherif Hetata (1964; one son).

Career: Medical officer, Cairo Hospital University (1956–8); village doctor (1958–9); director general of public health, Egyptian ministry of health (1966–72); head of UN women's programme in economic commission for Africa (1978–90); president, Arab Women's Solidarity Association (1982–).

Select bibliography: (English translations): *Women and Sex* (1972); *The Hidden Face of Eve* (1980); *Woman at Point Zero* (1982); *God Dies by the Nile* (1984); *The Fall of the Imam* (1987); *Memoirs from the Women's Prison* (1985); *The Well of Life* (1992); *A Daughter of Isis* (1999).

W. G. SEBALD

Recovered memories

Maya Jaggi

Under lowering skies in East Anglia, days after the Manhattan apocalypse, Max Sebald is troubled by Hitler's fantasy of setting New York ablaze, as the Blitz did London. The spectre of the past haunts Sebald, a German born under the Third Reich, though he was a babe in arms on VE Day. 'I was born in May 1944 in a place the war didn't get to,' he says of the Bavarian village of Wertach im Allgau. 'Then you find out it was the same month when Kafka's sister was deported to Auschwitz. It's bizarre; you're pushed in a pram through the flowering meadows, and a few hundred miles to the east these horrendous things are happening. It's the chronological contiguity that makes you think it is something to do with you.'

Sebald has lived in Britain since 1966, forsaking the Alps for the flatlands of Norfolk, where he is professor of European literature at the University of East Anglia in Norwich. Wearing a corduroy jacket with elbow patches, he sits in a modest office in a squat concrete block. Now fifty-seven, he began publishing what he terms 'prose fiction' only in his mid-forties, writing as W. G. Sebald (his third name is Maximilian), and always in German.

His first book to be translated into English, *The Emigrants*, published in 1996, came garlanded with awards from the German-speaking world and was one of the most lauded British debuts of the last decade. Susan Sontag acclaimed him as the 'contemporary master of the literature of lament and mental restlessness'. Translations of *The Rings of Saturn* in 1998 and *Vertigo* in 1999 – again by the poet Michael Hulse – sealed his reputation as one of the most original literary figures of our age. For Michael Ondaatje, Sebald is 'the most interesting and ambitious writer working in Britain today'.

Sebald's fiction is an innovative hybrid of memoir, travelogue and history, its text scattered with grainy, black-and-white photographs without captions that lend an unsettling feel of documentary. He often uses real names, in an endless journeying saturated with European cultural allusions and metaphysical meditations on loss, exile and death. 'At a time when everything is classified and marketed cynically, Sebald defies all genres,' says Bryan Cheyette, professor of twentieth-century literature at Southampton University. Cheyette sees him as a 'post-Holocaust writer', obliquely exploring the long aftermath of the Third Reich.

His new book, *Austerlitz*, which came out in Germany last spring, is published next month in an English translation by Anthea Bell. It was bought by Penguin as part of a three-book deal worth more than £100,000. The story concerns Jacques Austerlitz, who is brought up by Welsh Calvinist foster-parents and in his fifties recovers lost memories of having arrived from Prague on the *Kindertransport*, the lifeline to Britain of some ten thousand unaccompanied

Jewish children in 1938–9. It was spurred by watching a Channel 4 documentary on Susie Bechhofer, who in mid-life remembered coming to Wales on the *Kindertransport*. She shared a birthday with Sebald, 18 May, and was from Munich. 'That was very close to home,' he says.

Yet for the first half of the book the past is skirted, as Sebald explores the 'effects political persecution produces in people fifty years down the line, and the complicated workings of remembering and forgetting that go with that'. He is interested in the long-term effects on émigrés who 'may appear well adapted but, especially as they move towards old age, are still suffering from having been ostracized, deprived of country, family, language. There are damages to people's inner lives that can never be rectified.'

Austerlitz is also partly based on a real architectural historian, a friend whose boyhood photograph is on the cover. Austerlitz senses that buildings bear witness to the past, as unquiet ghosts in our midst demand redress. 'Places seem to me to have some kind of memory, in that they activate memory in those who look at them,' says Sebald. 'It's an old notion – this isn't a good house because bad things have happened in it. Where I grew up, in a remote village at the back of a valley, the old still thought the dead needed attending to – a notion so universal it's inscribed in all religions. If you didn't, they might exact revenge upon the living. Such notions were not alien to me as a child.'

Winfried Georg Maximilian Sebald was born the only son, with three sisters, of Rosa, daughter of a 'country copper', and Georg, from a family of glassmakers in the Bavarian forest. At eighteen, his father joined the army, amid mass unemployment in 1929. When the National Socialist party took power in 1933, he 'stayed and marched with it'. Sebald's parents were from 'conventional, Catholic, anti-communist, working-class backgrounds. They experienced upward mobility in the 1930s, like so many Germans; my father finished the war as a captain. Fascism did away with the class system – as in France under Napoleon, and in stark contrast to Britain, where it dominates the army to this day.'

Georg was a prisoner of war in France. When he returned to Bavaria in 1947, Max was three. 'I found it odd that this person turned up and claimed to be my father. Then he got a job in a small town and was only home on Sundays. He was a detached figure for me.' Sebald doted on his grandfather, an 'exceptionally kind man', who took care of him. 'As a boy I felt protected. His death when I was twelve wasn't something I ever quite got over.' It brought an early awareness of mortality and that the other side of life is something horrendously empty.'

Like most of his generation, Sebald grew up in the 'seas of silence' over the war. 'It was an idyllic environment, and only at seventeen or eighteen did you get inklings. All I knew was that there were families where, out of five sons, none returned.' His father's albums had photographs of the Polish campaign of 1939, first with a 'boy-scout atmosphere' and culminating in razed villages. But the images seemed 'normal' to Sebald as a child. At grammar school in the ski resort of Oberstdorf they were shown a film of the liberation of Belsen. 'It was a nice spring afternoon, and there was no discussion afterwards; you didn't know what to do with it. It was a long drawn-out process to find out, which I've done persistently ever since.'

While Sebald was at Freiburg University in 1965, the Frankfurt trial of

Auschwitz personnel began. 'It gave me an understanding of the real dimensions for the first time: the defendants were the kinds of people I'd known as neighbours – postmasters or railway workers – whereas the witnesses were people I'd never come across – Jewish people from Brooklyn or Sydney. They were a myth of the past. You found out they too had lived in Nuremberg and Stuttgart. So it gradually pieced itself together, along with the horrific details.'

While Sebald discounts the notion of inherited guilt, he says: 'If you know in the generation before you that your parents, your uncles and aunts were tacit accomplices, it's difficult to say you haven't anything to do with it. I've always felt I had to know what happened in detail, and to try to understand why it should have been so.' He was appalled by a 'concerted attempt in the first years after the war not to remember anything, for the obvious reason that those in office were implicated'. A sea change in the late 1960s was spurred by an 'uprising of the next generation; there was generational war for half a decade that culminated in terrorism in Germany, which was brutally eradicated'.

Yet Sebald found the resulting 'official culture of mourning and remembering' flawed. 'There's always an undercurrent – "Isn't this being forced upon us? Haven't we suffered also?" He disparages literary efforts in the 1970s and 80s to address the Nazi years, by such German writers as Alfred Andersch and Heinrich Böll. 'They felt they had to say something, but it was lacking in tact or true compassion; the moral presumption is insufferable. Andersch was married to a Jewish woman from Munich, and he divorced her in about 1936, exposing her to danger. I don't think one can write from a compromised moral position.' As a student, Sebald read works 'from the other side of the divide: people who'd escaped by a hair's breadth, writing usually after a twenty-year gap', German-Jewish writers such as Peter Weiss, and the Auschwitz survivor Jean Améry. 'There was a huge chasm between those voices and the immediate postwar German writers.'

After studying German literature in French-speaking Switzerland, Sebald came to Manchester University as a language assistant in 1966. 'I scarcely spoke English, and coming from a backwoods, I found it difficult to adapt. But I stuck it out; I got to like the place.' He relished the 'anti-hierarchical' new universities ('nobody bossed you around'), and moved to the fledgling University of East Anglia in 1970 to teach modern German literature. Michael Robinson, now professor of drama at UEA, remembers him as a 'sardonic and challenging' lecturer. Sebald was the founding director in 1989 of the groundbreaking British Centre for Literary Translation at the university. Peter Bush, the present director, says 'it took someone with Max's vision to say we needed this in Britain'.

Sebald published literary criticism on figures such as the Swiss Gottfried Keller and Robert Walser. But dismay at the Thatcherite 'so-called educational reforms' of the early 1980s drove him to other forms. 'The pressure of work got inexorably greater, partly to do with moving up the ladder [he became professor of German] and partly because we lost staff right, left and centre. What was once a very congenial workplace became very trying.'

He began with a prose poem, *After Nature* (1988), to be published in English next spring. (*For Years Now*, poems with images by the artist Tess Jaray, will be published in December.) His first prose fiction was *Vertigo* (1990), which spliced travels in Austria and Italy with fragments on Stendhal, Kafka, Casanova. Sontag praised it as a self-portrait of a 'restless, chronically dissatisfied, harrowed mind', one 'prone to hallucinations'.

As in all his fiction, Sebald's narrator is one 'W. G. Sebald', who lives in Norfolk, comes from the German village of 'W', and has a companion, 'Clara'. Max Sebald lives in an old rectory outside Norwich with his Austrian wife, Ute. They married 'very early', in 1967, and have one daughter, a schoolteacher. But Sebald ('I'd prefer to keep them out of it') gives only rare interviews and is obsessively private. 'I don't want to talk about my trials and tribulations. Once you reveal even part of what your real problems might be in life, they come back in a deformed way.' Robinson, a friend, sees the narrator as a distinct persona. 'He has obvious affinities with Max, but it's playing on our naivety, because the reader is always tempted to identify the narrator with the writer. He's taunting us.'

For Sebald, *Vertigo* is about the 'problem of love, but not in a standard way'. He scorns 'standard novels – about relationship problems in Kensington in the late-1990s', and is irritated by 'pages whose purpose is just to move the action along'. Prose fiction 'means each line has to be weighed as carefully, and with as much energy, as in a poem of half a page'. Anthea Bell, who describes her translations as very much a collaboration with the author, finds 'every word is weighed, nothing is careless in his writing'.

As in Stendhal's memoir, *The Life of Henry Brulard*, Sebald uses pictures, often photographs taken with 'cheap little cameras'. He says: 'In school I was in the dark room all the time, and I've always collected stray photographs; there's a great deal of memory in them.' Pointing out a small boy in an old family photograph on his office wall, he says: 'He returned from the First World War mentally disturbed after electric shock therapy. This is before he knew. I find that frightful: the incapacity to know what's round the corner.'

The images are tantalizing relics of a past that can never be known: 'There are always versions of history; the real thing we shall never grasp.' A. S. Byatt, who sees Sebald's subject as 'memory: its tenacity and fallibility', says: 'He connects with immense pain, only to say you can't connect; he tries to make you imagine things that he then delicately says are unimaginable.'

On his approach to factual 'material', Sebald says: 'There was a vogue of documentary writing in Germany in the seventies which opened my eyes. 'It's an important literary invention, but it's considered an artless form. I was trying to write something saturated with material but carefully wrought, where the art manifests itself in a discreet, not too pompous fashion.' The big events are true, he says, while the detail is invented to give the 'effect of the real'. 'Every novelist combines fact and fiction,' he insists. 'In my case, there's more reality. But I don't think it's radically different; you work with the same tools.'

For the writer Eva Hoffman, this blurred boundary between artifice and reality, memory and history, is 'embedded in his tone – one doesn't know what's fact or fiction'. That uncertainty, fuelled by forged documents or suspect portraits, is Sebald's aim. 'It's the opposite of suspending disbelief and being swept along by the action, which', he says drily, 'is perhaps not the highest form of mental activity; it's to constantly ask: "What happened to these people, what might they have felt like?" You can generate a similar state of mind in the reader by making them uncertain.'

The impulse to question, fostered by his work, is a virtue not only of the reader but the citizen. Passages in *Austerlitz* on the infamous ghetto of

Theresienstadt, northwest of Prague, which the Nazis passed off as a model town to the Red Cross, draw on the painstaking record of H. G. Adler. 'When you read the fascist jargon they evolved in ten years, you can't believe your ears. You need that tension between documentary evidence and questioning in the reader's mind: "Can it really have been so?" To read with vigilance is to question authority. In contrast to nineteenth-century novelists, who were 'at pains to tell you this was a true story', Sebald layers his narration; we learn things indirectly, unreliably: 'I try to let people talk for themselves, so the narrator is only the one who brings the tale but doesn't instal himself in it. There's still fiction with an anonymous narrator who knows everything, which seems to me preposterous. I content myself with the role of the messenger.'

The Emigrants (1993), which gradually links the stories of four displaced Germans to the Holocaust, emerged when Sebald learned of the suicide of one of his teachers not long after Jean Améry killed himself in 1978. In the tale of the schoolmaster, who is 'one-quarter Jewish, as they used to say', he sifted memories of the silence and 'normality' of his own village, mindful of the 'great time lag between the infliction of injustice and when it finally overwhelms you'.

The writer Linda Grant was struck by 'calm prose that packed an extraordinary emotional charge, but you couldn't see how it was done. There are no fireworks, he's the opposite of showy, but he does something magical.' He is free, she adds, of a 'tendency to sentimentalize when non-Jews write about the Holocaust'. Byatt finds the tone 'perfectly judged: it's a mournful, crab-wise, tactful way of getting at history, making tiny steps before he puts the knife in. The primary emotions are not anger but grief and tragic terror.' By contrast, the German novelist Georg Klein detests what he sees as Sebald's 'sweet melancholic masochism towards the past', which claims a 'false intimacy with the dead'.

Sebald has his own scruples about the 'morally questionable process of falsification. We're brought up to tell the truth, but as a writer, you're an accomplished liar. You persuade yourself it's to achieve a certain end. But there's a problem in departing from the literal truth to achieve an effect – in the worst case, melodrama, where you make someone cry. It's a vice.'

He is conscious of the danger of usurping others' existences. While all four emigrants are based on real people, the painter Max Ferber, who obsessively scratches out then redoes his work, is a composite of Sebald's Mancunian landlord ('I found out he'd skied in the same places as I had') and the London-based artist Frank Auerbach. Without naming Auerbach, Sebald says he felt he had the right – 'because the information on his manner of work is from a published source'. Auerbach, however, refused to allow his paintings to appear in the English edition. Sebald modified the character's name from Max Aurach in the German. 'I withdraw if I get any sense of the person's discomfort,' he says.

Hoffman admires Sebald's delicacy. 'He doesn't feel an entitlement to go at history frontally; he goes at it from an oblique angle.' As Sebald says: 'Do I, who carry a German passport and have two German parents, have the right? I try to do it as well as I can. If the reactions were different, I would stop – you do take notice.' (That tentativeness perhaps carries to his view of Israel. 'The situation is deplorable, there's no question. But it's an issue I've avoided.') In Byatt's view, 'Sebald's generation weren't involved in the war, but they've had to look at their own parents with horror. They're a wandering, lost generation that felt they had no right to speak. He's started speaking painfully out of that silence.'

One strategy is to avoid the sensational. 'The details of Susie Bechhofer's life, with child abuse in a Calvinist Welsh home, are far more horrific than anything in *Austerlitz*. But I didn't want to make use of it because I haven't the right. I try to keep at a distance and never invade,' Sebald says. 'I don't think you can focus on the horror of the Holocaust. It's like the head of the Medusa: you carry it with you in a sack, but if you looked at it you'd be petrified. I was trying to write the lives of some people who'd survived – the "lucky ones". If they were so fraught, you can extrapolate. But I didn't see it; I only know things indirectly.'

Sebald loathes the term 'Holocaust literature' ('it's a dreadful idea that you can have a sub-genre and make a speciality out of it; it's grotesque'). While he commends Claude Lanzmann's documentary *Shoah* (1985), he is doubtful about recreations. 'It can only become an obscenity, like *Schindler's List*, where you know the extras who get mown down will be drinking Coca-Cola after the filming.' In *The Emigrants*, it is the slow accretion of fictional details of an annihilated culture that fuels an overwhelming sense of loss. 'It's full of an ache for the past,' says Grant, 'something destroyed, not just for Jews but for Germans.' It may partly be an awareness of that lingering absence that repels Sebald from Germany. 'As a consequence of persecution, the country is much poorer,' he says. 'It's more homogeneous than other European nations.'

He has turned down job offers at German universities, but says: 'The longer I've stayed here, the less I feel at home. In Germany, they think I'm a native, but I feel at least as distant there. My ideal station,' he half smiles, 'is possibly a hotel in Switzerland.'

He travels almost monthly to the continent, 'digging around' in archives, 'servicing' his books with readings and appearances ('I try to keep this to a minimum') or visiting friends and relatives. His sisters live in French- and German-speaking Switzerland, while his mother is still alive in Sonthofen, Bavaria. 'Going home is not necessarily a wonderful experience,' he says. 'It always comes with a sense of loss, and makes you so conscious of the inexorable passage of time.' He adds: 'If you're based in two places, on a bad day you see only the disadvantages everywhere. On a bad day, returning to Germany brings back all kinds of spectres from the past.'

In *The Rings of Saturn* (1995), subtitled in German 'An English pilgrimage', W. G. takes a rucksack on a walking trip across East Anglia to 'dispel emptiness'. He discerns destruction and the dark undercurrents of European history all around. His mind travels from Conrad's sojourn in Lowestoft to the Belgian Congo, whose slave labour foreshadowed the concentration camps. Britain has its own amnesia about an imperial past, and Sebald has said he finds the English 'not so obviously guilty'.

The Rings of Saturn reveals links between beauty and brutality. 'Culture is not the antidote to the mayhem we wreak – expanding the economy or waging wars,' says Sebald. 'Art is a way of laundering money. It still goes on.' He cites the slave-driven sugar profits that built the Tate. 'It's more obvious with art because it's an expensive commodity. But literature is also affirmative of society – it oils the wheels.'

Austerlitz too explores the link between architecture and fascism. 'The Nazis had megalomaniac fantasies which Speer, the court architect, was going to realize,' says Sebald, who grew up near the Sonthofen Ordensburg, a former college for the Nazi elite. 'There were concerts, and you were dwarfed by the architecture of power-crazed minds. It was prefigured by the bombast of the nineteenth-century bourgeois style – it always comes from somewhere. These vast edifices depended on slave labour. The SS ran quarries next to concentration camps. It's not an accidental link.'

A year after his travels along the coast, the narrator in *The Rings of Saturn* is 'taken into hospital in Norwich in a state of almost total immobility'. While one reviewer assumed he had been incarcerated in a mental asylum, Sebald explains: 'Walking along the seashore was not comfortable – one foot was always lower than the other. I had a pain, and the following summer, I stretched, and something broke in my back.' Threatened with paralysis, he had a four-hour operation for a shattered disc. 'They mended me pretty well.'

Some found comedy in the morose narrator, an afflicted writer battling foul weather and fouler hotels, who was parodied in *Private Eye* as an Eeyore-like figure of gloom. It is an image Sebald himself laughs at. Evoking a boyhood photograph of his mother looking brightly at the camera and 'me being my usual self', he pulls an absurdly lugubrious face. His sombre reserve is relieved by a kindliness, deadpan wit and occasional flashes of laughter. Self-deprecation builds with comic force as he mocks his late starts in life.

While Hoffman says his 'mode of ironic melancholia' is in a 'vein of English eccentrics, and entirely consistent with his personality', for Robinson, Sebald is 'not so much melancholic as burdened by history: the wryness, the sardonic humour, is how he engages with experience he'd otherwise find too painful to contemplate'. Byatt, for whom Sebald's narrator 'journeys in great circling spirals in order not to go home, to get away from his origins', sees melancholy as a 'cover for something more savage: he suddenly puts the knife in about the Germans'.

Sebald, who relaxes by 'walking and taking the dog out', travels alone: 'You can't see anything as a pair; you have to be by yourself.' He is clearly burdened by his writing. 'You have no conception when you begin; it seems like an innocent occupation, but it's not easy. You become a boring person for those around you. It must be extremely uncomfortable to live with a writer – all that preoccupation and brooding.' He revises both his English and French translations, scans his Italian ones, and has 'intervened massively' in the past ('I literally rewrote them'). He is also oppressed by growing fame. 'The phone calls and letters could drive you out of writing. I'm on the brink of saying, no more readings. At the same time, one doesn't want to be too capricious.'

His celebrity in Germany spread beyond literary circles with the non-fiction *Air War and Literature* (1999), which will be published in Britain next year. It attempted to broach what he sees as a 'muteness' in Germany about the Allied firebombing of German cities in the final stages of the war. 'We didn't want to be reminded partly because of the shame,' he says. 'The country was reduced to rubble, and people were scavengers in the ruins – the same people who were "sanitizing" Europe were all of a sudden among the rats.' There is still resentment that it remains a taboo, says Sebald, 'but we should know where it came from: we bombed Warsaw and Stalingrad before the US came to bomb us. When Dresden was bombed and there were countless corpses, special commanders were brought in from Treblinka because they knew how to burn bodies.'

Amid TV debates spawned by the book, he recalls, 'it was very disagreeable to get a hundred letters every day at breakfast. Nobody had had an outlet for these feelings before. Some wrote hysterically about their experiences. It took the lid off. Others said the bombing had been masterminded by Jews abroad. There's a danger of getting applause from the wrong side.'

Sebald prefers his British readers to his German ones: 'I get very odd letters from my native country, horrified that there aren't any paragraphs in *Austerlitz*, or taking me up on errors of fact. It's an attitude problem, an inability to put yourself into the place of another person. There's definitely something like a national character, even though it's frowned upon to say so.' He thinks ambivalence about the 'official culture of memory' remains widespread, and suggests his books make a splash but then sink with little trace. 'After that, there's silence. It's an indication of resentment that somebody is making you think about all that again. People are saying: "It's enough – it's time to think about ourselves."'

Although his claims for the act of writing are so tentative, so doubt-ridden, Sebald feels writers have an obligation to air what others cannot bear to remember. Writing may even be a minute step towards expiation. 'It would be presumptuous to say writing a book would be a sufficient gesture,' he reflects. 'But if people were more preoccupied with the past, maybe the events that overwhelm us would be fewer.' At least, he adds, 'while you're sitting still in your own room, you don't do anyone any harm'.

22 September 2001

Life at a glance

WINFRIED GEORG MAXIMILIAN SEBALD

Born: 18 May 1944, Wertach im Allgau, Bavaria, Germany.

Education: Grammar school in Oberstdorf; Freiburg University, Switzerland; Manchester University.

Married: Ute (1967; one daughter).

Career: Language assistant, Manchester University (1966); lecturer, University of East Anglia (1970–87); professor of European literature, UEA (1987–2001); founding director, British Centre for Literary Translation, UEA (1989–93).

Select bibliography (German dates): *After Nature* (1988); *Vertigo* (1990); *The Emigrants* (1993); *The Rings of Saturn* (1995); *Austerlitz* (2001).

W. G. Sebald died on 14 December 2001.

MURIEL SPARK
The genteel assassin

Emma Brockes

For half a century, Muriel Spark has been stripping away human vanity with the force of a blowtorch. 'You will end up as a girl-guide leader in a suburb like Corstorphine,' withers Jean Brodie, Spark's most famous heroine, to one of her young charges. And her now infamous demolition of Marie Stopes, an adversary during Spark's time as editor of the *Poetry Review*, vibrates with her signature tone: 'I used to think it a pity that her mother rather than she had not thought of birth control,' Spark said, with an irony so delicate there is no sound of tearing as the knife goes in.

Because of this, her polite curiosity comes across in conversation as a front for more ruthless operations, her generous manner as a ruse to draw out pretensions. Naturally, this is absurd. Now eighty-two, she sits in her study in Tuscany with her wicked red hair and her merry eyes, the very incarnation of her novels: quick, compact, like a sparrow with its head to one side, prospecting for worms. She smiles, revealing small white teeth, perfectly cut. 'Now,' she says, after dispensing with preliminaries, 'what is it you are wearing?'

She has lived here, an hour from Florence, for the last twenty years. It is not an idyllic hideaway in Tuscany's New Labour belt, but a dark, crumbling presbytery conversion on a hilltop outside Arezzo, an industrial town where the outlying villages are one generation removed from poverty. It is a fitting backdrop for a woman to whom dark and dramatic things seem to happen, or at least, who presents them as such in the retelling. Over the last decade, five of Spark's pet dogs have been poisoned, in a case that made the front page of the Italian newspapers. 'Who killed Muriel's dogs?' demanded *La Repubblica* last March, while Spark rallied international attention and sealed her reputation among locals as a 'mad Englishwoman'.

Back in 1939, Nita McEwan, an old schoolfriend to whom she bore a striking resemblance, was shot dead in a boarding house in Rhodesia. Spark, boarding there also, entered the sitting room the following day and was perceived, amid much screaming, to be the ghost of the dead woman.

Perhaps to protect herself from these bizarre confrontations, Spark derives a brittle energy from working them into her fiction and consoling herself with the belief that, as John Masefield once told her, 'all experience is good for the artist'. It is possible that she welcomes a good fight as fuel for her eloquence; she is at her finest when under siege. For the last three years, she has maintained a high-profile dispute with her son, Robin, in which she has referred to him as a 'lousy' artist, consumed by 'jealousy and resentment'. There may be some teasing in this, not of Robin, but of the pious observers, to whom displays of 'bad motherhood' are kindling for moral outrage. None the less, friends wince at her forthrightness and she is reputed to be 'difficult', infuriated by sloppy reasoning and poised, cat-like, to strike at anyone who subjects her to it, even her own son. She is not a woman restrained by sentiment.

This is not to say she is without close friends. She shares her home with its owner, Penelope Jardine, a sculptor who has been her companion and assistant since they met in Rome in the 1960s and is, like Spark, a person to whom the sinister has a full-bodied presence in daily life. When Jardine lived in London, she was troubled by a man who persistently called her flat, asking to be put in touch with the previous occupant. 'It was plain from the questions he asked that he was intending to rub him out,' she says over tea. This is exactly the kind of scenario that Spark swoops on for her fiction: the hit man on the phone, the diamond smuggler down the street, the vast improbability that forces readers to reassess, mid-flow, what kind of book they are dealing with.

Spark is equally disorienting in person: 'I had my bag stolen from the back of my chair in a restaurant in Florence,' she recalls. 'It had an unfinished poem about a hat in it. When I went to the police, they asked me what was in the bag, and I said there was a poem. The policeman said can you describe the poem? I said, it was about a hat. I didn't get the feeling he took it seriously at all.'

Not taking Spark seriously is an error that critics have been sporadically making since her first novel, *The Comforters*, was published in 1957. 'Brief, brittle and nasty in an arch kind of way,' the critic Robert Nye wrote of her in 1971. A bad-tempered review of *The Hothouse by the East River* in 1973 called it 'elliptical and dotty'. In 1992, when her autobiography, *Curriculum Vitae*, was submitted for publication in America, word reached Spark that one of the editors had condemned it as 'so full of calculated madness' that they couldn't publish. Spark was swift in her assassination. 'I said: "She has dedicated her menopause to me." I left it at that.'

The huffy reviews were possibly provoked by Spark's talent for toying with her readers' expectations. It is an approach she occasionally takes too far: at the end of *Hothouse*, readers discover with a dizzy plunge that all the protagonists are dead and have been since the opening page. The characters in a Spark novel are held within a symbolic order that is not altogether reliable.

'What made her fiction in the sixties very important and exhilarating is that she seemed to have found a way of making it new,' says David Lodge, the novelist and academic who numbers Spark among the most influential of the postwar novelists. 'She uses the omniscient authorial voice, not as it appears in the classical novel, but in a very playful, whimsical, unexpected way, jerking the reader about on the end of a string. The first time I read *Jean Brodie*, I was baffled. The technique has become familiar now, but at the time it seemed extraordinary.'

'There is an intellectual energy that is staggering and touching and amazing,' says the poet Iris Birtwistle, whose work Spark first published in the *Poetry Review*. 'She carves with a very sharp knife. Muriel Spark was the keenest, sharpest, most agile brain that I ever came across. She is light years more intelligent than most people.'

The greatest non sequitur pulled off by Muriel Spark has been that of her own life. She knew that she wanted to write and she knew how she wanted to write, but it was many years before she was in a financial position to do anything beyond getting by. From the outset, however, she had a sort of damn-you self-assurance that kept her from editing her style to suit publishers' fancies.

'I was very much myself,' she says. 'I felt I should be getting as much money as people like Kingsley Amis, who was my contemporary.' Spark, however, was from a background quite at odds with the tenor of her prose – that glittering levity enabled by not having to worry about paying the gas bill. 'I had a certain throwaway attitude which really didn't belong to my upbringing. I had to adapt it to a life that was totally different from that of the people who had used that kind of prose style before. It usually belonged to people of leisure and I had always had to struggle.'

She was born Muriel Camberg in Edinburgh in 1918, to a Scots-Jewish father and an English mother, a fact that her own son, Robin, would contest seventy years later in a bid to vindicate his own religious choices by claiming that both his grandparents were Jewish. 'My mother and father were both religious,' says Spark, 'but not along any sectarian line. They believed in the Almighty.' Her confidence in her own talent was formidable. As a child she liked reading Sir Walter Scott's *Border Ballads* and eavesdropping on adult conversations, both of which stimulated what she later called, her 'literary sense', a highly-tuned ear for language.

Her precocious interest in literature (she was reading Browning and Swinburne at eleven) was not shared by her parents, an engineer and a music teacher, although they encouraged Spark and her brother to pursue their own interests. 'My mother wrote a nice letter, that was all. My father read the racing papers. My mother, however, liked to play the piano and was a music teacher, so maybe I get the musical side and imagination from her.'

When her first novel, *The Comforters* – an exploration of the mechanics of writing in which a woman hears the text of the book being narrated in her head – was published in 1957, Spark's parents were bemused. 'They didn't know what it was all about really,' she says, giggling at the memory of her mother's startled reaction. "Oh darling!" she said. "You've written a novel!" She didn't take it in.' Spark, however, had never doubted that she would be a writer. At eleven, she came under the influence of Miss Kay of James Gillespie's School in Edinburgh, a woman on whom the character of Miss Jean Brodie would eventually be based. Miss Kay taught Spark and her classmates that they were 'not to be carried away by crowd emotions, not to be fools', a lesson that Spark would remember and translate into the cool-headed, unsentimental slant of her own literature.

While she was still at school, five of her poems were accepted for an anthology, and in 1932, at the age of fourteen, she won first prize in a poetry competition to commemorate the death of Scott. 'The *Border Ballads* were a heavy influence on her,' says Alan Taylor, managing editor of the *Scotsman* and a frequent visitor to Spark's home in Tuscany. 'They have these summary ways of dispatching people, and she does this all the time.'

'I still take a poetic view of life as I see it through the novel,' says Spark, explaining that she views her novels as long prose poems, a claim that might inspire eye-rolling cynicism if it came from a less disciplined writer. Spark, however, refers not to the use of poetic language or to flowery imagery, but to the hard-boiled matter of rhythm and cadence. 'It is a question of construction, of lyricism – lyricism in that poetry has music in it. There are repetitive motifs; repetitive little phrases, themes, always returning and a complete reversal of circumstances towards the end.'

The repetitive motif beats time not only in her writing, but in her speech. She has a talent for packaging statements in such a way that they have a theatrical momentum, a spontaneous rhythm and suspense that explains how she writes her novels in a single go, without returning to edit them. She punctuates her spoken word as exactly as her written. There is a full stop at the end of each statement that she indicates by staring into space and tuning out. She has it first time.

She observes a writing routine that goes beyond strictness into the realm of superstition, pouring out each novel, in longhand, onto yellow note pads she buys from James Thin, the Edinburgh stationer. 'I have an absolute will to write,' she says. This can leave the impression of a chilly character, a woman meticulous in her enthusiasms, who regards people as if they appear on the end of a pin. Critics have marked her as 'cold' and 'highly calculated', a writer whose faculties, like a set of surgical instruments, ensure that 'every stitch is small and perfect'.

'She has a sense of humour but I don't think she has a sense of the ridiculous,' says Iris Birtwistle. 'I've never heard her do a hearty laugh, ever. All her conversation is spiked with merriment, but in the old-fashioned way. I think the ridiculous would probably be lowbrow for her.'

'I simply can't take the jocular,' Spark has said, 'either in life or art. A well-brewed send-up is delightful. Derision is boring.' Friends insist that her steely composure should not be mistaken for aloofness. 'She thinks before she speaks,' says Auberon Waugh, whose father Evelyn was a great promoter of Spark's work before it became well known. 'But she is terribly warm, terribly affectionate.'

After leaving school, Spark wanted to go to university but the family couldn't afford it, so she enrolled on a course in precis writing at Heriot-Watt College (now university), a natural home for her writing style. 'I do like to be brief,' she says. She didn't mope for her lack of a degree. It was regrettable, of course, but with her trademark defiance, Spark did not feel it diminished her. 'I thought all the books of the world are open to me if I can get at them. I could read all that I wanted.'

The war hadn't yet started and as nice girls didn't have sex before marriage, Spark made the practical and hasty decision at nineteen to get engaged to Sydney Oswald Spark – SOS as he was known – thirteen years her senior, whom she had met at a dance and whose history was largely unknown to her. He was going to Rhodesia as a schoolteacher and, keen for adventure, she grabbed at the chance to go with him. They were married on 3 September 1937. Within six months of arriving, she knew she had made a terrible mistake. Spark talks about this phase of her life with the same unblinking detachment she turns on everything: she is faintly amused, mildly astonished, forever precise and indignant at this, the crazy narrative of her twenties.

'My husband had an unbalanced family, and his sister had to go in a loony bin because she attempted to murder my mother. And then I realized that I had been taken in. But by that time I was expecting a baby.' Spark was in a genuinely precarious position. When Nita McEwan's husband killed her in the boarding house, Spark was rattled enough to hide the gun that her own husband liked to wave around and occasionally point at her.

And she hated the colony. 'The white people were not very nice,' she says. 'There was a feeling of people coming in just to exploit and I felt uneasy and frightened. I could see this myriad of blacks against 50,000 whites who wouldn't have a chance if it came to a showdown. And I could see that it was wrong. It was their house, not ours.'

Her husband became more manic and increasingly more violent and when Spark eventually left him, two years into the marriage, he was committed to a mental institution. She tried to get passage home, but the Second World War had broken out and there were no passenger ships sailing. 'I had to stick it out as much as possible, but it was all very much life and death for me.'

Throughout this time, she had not stopped writing. She twice won Rhodesia's annual poetry competition, and her appreciation for a strong narrative made her desperate to return to Britain to experience the war. She enrolled Robin, then five, in a convent in Rhodesia, and eventually sailed for England, not a decision she regrets, she says, because there was little alternative.

'There was almost no work for me to do there. I thought the war would be over in six months. Instead, it was eighteen months. It was quite a separation.' Friends have since raised eyebrows and muttered that she is not very maternal, that writing always came before her son, who she never quite seemed to identify with.

When Robin returned from Rhodesia, he went to live with his maternal grandparents in Edinburgh and decided, as a teenager, to embrace his grandfather's religion, Judaism. As an adult, he started campaigning for his late grandmother (Muriel's mother) to be recognized as a Jew, a cause taken up, to Muriel Spark's immense annoyance, by the *Jewish Chronicle*. 'They are really like hounds,' she says. 'Absolute hounds.' What is at least probable, in this pedantic and irritable dispute, is that her mother, Sarah Uezzel, signed a false Jewish name on her wedding certificate in order to be allowed to marry Spark's father in a synagogue.

Spark is at her haughtiest, her uncrushable best on this, the subject of her own contested heritage. 'The very strict Jews such as those at the *Jewish Chronicle* refuse the word "half-Jew" altogether, which is, of course, in the dictionary. One knows what half-Jew means. Hitler didn't care one damn what the Jews' definition was.' She pauses. 'They say there is no such thing as a half-Jew and I say there is, because I experienced it.'

There is a sense that this episode infuriated Spark less for its content than for what it did to her perception of Robin: that he appeared feeble to her, relying for his identity on some bogus interpretation of his ethnic background rather than his own convictions; that he was not like his mother at all.

Spark's own religious convictions were cemented in 1954 when she converted to Catholicism, a faith she practises, like all things, on her own terms. She is anti-clerical, dislikes dogma and will not remain silent on church matters she finds absurd. She doesn't believe in good and evil, but in absurdity and intelligence – in the fact that people who do 'evil' acts are pursuing a logic that intelligent people call absurd. 'I like to speak out,' she says. 'If the Catholic religion, to which I belong, can't allow me to speak out frankly, it is no religion for me.'

Her reasons for converting are deeply embedded in her prose. She speaks of the importance of recognizing a 'life beyond this life', of acknowledging the supernatural and, in a rare concession to poetic fancy, of believing in angels. 'I do think the whole of nature is impregnated with spiritual life. There is no substance without some spirit and no spirit without substance.'

It is possible that as a writer, she was attracted to Catholicism for its strong narrative, its seductive rituals and repetitive motifs, the sheer theatrical force of its history. It is also possible, as Auberon Waugh observes, that Spark's mental filing system required a repository of faith. 'The thing about Catholicism,' he says, 'is that there's no bloody nonsense – something is right, something is wrong.'

After she returned to London, Spark fulfilled her wish to 'see' the war, by working as a duty secretary at a military intelligence base in Milton Bryan, Bedfordshire, taking down telephone messages from Allied bombing crews and passing them on for use as black propaganda. It was not until after the war that she started writing in earnest, for a jewellery trade magazine called *Argentor*, a political magazine called *European Affairs*, and, after distinguishing herself in a number of its competitions, as editor of the *Poetry Review*. She was twenty-nine, and determined to rescue the magazine from ignominy as a forum for weak and vain poetry.

'I started publishing modern poems rather than Christmas card-type poems,' she sniffs and, not shy to admit it, she made enough enemies to be dismissed from the post after two years of constant assault from lecherous board members and bitter poets. 'They would do anything to get published. Those that weren't queer wanted to sleep with me. They thought they were poets and there should be free love or something. I've never known anything like it.'

Spark's friendship with Penelope Jardine has since provoked speculations about her own sexuality, although both she and her friends reject them as fanciful. 'She had enormous vitality and great appeal to the opposite sex,' says Iris Birtwistle. 'We had masses of boyfriends, and why not?' Theirs is an old-fashioned friendship, Spark says, although one that has evolved into a peculiar intensity. 'Penelope is like the archetypal novelist's wife,' says John Mortimer, who rents a summer house near their home. 'She is protective of Muriel.'

Spark's stint at the *Poetry Review* gained her a reputation as a stylish editor and she built on it with her biographies of Mary Shelley (1951) and Emily Brontë (1953). The real break, however, came on 5 November 1951, when she entered a short story competition in the *Observer*. The subject was 'Christmas' and the prize £250, big enough to attract 6,700 entries. Spark was thirty-three, renting a room in London's Old Brompton Road and earning £134 a year as a jobbing writer – of poetry, journalism and speech material on industrial relations, a subject about which she knew nothing but, with her customary flair, managed to pull off.

'It was on a Saturday that I finished writing the short story,' she recalls, in a polished anecdote. 'I was going to type it out and I found that I had no typing paper, and all the shops were shut except for one, a picture framer's. And so I said to him: "Just give me twenty pieces of paper, that's all I want." He said: "I don't sell paper." I said: "I can see you've got a typewriter there, I just want paper." I said: "I'm going to go in for this prize and if I win it I'll buy a picture off you."' She smiles sardonically. 'I bought a picture.'

The success of the story, 'The Seraph and the Zambesi', based on her time in Rhodesia, prompted a commission for a novel from Macmillan. Spark, still desperately poor, was only able to write it thanks to the patronage of a kindly Graham Greene. He had read and admired her non-fiction, and learning from her boyfriend, the critic and literary schmoozer Derek Stanford, that she was poor, offered to pay her an allowance.

Iris Birtwistle was one of the first people Spark knew intimately to have come from a background of private means. 'She was quite intrigued by it,' Birtwistle says. 'She was hooked on class, fascinated by the structure and interplay.'

'She has ideas of grandeur,' says Auberon Waugh. 'She has to be driven in a car everywhere.' She is acutely interested in the dynamics of snobbery, a subject that she examines in the novel she is currently writing. It will be called *The Finishing School* and she is reading *Debrett's Peerage* and a book on social manners for it, which she finds 'killingly funny'. Spark's own social position changed radically, not with the publication of her first novel – which was generally well received but didn't make her fortune – but with the success of *The Prime of Miss Jean Brodie*, the fictional schoolteacher who incinerates her enemies with a sharp tongue.

That 1961 hit was the turning point for Spark: William Shawn, then editor of the *New Yorker*, printed the entire manuscript of *Jean Brodie* in one issue of the magazine and offered Spark the use of an office overlooking Times Square. She took up his offer in 1963 when she moved to New York and, with the stage and film versions of *Jean Brodie* bringing her international acclaim, started knocking around the celebrity circuit with Norman Mailer and Mary McCarthy.

This is the glamorous period, full of parties and salons, which she revelled in, briefly, before shunning it to get back to writing. Even during the headiest days, however, she remained sceptical of Hollywood's interest in her and is critical of all the film versions of her work, considering Geraldine McEwan in the stage version to have been the best Jean Brodie. 'The colours in the film [directed by Ronald Neame, 1969] were much too bright for Edinburgh, which has a sort of pearly light. And everyone's hair was too red. Apart from that, I thought it quite well written.' It tickles her, however, that all the actresses who have been in dramatizations of her books have become dames: Judi Dench, Maggie Smith, Vanessa Redgrave, Elizabeth Taylor and Spark herself, in 1993. 'We are all dames together,' she says, and smiles.

The attention didn't change her; in fact, the moment the publicity circus threatened to interfere with her writing she fled, from London to New York, New York to Rome and finally to Arezzo. 'She has made a career of escaping when she thinks something is going to stop her writing,' says Alan Taylor.

To Spark, everything comes second to the story: sons, lovers, health and welfare. She gets up at seven every morning to write, aware in that unflinching way of hers that every novel might be her last. 'When I begin a novel, I want to absorb it through my pores,' she says, and this is apparent in the words that she uses, in the tiny shifts in temperature she records. Her defiance is in her detail, her precision driven by the knowledge that by fixing things exactly, we widen their possibility.

The novel she has just submitted is called *Aiding And Abetting*, a fictional account of what happened to Lord Lucan after he murdered the family nanny. (There are a few legal wrangles to negotiate, although Spark, poised as if at the head of an army, declares: 'Let him come forward and sue me.')

It is part of her resilience that she finds dramatic potential in everything. At the end of the interview, she is asked if she would mind being photographed outside in a gale. Spark bobs about in huge red hockey socks and yellow anorak, blinking gamely into the wind, throwing her bird-like frame against the elements with a wicked smile. It might be that she is content to suffer a little discomfort for the story she will tell when the door shuts behind her.

27 May 2000

Life at a glance

MURIEL SARAH SPARK, NÉE CAMBERG

Born: 1 February 1918, Edinburgh.
Education: James Gillespie's School for Girls, Edinburgh; Heriot-Watt College.
Married: Sydney Oswald Spark (1937, divorced; one son, Robin).
Career: Foreign Office (1944); general secretary, Poetry Society, editor, *Poetry Review* (1947–9).
Select bibliography: *Child of Light: A Reassessment of Mary Shelley* (1951); *The Comforters* (1957); *The Go-Away Bird* (1958); *Memento Mori* (1959); *The Ballad of Peckham Rye* (1960); *The Prime of Miss Jean Brodie* (1961); *The Girls of Slender Means* (1963); *The Mandelbaum Gate* (1965); *The Abbess of Crewe* (1974); *Loitering with Intent* (1981); *A Far Cry from Kensington* (1988); *Curriculum Vitae* (autobiography, 1992); *Reality and Dreams* (1996); *Aiding and Abetting* (2000).
Honours: Dame of the British Empire (1993).
Awards: David Cohen British literature prize for lifetime acheivement (1997).

JOHN UPDIKE
Indiscreet charmer of the bourgeoisie

Nicholas Wroe

John Updike has always said that he wanted to be a writer in the way other people are dentists and lawyers. To see him at his discreetly old-moneyed New England golf club is to see a man whose ambition has been fulfilled. With his courtly good manners and dogged nineteen-handicap swing, the imperfections immovably grooved after forty years of struggle, he is every inch a distinguished member of Boston's suburban professional elite.

Where he differs from some of his fellow rich businessmen is that he rarely talks shop on the course, but for someone who so efficiently recycles his life and the world around him into his art, there is always the occasional twitch of the literary antenna. He notes the 'sinister rattle' of spiked shoes on concrete and a six on a par four is still a six, 'but a gallant six', he thinks.

When his playing partners talk about the club's plan to close a road that runs through the course because it is being used as a lovers' lane he quietly nods. Then as they move off down the fairway you hear the definitive chronicler of middle-class American sex musing to himself: 'So where can people go to neck these days?'

Updike has successfully combined the self-consciously bourgeois and the self-consciously literary ever since he resigned from his job on the *New Yorker* magazine in 1957 and moved to Massachusetts to live as a freelance writer. He had a wife and two young children to support and set out to write two pages a day, six days a week. 'It was a modest target,' he says, 'but if I did it I thought I would accumulate manuscripts.' He has.

The years since then have witnessed an almost unparalleled surge of prolonged creative literary energy. Perhaps Anthony Burgess was similarly productive across such a range in recent times, but Updike's seemingly endless fecundity is really more reminiscent of Dickens. His quartet of novels featuring Harry 'Rabbit' Angstrom have provided a running commentary on contemporary middle America and are one of the great works of post-war fiction. His bed-hopping assault on American history, *Couples*, was a key novel of the 1960s and his short stories will eternally be anthologized. He has simultaneously maintained a barrage of erudite and thoughtful literary and art criticism, collected together a 350-page volume of poetry, and written a play.

As if that were not enough, every week seems to bring a new piece in some magazine or other; 'My Life in Cars' (he currently drives an Infiniti) or his happiest hour of the day (11 a.m., 'the hour for optimists'). There is a whole book about his tortured love affair with golf, and this month sees the publication of his fiftieth book, *More Matter*, a collection of his journalism from the last eight years. It is nine hundred pages long.

'But it is only the fiftieth if you count five children's books and several short-story collections,' Updike explains with a characteristic scrupulousness. 'My publishers like to say it is fifty but I think it's forty-four real books. Although perhaps I'm being hard on myself.' Perhaps he is, but however you do the arithmetic, it remains a phenomenal achievement of both quantity and quality.

The writer Nicholson Baker, in *U & I*, his odd little memoir about being obsessed with Updike, noted once seeing him on television. Updike was up a ladder at his mother's house fixing storm windows. 'He tossed down to us some startlingly lucid felicity,' recalled Baker, 'something about "these small yearly duties which blah blah blah", and I was stunned to recognize that in Updike we were dealing with a man so naturally verbal that he could write his fucking memoirs on a ladder!'

Roger Angell, the fiction editor at what remains Updike's spiritual home, the *New Yorker*, says, 'No one else in the world does as much writing of high quality as he does. It takes the breath away. He is constantly in our pages, and so when I looked at his new collection, I was astounded to see how much work he had done elsewhere.'

The writer and critic Malcolm Bradbury is preparing a single-volume edition of Updike's Henry Bech stories and novels. He sees Updike as 'the most enduring of that generation of American writers – J. D. Salinger, Norman Mailer, Saul Bellow – who emerged after the war. Perhaps Bellow has a greater grandeur and splendour, but Updike has had this sustained and varied career that has been filled with writing. An obvious contrast is with Salinger. In the late fifties and early sixties, they looked very much a pair; both *New Yorker* writers and both brilliantly developing the short story. Then Salinger goes one way, towards silence, and Updike goes the other way towards plenitude and to enormous adventures in fiction.'

Another writer who came to prominence in this era was Joseph Heller. When told of Heller's death this week, Updike said that although as a novelist he wasn't 'top of the chart, he was a sweet man' and *Catch-22* was an important book. 'It set the comic tone for a lot of fiction,' said Updike. 'It also sanctioned anti-war feeling about the Second World War, which was supposed to be the war we were all happy to fight.'

Heller, unlike Updike, found writing a slow and difficult process, but while Updike continues to produce at the rate he did twenty or thirty years ago, there is some doubt as to whether people are listening like they used to. The critic Sven Birketts claims that 'Philip Roth, Updike, Mailer and Bellow were all together on the great ride. They were there when fiction mattered, and fiction mattered, in part, because they were there. Only, the very thing that made these artists avatars of the self-seeking liberation culture is now their unmaking. Not because we, as a culture, have ceased to focus upon ourselves, but because they, as writers, have fallen victim to the law of diminishing returns. The self, however grandiose, is finite; the wells dry up.'

Updike's ability to utilize seemingly every single aspect of his life in his work has been a model of literary thrift. His childhood and his family, his marriages and his children, his psoriasis and his stammer have all been worked and reworked. We know about his cautious support for the Vietnam war and his Christianity. And just in case we miss anything, he periodically interviews himself in the guise of his alter ego, the Jewish Nobel prize-winning author

Henry Bech. But despite all this apparent openness, doubts remain as to who is the 'real' John Updike.

These doubts, it seems, are shared in part by Updike himself. In a wryly clever essay called 'Updike And I' he wrote: 'I created Updike, out of the sticks and mud of my Pennsylvania boyhood, so I can scarcely resent it when people, mistaking me for him, stop me on the street and ask me for his autograph.' He goes on to note: 'I feel that the fractional time of day he spends away from being Updike is what feeds and inspires him, and yet, perversely, he spends more and more time being Updike, that monster of whom my boyhood dreamed.' The piece ends with him wondering: 'Suppose, some day, he fails to show up? I would attempt to do his work, but no one would be fooled.'

This curious sense of distance is recognized even by long-time friends and colleagues. Roger Angell has been Updike's fiction editor at the *New Yorker* since 1976 and has known him since Angell's mother, Katherine White, then the fiction editor, introduced Updike to the magazine in 1955. 'We've been friends for a long time, but I can't say that I really know John,' he says. 'You can have a long, intense and complicated conversation with him, but then, as he leaves, you feel him sort of fading away. It's a strange phenomenon. He goes back into the thing that he really is and that makes all this possible.'

The facts of his life are straightforward enough. He was born in 1932 in Pennsylvania. His father, Wesley, was a mathematics teacher and his mother, Linda, an aspiring writer whose fiction was eventually published under her maiden name, as Linda Grace Hoyer. Her stories are as autobiographical as her son's, with John represented by a character called Christopher, a successful illustrator who has four children. Updike returned the compliment when he 'opportunistically transposed' details of her hospital treatment towards the end of her life into that of Harry Angstrom.

The Updikes lived in Shillington – pop. 5,000 and the model for his fictional Olinger – until he was thirteen, when they moved a dozen miles to a farm that had been his mother's birthplace. The Depression had hit the family hard. Updike remembers the 'bleak, brown' winter days being like something out of an Andrew Wyeth painting. His father lost his job, and his grandfather was forced to work on a road crew. 'We all took our lumps then', he says.

The experience helped prompt a lifelong reverence for hard work – 'work was sacred'. Barry Nelson, who worked with him on the school newspaper, recalls him even then as a conscientious worker and writer. 'He definitely stood out as someone who was talented,' says Nelson, now a retired teacher. 'He'd be the one who wrote most of the material for class shows and events. You'd think from his stories that he didn't fit in at school, but I never got that impression. He was class president and was generally popular.'

Updike says: 'Happy is not quite the right word for those years, but it was active. I was an only child and the son of an only child. There was an embattled, lonely feeling about our family as I grew up. But that was also good in some ways, it made me a reader, which made me a writer.'

His mother's literary ambitions meant that his own aims were always treated with respect. Aged eleven, he was given a subscription to the *New Yorker*, which fulfilled his need for cartoons – his first love and talent – as well as for good writing. Even at this stage, he had a vision of what a literary career could be. 'I saw it as glamorous, and imagined that a successful life would take me to New York where I would live in some sort of penthouse, dress glamorously and do glamorous things.'

Updike's journey towards New York started in 1950 when he won a scholarship to Harvard. His mother promoted the idea, having noted that many American writers had gone there. Austin Briggs met him at a poker game in the first term. 'He was wearing a green eyeshade and was smoking heavily, it was very impressive. He was very funny and spoke in the same ironic mode, with a good deal of that defence that irony puts up, as he does now. And of course he was very unusual because he got married as an undergraduate.'

That was in 1953. His wife was Mary Pennington, a fine arts major and the daughter of a Unitarian minister. They had four children before separating in 1974. The couple were granted a 'no fault' divorce two years later. 'Leaving my wife and family was the hardest thing I have ever done,' he says. 'It felt the worst thing I have done. For me, creating a family and having four children and a wife was not to be taken for granted. I was proud of it as if it was an achievement to become a family man.' He has said that 'sexual liberation' ended the marriage, 'but maybe it made it more fun at the time than it would have been otherwise. If it hadn't ended, my wife and I would have been the poorer for it.' In 1977, he married Martha Bernhard, a psychologist. They live together in a large home near the Massachusetts coast.

Updike was an outstanding student, edited the *Harvard Lampoon*, and graduated *summa cum laude*. At this time, he was still as interested in graphic arts as he was in writing and spent a year at the Ruskin School of Fine Art in Oxford. His time there was spent drawing from antiquities in the Ashmolean Museum and from still life. 'The drawing still helps me with my writing, in making an image in my mind of what the total work will be.' He rarely draws or paints now, but says that a few birthdays ago his children banded together to buy him paints and canvasses. 'They wanted to try and revive that innocent painter in me,' he smiles. 'I haven't actually used them yet, but I do know where they are.'

It was while at Oxford that he met E. B. and Katherine White of the *New Yorker*, who offered him a job. Roger Angell characterizes Updike's long relationship with the magazine as a 'friendship', one that provides a healthy stimulus for the still-competitive Updike. 'Sometimes he will see a piece in the magazine by a younger writer that he thinks is good. A few weeks later we'll get a story,' laughs Angell.

'As a boy I wanted to get into the magazine, and then as an adult I did,' says Updike, who wrote the 'Talk of the Town' column as well as contributing fiction. 'Then I realized that the kind of work I was doing was basically dead-end.' So two years after becoming a staffer, he set out on his own to concentrate on his fiction and his poetry in Ipswich, the small town in Massachusetts where he had spent his honeymoon. The town would later be immortalized as Tarbox, the location of *Couples*.

'Even though I resigned, I kept the magazine's good will, so that I didn't feel totally isolated financially. Instead of a college backing me and supplying me with faculty housing and all the other amenities an academic gets, I had the *New Yorker*. I counted on them for basic supplies.' Soon the Updikes had four children. 'It was much less expensive to live here than in New York, and there were much less demands. For one thing, you didn't have rich neighbours. If a writer can avoid rich neighbours, he's better off, because you can't help but try to get rich yourself. A writer has to embarrass himself. If you have all the money you need, why do that? So a little financial need is a good thing.'

Updike's approach was to mix idealism and professionalism and follow the example set by the likes of Sinclair Lewis and Ernest Hemingway. 'They did their best and were adequately rewarded for it. I thought that was possible for me then, but it may be getting impossible now. But to see your words actually making it into metal type – which of course it doesn't any more – was one of the thrills for a primitive boy like me. I came from farming and manufacturing country and the notion that you have to produce or make something is in my blood.'

He published a collection of poetry in 1958 and then a novel, *The Poorhouse Fair*, in 1959. The *New York Times* said it was 'brief and concentrated, punctiliously observed, and written in sentences shaped and mortised to an astonishing tightness'. The great prose stylist had arrived. 'There is something about making an artefact, with corners and nice bevelling and shiny varnish,' explains Updike. But not everyone shares his enthusiasm. Norman Mailer has called his sentences 'precious, overpreened, self-indulgent'. Another critic accuses him of treating language, particularly in his occasional journalism, as if it were a meaningless bill to a very rich man, 'adding a lazy 10 per cent tip to each sentence'. But Malcolm Bradbury praises the, 'extraordinary quality of the prose. It was there from the start. Here was someone who had learned to be a beautiful writer. As a former art student he is fascinated by the aesthetics of writing and the elegance of the prose.'

In Ipswich, the Updikes threw themselves into the civic and social life of the town. 'At school, I had charisma when I was about nine,' he says, 'but I lost it when I was about eleven, when sex started to play a part. So a lot of my high school career was spent trying to win back popularity and a sense of belongingness. I was a good student, but I felt I was on the fringes of the hot set, the clique that mattered.' When he went to Ipswich, he says, 'I did feel I'd made it, into an inner circle of young marrieds. And it was the sixties so there was a current of rebellion and doing different things.'

Updike says his contribution to the radical sixties was to grow a beard, but he also expresses a fondness for 'bell bottoms, love beads and the Beatles. And sex was seen as a duty, something you ought to do, which was fun. There was a little pot, although we were too old for that really. We were the generation older than the generation who had the revolution, but we were young enough.'

In some ways these years were his classic writing time: 1960 saw the publication of *Rabbit, Run* in which scenes of oral sex and of infanticide prompted equal acclaim and uproar. Austin Briggs remembers the *New Yorker* being, 'a bit skittish' about Updike's increasing sexual frankness, and a time when Updike himself was wary of being as explicit as he would want for fear of horrifying his mother. But he persevered, and when *Couples* was published in 1968, with its minutely detailed descriptions of genitalia and endless, if ultimately shallow, partner swapping, he was put on the cover of *Time* magazine with the headline 'The Adulterous Society'. The book was a massive seller and the film rights alone brought him half a million dollars.

Austin Briggs remembers Updike giving a tantalizing glimpse into his mindset at this time. He was staying with Briggs, and over dinner said he thought that fidelity was one of the most important virtues, 'which in the wake of *Couples* was fascinating', says Briggs. 'Then there was a pause and he said: "That's why I've continued with the same publisher all along."'

Updike says that *Couples* did satisfy his immediate yen to have a bestseller, but was still put out that it was number one for only a couple of weeks. '*Airport*, by Arthur Haley, knocked it off,' he recalls. 'You can be nagged by insufficiency at any level.'

With the novel set so obviously in his home town, among a group of people not unlike the ones he knew, it provoked some tension in Ipswich. 'It was a little hairy that way, but I wasn't attacked,' he says. 'There was a lot of exaggeration and simplification in the book. But because I describe a small town as teeming with sexual passion and people having no purpose in life but fornication, it did, as we say, ruffle some feathers.'

In theory, fiction allows you to be honest, he says. 'And I've nothing to lose by being honest, except for a few friends. You invent names and appearances, and once you've done that, you're free to be as honest about people as you can. There's no point in not being honest about yourself. If you only have one go at it why be shy or tactful?'

Being honest about neighbours is one thing, what about writing about family? 'Of course your children are children and don't read, bless them,' he smiles. 'Your wife maybe is hurt and offended, but she's getting something out of it. You're supporting her. This is what you live by, this is what you do. It's an unspoken contract. I was not a published writer when I married my first wife, but she believed in art, was herself an artist and not everything I wrote was about her of course. She was enough of an artist herself to give me a long leash.'

Another long leash was provided by his mother, who 'raised me to be a writer. When she wrote about me, I found her representation of me very unappealing; a kind of goody-goody, sickly, unreal guy. I know it's not necessarily pleasant to see yourself in fiction, but it is fiction. I've managed to limp along and maybe I have offended a few people, but less have complained to me than you would think.'

Nevertheless, people increasingly do complain. The American novelist David Foster Wallace, as part of a wider attack on what he called Great Male Narcissist writers said that 'most of the literary readers I know personally are under forty, and a fair number are female, and none of them are big admirers of the post-war Great Male Narcissists. But it's Updike in particular they seem to hate. And not merely his books, for some reason. Mention the poor man himself and you have to jump back: "Just a penis with a thesaurus."'

Austin Briggs teaches English at an American university: 'Students hear that I know John, and a good many female students go out of their way to say to me that they don't read Updike. I'm not sure what I'm supposed to do about this, but they like to make the statement.'

Updike has also recently been in trouble with the gay lobby in New York, following his review of Alan Hollinghurst's novel, *The Spell*, in which Updike noted that 'after a while you begin to long for the chirp and swing and civilizing animation of a female character'. But he has been defying PC since long before it was invented. In 1966, he was identified in the *New York Times* as the only author to come out in favour of America's intervention in Vietnam.

'The war was upsetting, but the protests against the war were also upsetting,' he says. 'It flushed out all of my conservative, vitriolic, I guess Shillington instincts.' He says that many of his new, upper-middle-class friends were Democrats out of human sympathy. His own family had been Democrats because they had been poor. He identified with the president, Lyndon Johnson, 'meaning so well. And this country, that had been so good to me, was being called a fascist state. It shocked me. America had become so abrasive and unpleasant.'

In contemporary politics, he has been associated, tangentially, with another presidential meltdown. There is a line of argument that blames Updike for Monicagate because it was Nicholson Baker's phone-sex book *Vox*, said to be influenced by *Couples*, which Monica Lewinsky gave to the president. Baker said of his own tangential involvement in the scandal that it was ' like manufacturing some little bolt, and then finding it was being used on the Manhattan Project'. Does Updike feel, therefore, that he played a part in the story? He says he would 'field the blame for the crumbling presidency', before adding, 'if I had any fear that Clinton had read me'.

In 1968, Updike moved his family to London for a year. Diana Athill was his English publisher and she arranged a rather grand house for him and his family off Regent's Park. 'I remember ringing up and telling him it was frightfully expensive. John was extremely frugal in small matters – he'd always use a bus rather than a taxi – but in big matters he could be very dashing. He said "let's be devils", and as he had the *Couples* money he must have been feeling dashing.'

'England was kind to me', he says, 'and when I returned home, all those issues hadn't gone away but they were going away. Everyone was so beastly to Lyndon Johnson, but now Nixon was president and I didn't much like Nixon, so being beastly to him didn't seem to me so bad. The pressure was off.'

And so Updike settled into the life he has, by and large, maintained ever since. He has taken Flaubert's words to heart and lived like a bourgeois, from the 'anti-bohemianism gesture of deadpan churchgoing' to his golf to his forty-year relationship with the same publisher. His long-time editor, Judith Jones, still recognizes the perfectionist who would change the typeface, the margins and the spacing, let alone the words in his pieces right up to the very last deadline. 'He still comes into my office and whacks something out of the typewriter in three minutes that would have taken me three hours.'

He has strictly followed a formula of a novel every other book. A new novel called *Gertrude and Claudius*, a prequel to Hamlet – 'Tom Stoppard is not the only one who can play this game' – has already been delivered to his publishers. 'I know people think I turn them out as easily as a bird lays eggs, but to me they seem to be slow accretions and I would feel guilty if I didn't produce a reasonable amount most days. I can lose a day now and then to illness or to golf, but generally I do like to keep the flow coming on something.'

His health is actually pretty good. He gave up smoking in his early thirties and stopped drinking about ten years ago when it disagreed with a psoriasis pill. 'And I get a little exercise with the golf, so I won't retire until some doctor comes and tells me that I'm gaga.'

So we can expect more journalism – in a magazine this month he chooses his favourite year of the century, 1946 – and more novels. 'Undoubtedly the novel has taken some hits recently, but when you do write you feel that momentous possibilities are still there, even after Tolstoy and Stendhal. There are still things left unsaid. Novels still deliver the actual feeling of being alive better than any other medium. Better than sociology, more accessible than poetry, more plausible than the movies. For those that are curious about the human condition the novel will always occupy a place in the budget of the bourgeoisie.'

And who is better suited to mop up that small contribution from Middle America's pocket book? 'I have been very lucky in that I know I won't go to the grave regretting that I never gave it my best shot,' he says. 'Whatever my shortcomings as a writer have been and are, it's not something that more work could have corrected. I've had a very fair chance at being my best self as a writer, an indulgent publisher, indulgent parents and two spouses who supported me. I had all the breaks you could ask for. It doesn't make you good but it means that you are not nagged by excuses. I'm very grateful that I've had every opportunity not to let myself down.'

18 December 1999

Life at a glance

JOHN HOYER UPDIKE

Born: 18 March 1932, Reading, Pennsylvania.

Education: Shillington public schools (1936–50); Harvard University (1950–54); Ruskin School of Art, Oxford (1954–5).

Married: Mary Pennington (1953, divorced 1976; four children: Elizabeth, David, Michael, Miranda); Martha Bernhard (1977).

Career: Staff writer on the *New Yorker* (1955–7).

Select bibliography: *The Carpentered Hen and Other Tame Creatures* (poetry, 1958); *The Poorhouse Fair* (1959); *Rabbit, Run* (1960); *Olinger Stories – A Selection* (1964); *Couples* (1968); *Rabbit Redux* (1971); *A Month of Sundays* (1975); *Rabbit is Rich* (1981); *Bech is Back* (1982); *The Witches of Eastwick* (1984); *Trust Me* (1987); *Just Looking* (essays on art, 1989); *Collected Poems* (1993); *Brazil* (1994); *More Matter: Essays and Criticism* (1999); *Gertrude and Claudius* (2000).

Awards: National Book Award (1964), American Book Award (1982), National Arts Club Medal of Honor (1984), Pulitzer prize *Rabbit is Rich* (1982) and *Rabbit at Rest* (1991).

GORE VIDAL

Ice in the soul

Roy Hattersley

Gore Vidal is the most elegant, erudite and eclectic writer of his generation – a stylist who would never descend to the vulgar alliteration with which this sentence begins.

Yet both his many admirers and his even more numerous critics react to the mention of his name not by recalling a novel, essay or film script, but with a description of what can only be called a performance. Admittedly, the memorable moments are all literary – they are built around apparently spontaneous aphorisms. But as every stand-up comic will agree, it's the way he tells 'em that makes all the difference.

It was a late-night argument on the law and morality that established him in the minds and memories of British television viewers who had never read a word he wrote. Vidal's opponent – Sir Cyril Osborne, a Tory MP with hardline views on family values – demanded a straight answer to a straight question: 'Do you or do you not believe in corporal punishment?' Vidal replied: 'Only between consenting adults.' The reply provoked delight and outrage in almost equal measure and was, therefore, a paradigm of Vidal's whole relationship with the world.

Ned Sherrin – producer, thirty years ago, of *That Was The Week That Was* – recalls a programme in which Richard Adams, author of *Watership Down*, told Vidal that his work was meretricious. 'I beg your pardon,' said Gore. 'Meretricious,' Adams repeated. 'Meretricious.' Vidal smiled – like many handsome men he smiles a lot. Then he replied: 'Meretricious to you and a happy New Year.' It is the sort of vacuous retort that is meant, by its vacuity, to be offensively dismissive. And it never fails. Norman Mailer was so annoyed by the style of Vidal's literary criticism that he hit him over the head with a glass tumbler. 'Ah,' said Vidal without rubbing his scalp, 'Mailer is, as usual, lost for words.'

Vidal is encouraged in that sort of behaviour by the knowledge that even some victims of his arrogance enjoy the experience – at least if they are the sort of people who find speed of thought and respect for language irresistible. More than twenty years ago, Susan Crosland, writing a profile for the *Sunday Times*, visited Vidal in his extraordinary Italian villa on the cliffs above the Gulf of Salerno at Ravello. She made the mistake of taking her husband with her. Tony Crosland (later to become Foreign Secretary in Jim Callaghan's government) was not a naturally emollient man. Paul Newman and Joanne Woodward – friends from Vidal's roisterous youth – were staying at the house. Susan Crosland did not recognize the silent lady who was working on her tapestry in the corner of the drawing room. Worse still, for some reason Tony Crosland believed Newman to be a baseball player. During and after dinner, relations deteriorated still further with Crosland – whose conversations were usually confrontational – expressing strong doubts about Vidal's literary judgment. Next morning, Vidal announced that Newman had recommended the interview be cancelled. After some persuasion, he agreed to carry on, but there was an immediate *frisson* when the subject of his sexuality was raised. Vidal still recalls the occasion with absolute horror. Susan Crosland, however, thought him delightful. 'He knows so much. He thinks so quickly and he has such good manners. How could you think anything else?'

Other visitors may have less happy memories. Martin Amis (with admirable honesty) began an interview with Vidal by making the admission that he was not familiar with all of his subject's work. Ten years on, Vidal still complains about his time being wasted. Some of his annoyance is the product of hurt pride. But it is also clear that he found it hard to understand how a respectable writer could approach his task so casually. And he made his disapproval clear. He always does. Whether he is expressing a political opinion, offering a literary criticism or just commenting on the weather, he says what he thinks. He has a rare talent for combining good manners with ruthless frankness. 'Gore,' Melvyn Bragg says, 'always takes you head-on. He never patronizes anybody. He assumes that we have all read as much as he has and that we will argue with him on his own terms.' He adds that Vidal is, in consequence, 'immensely attractive' to people who admire intellectual rough and tumble. The implication is clear. Gentler souls with a more tepid view of life find him intolerable.

Vidal accepts without question that he has a talent to annoy, and attributes it to an arcane cause. 'It's all because I talk in complete sentences and this is hateful to most people. There are a lot of people who can but won't, because it sounds arrogant. So they say "Isn't he arrogant?" and it's simply because he said: "Yes, I do think it is a nice afternoon, but I do believe it's going to rain."'

The complete sentences are normally used to express more controversial opinions. When a journalist enquired whether his first sexual experience was heterosexual or homosexual, he replied: 'I was too polite to ask.' Vidal is quick and therefore infuriates the slow. His defence is that such comments 'increase the joy of nations'.

Whether or not his style of speech adds to the offence of his *outré* opinions, it is certainly distinctive. There is no trace of the stammer he says he lost in his teens, but the Southern drawl is still audible beneath the clean-cut vowel sounds of Exeter – a college which its alumni claim, with some justification, is socially superior to Andover or Groton. Vidal was the child of a constantly broken marriage and was largely brought up by his maternal grandfather, 'the head of a Mississippi household, even though he represented Oklahoma in the Senate'. Old Senator Gore was blind. 'When he discovered a grandchild who had a passion for reading, I became his favourite. But after several hours of reading away at the Congressional Record, I used to get bored. I was the only child who understood bimetalism by the time I was seven...So I started reading Roman stuff because I liked it.'

His father, Eugene, was a US Army pilot in the First World War, who taught aeronautics at West Point Military Academy (where his son was born) before starting up three civil airlines – each of which failed. Then he briefly became President Franklin Roosevelt's secretary of aviation. Eugene and Nina Vidal were the handsomest (and almost the poorest) couple in Washington society. Both had innumerable affairs. Young Gore, in his grandfather's care, spent most of his time among the books – 'him at his desk, me sitting on the floor'. But the library was running out of stories. 'There was so much banking and currency that there was very little of what I liked. I liked narratives and the best way of getting to a narrative was to write one.'

So the literary career began – together with the other defining features of Vidal's life and work. It was during his school days in Washington that he met Jimmy Trimble – a young man who was subsequently killed while serving with the US Marines at Iwo Jima in 1944. In *Palimpsest*, Vidal's memoirs, he specu-lates on the hateful possibility that 'something had happened' between Jimmy and his stepfather. Vidal wrote: 'I had always thought that I had been the seducer, as I was to prove for the rest of my life, and so it had never occurred to me that it might have been the other way round. Like me, Jimmy would have been repelled at the idea of a sexual act with a grown man. But with another boy, an equal other half, it is the most natural business in the world.'

Vidal's most recent novel, *The Smithsonian Institution*, is the fantasy of a boy mysteriously called to Washington's great museum. After various encounters with the historic figures who are immortalized there, he is incorporated into a military tableau as the Marine killed by a Japanese hand grenade in an Iwo Jima foxhole. The boy is called T. Jimmy Trimble is clearly still in Vidal's mind if not in his heart.

In fact, despite the sharp, bright, quick persona, Vidal is clearly a man who values love and loyalty. Howard Austen has been his companion for more than forty years. Asked how they have managed to stay together for so long, he replied: 'No sex,' and he still insists that celibacy is the best guarantee for last-ing relationships. Sex, he insists, with an intensity that makes him sound sincere, is best gratified for money. His conviction that the rule applies to hetero- as well as homosexual relationships is reinforced by requests to con-sider the damage done to children in 'emotional break-ups'. Very clearly, Austen and Vidal are bound together by deep affection. He speaks bitterly of the way that Austen's career in advertising was held back by anti-Semitism until he changed the 'r' at the end of his name to an 'n', and boasts with something approaching uxorious pride about the days when Howard was one of the best half-dozen nightclub singers in America. Austen, for his part, speaks with a mixture of admiration and awe of the way Vidal 'reads for six or more hours every day'.

Despite a brief excursion into active politics in the 1960s, it is reading and writing that have filled Vidal's life. His novels, plays and essays have an invari-able polish that can only be the product of hard work. But he attempts to pre-serve the illusion of effortless superiority, speaking of *Myra Breckinridge* – a story of an apparent woman who turns out to be a biological man – as if the brilliant construction all happened by mistake: 'I was halfway through before I realized that Myra had been a man. A voice within me said: "I'm Myra Breckinridge, whom no man will possess." All this came thundering into my head and I just followed the lead.'

He is similarly dismissive about the great achievements of *Julian* – a novel that combines an historical understanding of ancient Rome with his views on the American twentieth-century imperium. Did he choose to write about Julian because he thought that particular emperor a great man? 'He tried to stop Christianity. So Julian was a great man in my book. Literally in my book and metaphorically in my book.' The Roman period came to an unhappy ending. He was employed to write the screenplay of *Caligula*, which 'was a serious movie that got taken over by *Penthouse* and turned into a travesty'. Litigation followed. Vidal wanted his name removed from the credits. Vidal has a high opinion of his own literary merit and an equally low one of most twentieth-century novelists. Ernest Hemingway 'never wrote a good novel. Even at fifteen or sixteen, I could see that *For Whom the Bell Tolls* is bullshit.' Even that is better than *A Farewell to Arms*. 'It's raining in the death scene between Katherine and Lieutenant Henry...It always rains in Hemingway to show the mood is dark.' Fitzgerald? 'He always puts a foot wrong...*Tender is the Night* is painful. *Gatsby* is a special category. That's a lovely work, but really a long short story.' Faulkner he dismisses with a bruising parody: 'Don't you remember when Aunt Nana was in the kitchen and the child had fits so they tied him to the stove? That was when the fire came but I don't know how it started. There are stories that she started it, but I don't know.'

Perhaps Vidal is so critical of others because literary success came to him early. *Williwaw* is one of the great novels of the Second World War. Vidal served mostly in the Aleutians at the wheel of Supply Ship *FS35*. He was a Warrant Officer (junior grade). For a man of his background, a commission would normally have been a formality. According to his version of events, his bad eyesight kept him in the ranks, though suspicions of homosexuality may well have contributed to the decision. However: 'In the forties, it wasn't so bad. They needed everybody in the Army. But by the fifties there was a real pogrom in the United States against what they called "fags". There could be a man with four children and twelve grandchildren, a good job in the Interior Department and he would lose it. He would be found with a man and his career would be ruined. This is the kind of thing I do speak on and I make myself extremely unpopular.'

He certainly made himself extremely unpopular – at least with a certain sort of person – when he published *The City and the Pillar* in 1948. But by then, he had already written *Williwaw* and it had brought instant critical acclaim to a young man still in his twenties. He 'had been all over *Life* magazine, all over the press were beautiful reviews. Then suddenly the blackout came.' The blackout was ostracism by the literary establishment in response to *The City and the Pillar*, a novel of homosexual life. The *New York Times*, 'the most powerful book reviewing in the United States until this day', ignored everything he wrote. 'The senior reviewer of the *Times* weekday edition told my publisher: 'I will not only never review him again, but I'll never read him after this disgusting book.' So I had to take about ten years off to earn a living, which I did through television, movies and the theatre.' He also did it by writing short stories under the name of Edgar Box, a part of his oeuvre that rarely intrudes into his conversation.

As he lay fallow he also developed a social life – more irregular in Paris and Florida than in Washington, but clearly highly enjoyable in every location. His biography includes a picture of Gore the groomsman at the wedding of his half-sister, Nina. All the men – including Senator John F. Kennedy, on the fringe of the group – wear the regulation marriage uniforms of the American upper class. In those days, Vidal looked, at least at first glance, the archetypal American gentleman – obviously rich, evidently suave, undoubtedly self-confident.

Then you notice the hair. The line of the classic cut is broken by a quiff of which James Dean would have been proud. The caption makes clear that Vidal did not, even then, think of himself as part of the Washington Establishment. 'Behind me stands my sister's next husband, Michael Whitney Straight. As family tradition required, "both marriages failed".' The man cannot help it. The ice is in his soul.

Sting, who got to know Vidal when one of his friends was making a film about Vidal's life and work, agrees that the ice is there, but believes that it hides 'a genuinely kind nature'. The rock star pays all the usual compliments – funny, intellectual, entertaining. But he says that what attracts him to the man is generosity of spirit. The compliment is probably justified, but Vidal would certainly reject and probably resent it. He works so hard to cultivate his brittle reputation.

Vidal's description of his sister's wedding is a perfect example of behaviour behind which (according to Sting) he hides his gentle nature. It includes an account (presumably secondhand rather than observed) of Jackie Bouvier Kennedy 'hitching up her gown to show the innocent Nina how to douche post-sex – one foot in the bathtub and the other on the white tiled floor'. Vidal's fictional sex is often followed by washing – ritual, erotic or purely hygienic. The wandering boy of *The Smithsonian Institution* is scrubbed clean by an Indian squaw from the museum's Native American tableau. The temptation to suspect something deeply Freudian – rather than mildly prurient – is irresistible. The suggestion that washing has some symbolic significance is met with the crushing response: 'I've noticed that the British are not given to it.' Then he corrects his own story.

'I left out the detail which betrayed Jackie as not the best Catholic on earth. She told Nina to put vinegar in the water. They believed in those days that if you sloshed around in vinegar and water you would not propagate. I left the vinegar out so the thing doesn't make such sense.'

He reacts with not-quite-mock-horror to the suggestion that the detail was omitted out of kindness and decency. 'Certainly not! I was so transfixed by the picture of primordial rites, that I forgot.'

For a moment, he becomes uncharacteristically defensive: 'I don't go into anybody's private life unless there is something irresistibly comic; it was a long time ago and they are dead.'

Now, with a lifetime of literary success behind him, it is impossible to tell how bruised he was by the Philistines' response to *The City and the Pillar*. But one thing is absolutely clear. It did not end his romantic attachment to America. For years, he has spent more time in Italy than in the United States – first in Rome and now looking out towards the blue Tyrrhenian Sea. But he rejects the notion that he is in any sort of exile. In fact his criticisms of his homeland are the sad cries of a disappointed lover. He believes in the Great Republic. And when its politicians – particularly if they are presidents – failed to live up to his high expectations, he turned on them with his customary tailored savagery.

'There is a great speech, which I can only paraphrase, from John Quincy Adams. He said: "You know America is not the paladin of the world. Yes, we have the power [this was in the 1820s and 30s] to conquer the world, but in the process we would lose our souls."'

Vidal adds that Adams's view was too intelligent for his time – speaking in a manner that emphasizes that it goes without saying that it is too intelligent for our time as well. His resentment at America's failure to heed the good advice has produced thirty years of philippics, eventually published in anthologies which switch, page by page, from obscure literary criticism to denunciations of the corruption which now infests Washington and the policy failures which are its results.

Reflections From A Sinking Ship (published in 1968) sets the tone in its preface: 'I have selected a title which seems to me altogether apt this bright savage spring with Martin Luther King dead and now Robert Kennedy. The fact that these deaths occurred at a time when the American empire was sustaining a richly deserved defeat in Asia simply makes for added poignancy if not tragedy.'

Since then, the tragedy has deepened. 'We have not declared war since December 1941 and we have fought about fifty wars since then. That means that the House of Representatives has given up its great powers and the power of the purse is now rather dubious, since the executive does all sorts of funny things when it wants to raise money without consulting the House if it feels the House won't go along. The constitution doesn't work.' The result, according to Vidal, is Pax Americana – the empire that rules where it has no right to govern. He will not even concede that there are occasions when the richest country in the world needs to spend its treasure and sacrifice its sons in a good cause.

'Who determines a good cause? The Croats might say it's good and the Serbs might say it's bad.' Pressed on the possible annihilation of Kosovo, he remains adamant. 'Of course we should not do anything. What is our national interest?' The suggestion that his high moral tone is not very different from his grandfather's isolationism is met with a response that is more philological than philosophic: 'I don't accept isolationists because now it means somebody who believes the Earth is flat and that flying saucers land in your backyard and abduct people...The word has been totally smeared... 'I simply say we have no moral responsibility. It may be for God to keep his eye on the swallow as it falls. But it is not for the United States of America, a country that always acts in bad faith.'

Not always – even by Gore's own account. There was a 'golden age' in American politics and *Burr* is his novel about those early days of the Republic. There is, in much of what he writes, a yearning for that mythical past – the age of primitive innocence before the fall of federal government. Now he is bitterly critical of the political system and of those politicians who depend on great corporations to pay their election expenses. Grandfather Gore was a survivor of that Elysian time – uncorrupted because he was incorruptible – who stood out against the vested interests in his state.

Vidal justifies his nostalgia with a literary parallel: 'Hazlitt said something quite startling. He said that all of art had its best in the beginning. Playwriting really is Shakespeare.' He will never be convinced that the rules of literature are not necessarily the rules of life.

He is, of course, on Clinton's side against the House of Representatives. It is, after all, 'the insurance lobby, who hate healthcare, and the tobacco companies' that are out to destroy the president. In any case, Vidal is not judgmental about anything except public matters. 'That's where you must exert judgment, a private matter is a private affair and one shouldn't, wouldn't, doesn't...' For once, he allows the incomplete sentence to hang in the air and moves on to praise Clinton's ability. 'He's a lot more intelligent than Roosevelt. He doesn't have the flair of Roosevelt or the look either, but he doesn't have the same country.' Vidal comes second only to William Cobbett as an exponent of the backward glance.

Forty years ago he wrote *The Best Man* – a play that became the one film that lived up to Vidal's expectations for his own work. In it, a mature and admirable presidential candidate contests his party's nomination with a young and handsome opportunist. The characters in some part reflect the battle between Adlai Stevenson and John Kennedy – which the best man lost. The play also contains a sideswipe at Richard Nixon, a Vidal hate-figure long before his failings were generally acknowledged in the United States. Sting believes that the play reflects Vidal's yearning for a life in active politics and insists that he really did once dream of occupying the White House. As he well knows, *The City and the Pillar* made that impossible fifty years ago. But he was still the best man in his own mind. Yet there was a brief flirtation with active electoral politics.

In 1960, he was the Democratic Party's candidate for a Congressional seat that he had no chance of winning. It was the year that Kennedy just won the presidency and Vidal polled more votes in his district than his party's presidential nominee. When he was offered the chance to fight a safe seat, he turned it down.

Journalist Christopher Hitchens – afraid that his admiration for Vidal is no longer reciprocated because of recent attacks on President Clinton – believes that he has regretted it ever since. 'He was delighted when Hillary and Chelsea Clinton went to see him. It was not just the Clintons trying to establish contact with literate America, it was Gore's reconciliation with politics.'

He has, of course, been in politics for the past fifty years. His essays – 'remarkable how well they stand up', says Hitchens – have provided a more intelligent critique of American policy than anything that has been written since the war. Often they are wrong. However he chooses to describe his foreign policy position, he is an isolationist. But he is also the living proof of a glorious truth: literature and politics are not necessarily at war with each other. It is still possible to forget the soundbite and have an elegant debate.

27 February 1999

Life at a glance

EUGENE LUTHER GORE VIDAL JR

Born: 3 October 1925, New York.

Education: Graduated from Phillips Exeter Academy in 1943.

Career: Served in the US Army (1943–6); New York Democratic-Liberal candidate for US Congress (1960).

Select bibliography: *Williwaw* (1946); *The City and the Pillar* (1948); *A Thirsty Evil* (1956); *Visit To A Small Planet* (1957); *The Best Man* (1960); *Julian* (1964); *Washington, DC* (1967); *Myra Breckinridge* (1968); *Homage to Daniel Shays* (1972); *Burr* (1973); *Myron* (1974); *1876* (1976); *Matters Of Fact And Fiction* (1977); *Kalki* (1978); *Creation* (1981); *The Second American Revolution* (1982); *Duluth* (1983); *Lincoln* (1984); *Empire* (1987); *At Home* (1988); *Live From Golgotha* (1992); *United States* (1993); *Hollywood* (1990); *Palimpsest* (1995); *The Smithsonian Institution* (1998). Vidal also wrote a number of plays for TV (*The Death Of Billy The Kid*), as well as Hollywood screenplays (*Suddenly Last Summer*).

IRVINE WELSH
The ecstasy and the agony

Andy Beckett

Until quite recently, in one of the quieter reaches of north London, a local book-shop was running a clever promotion. At Prospero's Books on Crouch End Broadway, the staff had set up a display of volumes endorsed by Irvine Welsh. There was a book about football hooligans, an account of the rise of Oasis, a study of rave culture, even a biography of Robin Friday, an almost-forgotten striker from the seventies. Welsh's praise rang from each cover, amplifying a matter of minority interest into something worth noticing: 'The best I've read', 'I read it again', 'buy, steal or borrow a copy now'.

The books sold. And handily, Welsh's own fiction was in stock too. There was *The Acid House*, with its short stories about council workmen and LSD, the three novellas that made up *Ecstasy*, riotous with stabbings and swearing, and the best-selling of all, *Trainspotting*, a novel about death and heroin.

Prospero's is not, generally, that kind of bookshop. It has half a wall of Penguin Classics and histories of the nearby Alexandra Palace. Smart young mothers park their pushchairs in the aisles. Outside, Volvos cruise past candle shops up the streets off the Broadway, restored Victorian gables march to the horizon. Yet it no longer seems strange that Welsh should do well in somewhere like this. *Trainspotting* sold more than 800,000 copies in 1996 alone, as many as the most mainstream thriller. It has become a film and two soundtrack albums and a play in several versions, and a poster so recognizable that newspaper cartoonists parodied it. Meanwhile, Welsh himself, with his shaven head and troublemaker's twinkle, his muttered Edinburgh vowels and drug-taker's wrinkles, had become as much of a celebrity, perhaps, as modern British literature produces.

He drinks with Damien Hirst and Damon Albarn. He confides with Jarvis Cocker. He gets asked to DJ at the most famous club in Ibiza. And all the while, by word of mouth and weight of promotion, his books keep circulating. For all their glaring covers, their rave-culture packaging, their appeal is also quite literary, even traditional: the evocation of a world, in seething detail, almost entirely missed by current British fiction. Welsh writes about the poor, the young and the very old, the wandering and reckless and feckless. He knows his kebab shops and council stairwells, his Scots dialects and dossers' strategies, but he is not simply a realist. His stories abruptly hinge and twist, throw up bizarre possibilities, upset the order of things: a policeman frames a fanatically prudish businessman as a pornographer; a teenager looks under his grandmother's bed for money, and finds she is a drug dealer.

'On a superficial reading, Welsh speaks for the dispossessed,' says Professor Douglas Gifford, who teaches Scottish literature at Glasgow University. 'But he has a wonderfully grotesque and inverting sense of humour.' This is attractive in unstable times. Few of Welsh's readers, most likely, have been junkies, as he has, or grew up on the same damp council estate, with the wind slicing off the North Sea. Yet these days, plenty of people have met a drug dealer, or plunged from comfort into poverty, or wasted whole years in dead-end jobs and nightclubs. They can understand what Welsh is writing about.

There is only one problem. *Trainspotting* came out in 1993, *The Acid House* in 1994, *Marabou Stork Nightmares*, another novel, in 1995, *Ecstasy* in 1996. Last year, Welsh contributed short stories to at least three collections, several pieces to magazines, a column for *Loaded*, and a foreword to a book about legalizing drugs. This year, he has done a play, *You'll Have Had Your Hole*, a screenplay for a forthcoming film of *The Acid House*, two records, more short stories, and now a novel, four hundred pages long, called *Filth*. Plus all those cover blurbs for other people. At Prospero's Books, after three months displaying Welsh's recommendations, they got rid of his section. Now, one of the staff says, 'We're going to put a new one up – books not endorsed by Irvine Welsh.' Some people are getting sick of him. *Ecstasy* got his first bad reviews. *You'll Have Had Your Hole* got his first terrible ones. Some of the critics were simply, predictably shocked – by the torture scenes in both works, the rape scenes, the calculated relentlessness of the violence – but others said something more damaging. Welsh was becoming boring.

Ecstasy showed all the signs – the obviousness of its title, the clumsy nudge of its cover (a man with the letter 'e' in his mouth), the rattled-off quality of the writing within. The tower block Dickens who wrote *Trainspotting* seemed to have shrunk to a much narrower talent, the in-house spokesman for that style magazine invention, 'the chemical generation'. Previously, Welsh had used drugs as a window on to his characters' lives and deaths – now he was just writing about drugs.

Welsh's publisher knows standards have slipped. '*Ecstasy* was a rushed job,' says Robin Robertson, who has edited all his books. 'The film of *Trainspotting* was about to come out, so we wanted a book. We were victims of his momentum...' The same, says Robertson, goes for some of the short stories: 'The magazines were besieging Irvine for new work. They wanted rave stuff, and he obliged them.' His new book, at first sight, looks just as predictable. The protagonist of *Filth*, brags the book's back cover, is 'one of the most corrupt, misanthropic characters in contemporary fiction'. The novel's milieu is 'the lower reaches of degradation and evil'. The cover copy concludes like the hard sell for a horror paperback: 'In an Irvine Welsh book nothing is ever so bad that it can't get worse...' Welsh is thirty-nine. He has recently recorded a rap record. His books still contain jokes about trainers. Two months ago, after being flown out for the Sydney Writers' Festival, he sabotaged a discussion panel in a fury of beery silences and swearwords. 'There's fuck-all to say about my books,' he said, 'other than what's written in them.' A career that once astonished now seems to be tottering over. The British Council, which was interested in taking *You'll Have Had Your Hole* overseas, has decided not to pitch it to foreign promoters. Edinburgh councillors have queued up to condemn *Filth* before it has even appeared. Plenty of other people – Welsh has never won a literary prize – would love to see the Scottish upstart disappear back to Leith. Even Robertson has his anxieties. 'I was worried at the time that *Ecstasy* came out. The bubble might burst.' Welsh does not seem particularly nervous. 'Writers will go through their whole lives to achieve what I did with *Trainspotting*,' he says, in his soft insistent voice, without a single pause for modesty. 'It's a passport, not an albatross, to do whatever I want.' His small sharp eyes shine with mockery. 'When *Trainspotting* came out, there was this idea of me as a noble savage...a thick fucker from a Scottish council estate. The idea that you could become a proper writer is more of an overt challenge.' He has not bothered to dress up for our meeting. His T-shirt is a black sack, almost grey with age; his jeans are dead straight, tight around his thin legs, not the sort his hipper readers would wear. At the back of the café, behind his chair, he has dumped a record bag and a baseball cap and a flying jacket, also black. He is quite tall; he looks like a slim, off-duty bouncer.

His face suggests the same: lines round the eyes, hair shaved to the skull, a raised web of veins behind one pointed ear. But when he smiles, which he does intermittently, with a wolfish flash of teeth for each boast or small confession, his profile changes. His cheeks become like a bright baby's, his wrinkles like the marks of a shrewd old man. Like everyone else in the room, Welsh has his tabloid and his mug of tea, his slouch and his easy patter, yet he is the man here who has made a name by watching others.

The café is in Islington; among antique shops, its Formica and tiles have the air of a listed interior. Welsh lives in London these days, up the road, in rapidly gentrifying Stoke Newington. He has just come back from Ibiza. There is a tinge of brown in his pale bare arms. What sort of records did he play there? 'A bit of house, a bit of techno, a bit of disco, just party tunes...Welsh's answer trickles away. This is the way the afternoon goes. He is polite, he replies to every question, he never tries to be tough or aggressive or silent. But he evades particularities, speeds chattily through areas of potential difficulty. Each issue gets thirty seconds.

No, he is not worried about being labelled as an author for ravers. 'There's nothing you can do...You just sort of go along with these sort of labels.' He takes refuge, as he likes to, behind a barricade of jargon: '*Trainspotting* has been appropriated so much it's like a Richard Branson product. A zone of identity that's used to sell products.' Does he think he's too famous? 'Celebrity is about swapping a lot of good friends for a load of acquaintances...I experimented with it for a few months, but it kills what I want to write about.' Nowadays, he adds quickly, 'I've got certain golden rules. I don't know how to find the Groucho Club. I keep out of places like that.' While he was writing *Ecstasy*, Welsh may have been having too much fun. 'I never sat down properly with it. I was doing the *Acid House* screenplay at the same time. *Ecstasy* was like somebody writing an Irvine Welsh exploitation book.' Had it damaged his reputation? Welsh almost says yes: 'With the first three books, I'd established something...' His hands are darting over the tabletop. But half an hour later, he knots his brow and suggests the opposite: 'Writing is something I've stumbled into. It's been lucrative, opened a few doors...Part of me is hoping that *Filth* doesn't do so well, that it bombs in a way. Because it's not something I see myself doing for ever.' In truth, *Filth* will probably extend his career a while longer. 'He's got such a huge fan base,' says Robertson. Even *Ecstasy*, he claims, has sold 230,000 copies. And *Filth* is better than that. 'I was determined with this one,' says Welsh, 'that I was going to put a bit more into it.' For one thing, *Filth* is his first full-length novel for more than three years. Its paragraphs are dense, worked-on. He has bothered to establish a world again.

His protagonist is an Edinburgh policeman. Detective Sergeant Bruce Robertson is not fashionable or young: he listens, lovingly, to heavy metal and Michael Bolton. He hates ravers, football hooligans, slackers and every subculture Welsh has previously treasured. He plots against his colleagues ('spastics') and for his own promotion with relentless ingenuity. In the background is the unsolved murder of an African diplomat's son, and, more promisingly, a minutely-drawn panorama of modern police unpleasantness. Freemasons rule. Crossword-solving comes before crime-solving. Drugs are planted to prompt informers. Hoarding overtime is the great goal.

'Organizations are like churches,' says Welsh. 'They are where people learn their behaviour.' The book's flaw is to argue this too fiercely. Robertson is almost nothing but a monster: always lying, abusing prostitutes, comparing women to milk cartons and kebabs. In this bleak lads' landscape, only scattered stumps of emotions are allowed to grow. 'Welsh has been trapped into a certain category,' says Professor Gifford. 'Struggling underneath, there is a very genuine humanity that he has to conceal, because the boys wouldn't like it...There is a guard there, a carapace that has grown very strong indeed.' Welsh shields his life story well. In interviews, a process he has called 'the manufacturing of passions', he usually offers a paragraph's worth of fragments, at best. At worst, he makes things up.

He was born, it seems fairly certain, in Leith in 1958. Leith is Edinburgh's port, a couple of miles to the north, incorporated into that city against its will in 1820. Leith natives have grumbled ever since. 'Leith and Edinburgh,' Welsh says, 'are quite analogous to Scotland and England.' From the tiered and elegant hills in the centre of Edinburgh, Leith looks drab, its horizon cluttered with cranes and silos and the odd sallow tower block. Only the pale sea glitters, behind the docks. Welsh's father worked in them until his health gave out. Then he became a carpet salesman. His wife waited on tables.

When Welsh was four, his family were moved by the council to a new housing estate in Muirhouse, a few miles along the coast, further from Edinburgh. Leith had been hard – the docks fading, prostitutes on the cobbles, Victorian relics all around – but this was much worse. At first, they lived in paper-thin prefabs, then in a maisonette in a two-floor block. Like all of Muirhouse, with its open spaces and avenues and sea views, the Welshes' house had been built for Marseilles or Morocco. It had underfloor heating that was too expensive to turn on.

There was one pub, a few shops, hardly anything to do. 'You'd get covered in dogshit when you were playing football,' Welsh says. 'As a kid, you were more or less tolerated, hanging around or roaming the streets. When you got to be a teenager, there was more of an air of menace...You'd go up to a police car and start banging the garden rails with sticks. The police would come, and you'd run away.' He left school at sixteen. 'I was only interested in English and art.' He went straight back to Leith – jobs in Edinburgh meant forty minutes in a juddering bus – to train as a TV repairman. Telectra House was a grey concrete box owned by the Co-op, but it was right in the busy middle of town, which was full of working-class families, as Welsh remembers it, escaping the estates they had been exiled to. Easter Road, the Hibernian football ground, was just up the hill. There were record shops and discos. Welsh lasted six months as a Telectra House apprentice, until an old valve set nearly fried him.

In the late seventies, he decided to be a rock musician. He played in bands at community centres, and collected Iggy Pop and Sex Pistols singles. But Leith's youth culture was not London's Punk scene. One night in 1978, Welsh went south, drunk on a bus. He slept in Green Park for a while. Then he shared squats and bedsits with other sunburned Scotsmen. He played guitar, and tried to sing, for The Pubic Lice and Stairway 13. He dug roads and washed saucepans. The way Welsh summarizes them, his twenties were nothing but drift: 'Go down to London, get some work, stay for a few months on someone's floor, go back up to Scotland, do the same thing.' But, every now and again, when he had run out of amphetamines, or was just plain bored, a self-improving impulse stirred. Welsh had already done a City & Guilds course in electrical engineering; in London, he began doing clerical work for Hackney council, then was sponsored to take a computing MSc by the Manpower Services Commission. He had money now, and an idea what to do with it. During the mid-eighties, Welsh bought up bedsits in Hackney and Islington and Camden, did them up, and sold them six months later. He made 'about £50,000', then lost some of it in the property slump, but the habit stayed. 'I'm always buying flats,' he says. 'I rent them through a property management agency. Edinburgh is a booming market, and I don't like to have too much cash...' Then again, this is not quite what fans of Welsh's dead-end dramas, or his frequent polemics against the gentrification of Edinburgh, might expect. Leaning forward over his café table, he lifts his voice a little: 'I get really schizophrenic about it. I didn't invent capitalism. It's not the best way of running things.' He pauses. 'But I'm not going to be a stupid martyr.' While Welsh was living in London and, briefly, Croydon (which he hated), and spending half of 1984 exploring Los Angeles, some of his Leith and Muirhouse friends were taking up heroin. The docks had long been a conduit; the disappearence of local factory jobs did the rest. Muirhouse, in particular, had all the right conditions for addicts: poverty, boredom, remoteness and a sense of decay, as the original plaster peeled and the pebbledash blackened, and the barrack blocks filled up with families displaced by the sell-off of other, more attractive council properties.

Welsh saw all this happening when he came back to visit friends. The extent of his actual involvement in the local heroin subculture has long been less clear. Two years ago he said: 'I don't claim to have experienced everything I write about. I was just in the area of those things for a time.' When we meet, he seems franker. 'I've got this friend who's been a junkie for twenty-five years. He said to me when *Trainspotting* came out, "Why have you written this book? You've only been a junkie for five minutes."' Welsh's eyes dim for a moment. 'Well actually, it was eighteen months.' He seems keen to go on. 'It was a stupidity and a weakness. I've not touched it for years, but it's in your vocabulary. If something bad happens in your life, it's always there in the background, waiting for you to trip up.' Welsh kept a diary when he was on heroin: sometimes the odd note, sometimes whole therapeutic pages about addiction – *Trainspotting* in embryo. But chasing round estates after China white was not the way to properly cook up a novel. He needed Edinburgh council to get him started.

In 1988, he got a job as a training officer in the housing department that had planned Muirhouse in the first place. The irony of his new role did not stop him being good at it. Welsh worked hard and won promotions – 'he could have gone right to the top in local government,' says one old colleague – and was offered time off to study at Heriot-Watt University. Here, on the other side of Edinburgh from Leith, among the business students and the campus trees, he studied for an MBA.

Welsh usually refers to his degree, when he mentions it at all, as 'a yuppie Daz-coupon qualification'. He says he was 'so bored I still had time on my hands to write'. But this rather undersells his studying. 'He was a super member of the class,' says Professor Zander Wedderburn, who supervised his dissertation. 'He was very very good at thinking his way into situations.' Welsh's dissertation was about using training to give equal opportunities to women. Professor Wedderburn found it persuasive in every way except, oddly, the writing style: 'It wasn't very forceful.' Instead, Welsh saved his fierceness – Wedderburn thought he might go into politics – for face-to-face seminars. 'We had one afternoon on assertiveness. He got us to walk in opposite ways round the table, and bang into each other. He wanted us to say, "Get out of my way!"...I remember having to ask him to tone the polemic down.' By late 1991, Welsh had finished at Heriot-Watt, and had strung together enough of *Trainspotting* to send it to a publisher. Who it went to first, and who made it take off, is a matter of controversy nowadays, but the most convincing claim comes from a big-boned Geordie called David Crystal. He runs a south London literary magazine called *DOG*. In December 1991, for his first, illicitly photocopied issue, he received about twenty unsolicited pages, in typed-up fragments, of Welsh's novel. 'I thought it was very funny,' says Crystal. He published the extract, without paying for it, in just a hundred copies. A few months later, when he had twenty-five left, an order came through: 'I thought, "They might as well have them all..."' Crystal pauses, mid-afternoon pint in hand. 'Some lucky punter's got them.' Between 1991 and 1996, *Trainspotting* swelled, via friends of Crystal's up in Scotland, small-press publishers there, and Robin Robertson in London, into an almost impregnable cultural leviathan. Welsh was not about to discourage the process – he had to keep working at the council until 1994, and even set up his own training company to supplement his income. Yet some of his book's subtleties, perhaps, were lost along the way. *Trainspotting*, as originally written, was morbid, almost gothic, and full of rage: an addict's shivers covered his back 'like a thin layer ay autumn frost oan a car roof'; another heroin user was a homeless Falklands veteran; even the novel's title came from a bitter joke about the abandoned Victorian cavern of Leith station.

'Irvine's knowledge of British politics is encyclopaedic,' says Duncan McLean, a Scottish writer who has known him for years. 'He and (James) Kelman and I went on an American tour during the general election last year. On election night, Irvine would keep saying: "I see Sir Henry Smithers in West Sussex North has had his majority reduced by 17 per cent."' *Trainspotting*-the-phenomenon, however, steered away from such seriousness. The film only set one scene on a housing scheme, dropped the hospice visits for drug capers, and brought forward the setting from the mid-eighties to the late eighties, making the characters into ravers. Welsh's next three books, produced in a rush, played along. *The Acid House* seemed to be called that for marketing reasons – there was no mention of the dance culture until past page 200. *Marabou Stork Nightmares* shoehorned in nightclub scenes, which were much less vividly written than the episodes around them. And *Ecstasy* was just chemical-generation clichés, many of them recycled from a Welsh novel that Robertson had rejected in 1994. It was called *The Chill-Out Zone*.

Irvine Welsh may need saving from his image. His music spin-offs have not been universally applauded, even in the dance music press. Remarks have been made about age and appropriate fields of activity, but he has already written an album. 'He can't help himself,' says Kris Needs, Welsh's main musical collaborator. 'Irv's got a younger attitude than these kids who slag off our records.' In the café, with his red record bag, Welsh is expanding on his activities as a DJ. 'It's a way of retaining an interest in the music,' he says. How much does he get paid? His grin pops up like a bright sliver of moon. 'Not that much...Well, to a lot of people it would be a lot of money.' Is he good? 'No. I can't fucking mix – or not very well yet.' He looks out of the window, towards the record shop he's going to after the interview. 'But it might be a way to go.' Douglas Gifford, for one, would be disappointed. To him, Welsh is the latest of an important line of Scottish literary experimenters, going back to Iain Banks and Alasdair Gray and Alexander Trocchi. Each has mixed up street lore and philosophy, the earthy and the existential, to better and more popular effect than most postwar English novelists. Professor Gifford is persuasive – in Irvine Welsh books, unlike ones by Martin Amis, the council wallpaper and cooked breakfasts really sweat, in a deeply felt detail that perhaps only experience brings. And Welsh, too, seems to know and think about all of modern Britain, not just the bits which dream of Manhattan.

But authenticity is not enough. *Filth*, for all its foul energy and texture, feels like a narrow achievement in the end. Were it not by Welsh, it would be a genre book. As in most of his writing since *Trainspotting*, the novel strains when plot invention or character justification is required; there is a sense that he is still happiest with his memories and notebooks. 'I've got another five hundred pages of *Trainspotting*,' says Welsh. 'I might sit down and rewrite it, as if it's five or ten years on, take the story on...' Or he could follow the example of his least-known book. *Marabou Stork Nightmares* has never sold heavily (Robertson blames the title), yet Welsh is protective. He has already sold the film rights to *Filth*, but he has refused all offers to shoot this earlier novel. 'I don't want it to be exploited,' he says. He is worried that the book's 'issues' – Scottish racism, his country's complicity in the British Empire, the consequences of all immoral actions – would be smoothed away. As he says this, for a few moments, Welsh's literary world-view opens up. He admits to being interested in apartheid, the Second World War, even Evelyn Waugh.

Then he stops himself. He says he can't remember which Waugh book he read. 'I've never been a great reader of fiction,' he says. Soon afterwards, he slips out of the door, record bag swinging, leaving a remark to linger. 'I'm not that reflective – it's good to remain a bit strange to yourself.' Irvine Welsh, the restless entrepreneur, with his compartmentalized life, and the wife he won't discuss, or even confirm as existing, has many projects to finish. He may be too busy for great literature.

25 July 1998

Life at a glance

IRVINE WELSH

Born: 1958, Leith.

Education: Comprehensive schools in Leith and Muirhouse (1963–74); City & Guilds course in electrical engineering, Edinburgh (1970s); MSc in computing, London (1980s); MBA, Heriot-Watt University (1988–90).

Career: TV repairman, clerical temp, computer trouble-shooter, training officer for Edinburgh council, freelance training consultant.

Select bibliography: *Trainspotting* (1993); *The Acid House* (1994); *Marabou Stork Nightmares* (1995); *Ecstasy* (1996); *You'll Have Had Your Hole* (1998); *Filth* (1998); *Glue* (2001); *Porno* (2002).

TOM WOLFE
Radical cheek

Andrew O'Hagan

When the elevator doors open, Wolfe is standing there. He's got the vanilla suit on; he's a good-looking sixty-eight in his shoes. He is framed there, in all his Tom Wolfeness. And right beside him is a grandfather clock: the old, burnished wood of the South, a painted face, and telling the right time. 'It belonged to my father,' he says. 'It came all the way from Virginia.'

If Tom Wolfe is the poet of anything, he's the poet of American aspiration. He's always been interested in people going up, and people coming down; people who want to go faster, and who suffer the slowness of retreat. In 1965, he threw out an account of people who make themselves over with cars, *The Kandy-Kolored Tangerine-Flake Streamline Baby*.

After that he was deep in the fizz of postwar America. People putting their fists in the air for a stylish cause (*Radical Chic*), people wigging out on acid (*The Electric Kool-Aid Acid Test*), people making journalism as if it were fiction (*The New Journalism*), people jetting to the moon (*The Right Stuff*). And in-between, he wrote pieces that got on people's nerves, about surfers, It-Girls, dress codes, and the Me, Me, Mes. He lifted his skirts to the art world, making fun, scoring points, in the face of all the nodding complicities, and he exhibited no meagre talent for ridiculing onanistic weirdos.

He wrote a novel, *Bonfire of the Vanities*, a novel of Manhattan society in the eighties, and he claimed all the realist tradition for himself. And now he has completed a second novel. It is a book about a property developer, and about the politics of the South; about aspiration, celebrity, redemption.

A Man In Full is the total Wolfe: every notion, every hunch that he has ever had about writing is there in the book; its grand lineaments, such as they are, might be seen to exist in the world outside the windows of Wolfe's big apartment. But that's not the main thing: those lineaments might also be there in Wolfe's eyes, and on the face of that old clock at his side. It might also demonstrate the central problem of his writing life: how to describe everything, and say nothing.

Tom Wolfe was named after his father, Thomas Kennerly Wolfe, an agronomist and editor of the *Southern Planter*. Wolfe Snr was never cut out to be a journalist, but he wrote a book, *The Production Of Field Crops*, and was a professor at Virginia Tech. But it was the other Thomas Wolfe, the novelist of the Depression – who wrote *Look Homeward, Angel* – whom the young boy felt must be his literary forebear. (They weren't related.)

Wolfe seems moved as he describes the house he grew up in, and the books there. 'A little painting of mine was featured in a newspaper when I was seven,' he says. 'I remember our house – 3037 Gloucester Road in Richmond. I can see that house in minute detail. It was white, three good-sized bedrooms, one bathroom. The garden is idealized in my mind; my mother really was a wonderful gardener. Magnolia trees. I used to say my prayers at night and thank God I'd been born an American.'

The other Thomas Wolfe once tried to pin down the oddness of being a writer in America. 'We're still more perturbed by the writing profession than any other people I have known on the earth,' he said. 'It is for this reason that one finds among a great number of our people, I mean the labouring, farming sort of people from which I came, a kind of great wonder and doubt and romantic feeling about writers, so that it is hard for them to understand that a writer may be one of them.'

Joseph Lewis Wolfe, our author's grandfather, fought as a twenty-something in the Confederate army. 'He was in prison at the end of the war,' Wolfe says, 'and when they were freed by the Union soldiers, no one was sure where his home was, or how to get there. My grandfather was never keen to talk about it, which was a huge disappointment to me.'

People remember the boy Tom Wolfe being just like many boys in Richmond, Virginia. He seemed to like attention, though. He studied ballet and tap. He wasn't slow to say what he thought of this and that. Wolfe always used to say that he hadn't written about his childhood, or the South, because he wanted 'a safe haven to come back to'. He spent the years of the Second World War at St Christopher's School, where he spoke well, and read well, and where he seemed like someone who would grow up white-suited and respectable, like his father, or his grandfather.

People say he had good manners too, the good manners of Helen Hughes, his mother. 'She was a voracious reader,' he says. 'Her first love was Dickens. There was a full set in our house, though I didn't start reading Dickens until about six years ago.'

Wolfe went from school to Washington and Lee University. This is the institution where Robert E. Lee served as president after the Civil War. Wolfe's family were not rich – they had a little – but the university was a favoured place for the children of wealthy families. Wolfe had a ton of energy. He helped found the literary magazine *Shenandoah* and excelled at anything to do with writing or American history.

In 1951 he graduated *cum laude* from Washington and went on to Yale, taking a PhD in American Studies, and writing a dissertation on 'The League Of American Writers: Communist Activity Among American Writers, 1929–1942'. A contemporary from around that time speaks of a sense of discomfort in Wolfe. 'He seemed somewhat out on his own,' he says. 'What was then called the white-shoe brigade at Yale, the liberal establishment, he never quite made it with them. He worked hard enough, but there was a feeling that he worked his own yard.' Wolfe occasionally wrote little poems at this time; under the pseudonym Jocko Thor, he wrote:

> I shall Revolt
> I shall burst this placid pink shell
> I shall wake up slightly hungover,
> Favoured, adored, worshipped and clamoured for.
> I shall raise Hell and be a real Cut-up.

'At college,' he says now, 'I hoped that I might be able to go off to a shack one day soon and write my big novel. But journalism seemed closer.' In his last months at Yale, he wrote to 120 newspapers. He started as a reporter on the *Springfield* [Massachusetts] *Union*. He tended to file very efficient, lively, but otherwise ordinary copy, and he took to wearing the reporter's hat and raincoat. He had something increasingly different though, a touch of elegance.

In 1958, he interviewed Senator John Kennedy, but Wolfe wasn't inclined to pin his colours to the young man's mast, or indeed any mast. He went on to do some reporting for the *Washington Post*. Then, in 1962, he decided to move to New York, a place he was scared of. In a letter to his young friend Hugh Troy, he wrote: 'The first thing I knew I was on the 1.20 a.m. bus, with fifteen coloured brethren, all of us, no doubt, out to make it in New York...Whether I am moving on to bigger and better things, I don't know, but I knew I wouldn't be happy until I gave it a try. This is one big sonofabitch of a town, but I guess they are used to boys from the foothills coming in here, and they are probably even tolerant.'

The boy from the foothills would come to love New York. There was a certain kind of Manhattan reporter that Wolfe was trying to be. A beat reporter, with style, a kind of Damon Runyon in a crepe-de-Chine necktie. He was also influenced by one or two contemporary reporters who lived close-in to their prose: Jimmy Breslin, Gay Talese.

Wolfe spent several years doing nothing but work. 'The idea of a day off lost all meaning,' he wrote. 'I can remember being furious on Monday 25 September 1963, because there were people I desperately needed to talk to, for some story or other, and I couldn't reach them because all the offices in New York seemed to be closed, every one. It was the day of President Kennedy's funeral. I remember staring at the television set...morosely, but for all the wrong reasons.'

Wolfe convinced Byron Dobell, the managing editor of *Esquire*, to let him go to southern California and write about the kids who were customizing hot-rod cars. Wolfe watched everything – he had an intelligent ear, a vivid sense of the surface of things. But he had a problem setting it down. He didn't know how to write the piece. Dobell eventually got him on the phone: 'Look,' said Dobell, 'we can't wait any longer for this piece. You just write your notes down, and we'll get a competent writer to put it into shape for you.' So Wolfe sat down and wrote, overnight, a memo of forty-odd pages. *Esquire* struck out the 'Dear Byron,' and ran it as it was: 'The Kandy-Kolored Tangerine-Flake Streamline Baby'. And the Hectoring Narrator was out of the garage for good (or ill).

Nineteen sixty-five was Wolfe's coming-out year. He published his first book, had a show of his drawings at the Maynard Walker Gallery, and wrote the first of his really spiteful pieces, a piece about the *New Yorker* called 'Tiny Mummies! The True Story of 43rd Street's House of the Walking Dead'.

He then wrote a second piece. Without interviewing any of the people at the magazine, or checking anything, he wrote what the writer Ved Mehta calls a 'pernicious attack', a style of attack that Muriel Spark says was 'plainly derived from Senator McCarthy'. Wolfe called the editor, William Shawn, 'a museum custodian, an undertaker, a mortuary scientist'. Mehta has never forgotten what he did. 'Wolfe's articles,' he says, 'were such murderous inventions and such a brutal caricature of Mr Shawn that all of us at the *New Yorker* felt that the random violence of the city streets had suddenly entered our lives.'

Another of Shawn's writers, and his lover, Lillian Ross, remembers the slur with a greater measure of calm. 'There was a reference to Mr Shawn and meeting in a restaurant,' she says. 'It was just one of those pieces written by someone who wasn't familiar with the subject. I remember Bill [Shawn] talking about his talent, and saying how he would have given him somewhat different guidance from what he was getting.' Wolfe says that writing that sort of piece was like 'laughing in church'.

The main person offering Wolfe editorial advice was Clay Felker, who worked on the *New York World Journal Tribune*, and who later went out on his own with *New York* magazine. He wildly encouraged Wolfe (and other contributors) to write those dingy pieces. He felt they were completely in tune with the times. Wolfe could write quickly, and make them read quickly too. 'It was a strange time for me,' Wolfe says, 'many rogue volts of euphoria. I went from one side of the country to the other and then from one side of England to the other. The people I met – the things they did – I was entranced.'

Felker saw how effective Wolfe was as a social shit-stirrer ('New Manners for New York') and let him go with his instincts. 'Wolfe anticipated the American conservative movement,' says Felker.

He is thinking of *Radical Chic*. Wolfe stole an invitation to a party Leonard Bernstein was throwing to raise money for the Black Panthers. Wolfe turned up and took notes. 'They assumed that since I was there, I must be in favour of what was going on,' he says. The piece he wrote described the whole Fifth Avenue plushness of the event, the incongruous, self-pleasing right-on-ness, the lavish phoneyness, the oozing profiteroles. It was an outrageous piece of description, a slap in the face of the liberal establishment, and it may have brought out a schism in Wolfe's style. Here was a writer who eyed the world like a liberal, but who didn't think like one.

It is the central plank in his development as a conservative writer, and nowadays, his salient feature as a novelist. 'A lot of people on the Left said that I'd caused money to dry up,' he says, 'by mocking a famous and generous fundraiser like Mr Bernstein. It was the greatest flak I ever got.' Hunter S. Thompson describes the difficulty Wolfe has engaged with. 'In order to write that punched-out stuff,' he says, 'you have to add up the facts in your own fuzzy way, and to hell with hired swine who use adding machines.'

Thompson says the people at the *Washington Post* hated Wolfe. He once wrote a positive review of one of Wolfe's books for the *National Observer* and they rejected it, admitting, as they did so, that 'there was a "feeling" around the office about giving him (Wolfe) a good review'. In those days, Wolfe liked to bandy words with his co-New Journalists ('Don't let the bastids squash you,' he writes in a letter to Thompson), but he was increasingly going his own way. Something deeply Southern in Wolfe would forever keep the oil off his cuffs.

Even his friend Thompson comes to admit it. 'Wolfe's problem is he's too crusty to participate in his stories,' he says. 'The people he feels comfortable with are dull as stale dogshit, and the people who seem to fascinate him as a writer are so weird that they make him nervous. All Tom Wolfe did – after he couldn't make it on the *Washington Post* and couldn't even get hired by the *National Observer* – was to figure out that there really wasn't much percentage in playing the old Colliers game, and that if he was ever going to make it in "journalism", his only hope was to make it on his own terms: by being good in the classical – rather than the contemporary – sense, and by being the kind of journalist that the American print media honour mainly in the breach.'

Wolfe can't see it that way. He believes that the New Journalism, in the sixties and early seventies at least, wiped out the novel as the main literary event. He believes it started 'the first new direction in American literature for half a century'. Out of the bear-pits and farting halls of Manhattan journalism a new kind of writing was seen to be born. Wolfe's idea of it was strangely grandiose.

'Sometimes I used point-of-view in the Jamesian sense,' he wrote in *The New Journalism*, 'entering directly into the mind of a character, experiencing the world through his central nervous system throughout a given scene.' Wolfe blinded himself to the tradition this sort of writing emerged from: it was 'new' only in the sense that mainstream journalism had been going through a boring period, a 'beige period' as he might have said himself. When it came to reversing the lesson in years to come – seeing how much good fiction could be influenced by the techniques of reporting – he was much quicker to mention Thackeray, Dickens, Balzac and Stendhal.

The New York writer Morris Dickstein has chosen to see Wolfe as a perennial opportunist. Wolfe, he thinks, was expressing this with this radical-seeming doctrine of New Journalism. His true opposition was to anything avant-garde or experimental in the American novel. It is Wolfe's strange reading of the sixties that – like Ronald Reagan's, like Bill Clinton's – gives clues to his power and his weakness.

'Wolfe's pretentious literary claims,' Dickstein says, 'make good magazine work seem disappointing, like failed literature...Wolfe seems incapable of exposing or involving himself. He seems to have nothing to say. Compared to all the great realists he admires, Wolfe has no sense of what makes society work, what greases the wheels, what makes it run. Only the colour and splash of fashion, the social surface, engages him. It's not that he's anti-radical: politics of any sort passes him by, except as spectacle. Wolfe's distortion of the New Journalism is rooted in his misreading of the sixties, when politics truly came to the fore.'

Not for Wolfe – at least not in that way. He thinks the Left was dying then, and finally pegged out in the seventies. (He calls Vietnam an 'idealistic war'.) In the middle of the sixties, there was a symposium at Princeton. Tom Wolfe was there with Günter Grass, Allen Ginsberg and an underground filmmaker. The discussion soon got on to police repression, the Gestapo atmosphere, and such like. 'What are you talking about?' Wolfe asked from the dais. 'We're in the middle of a Happiness Explosion!'

As if to prove the point, Wolfe once took Marshall McLuhan to a topless lunch in San Francisco. 'I found out,' Wolfe wrote, 'that a curious thing happens when men walk for the first time into a room full of nude girls. Namely, they are speechless.' Wolfe's interest in social surface prevails: there is no sense of what it might be like for the 'girls'.

At the very end of the sixties, he had lunch in London with Germaine Greer ('a thin hard-looking woman with a tremendous curly electric hairdo and the most outrageous Naugahyde mouth I had ever heard on a woman'). Wolfe says that Greer got so bored with what was going on that she set fire to her hair with a match. 'There's only one problem with that,' Greer says. 'It isn't true. The dinner we had together was completely uneventful. Indeed, I thought Wolfe and I had got on rather well. During the dinner, I told Wolfe of a meal I had had with someone else, during which my hair had caught fire. The point of the story was that my front hair has been burnt so many times, ever since I read books under the bedcovers by the light of a candle-end, ever since I started smoking, ever since I tried to heat my various kinds of sub-standard accommodation with damp wood, that I don't react to the occasional conflagration. Not so the waiters who beat my head so frantically with their napkins it was like being Leda attacked by the swan. I used to admire Wolfe. Nowadays I take him *cum grano salis* [with a grain of salt], if at all.'

There have always been notions of Wolfe's secret politics. Jose Torres, the former light-heavyweight boxing champion, remembers Tom Wolfe going around calling him 'Norman Mailer's pet primitive'. 'Norman and I were at Elaine's [a New York restaurant] one night, and I saw this guy wearing a white hat and suit and asked Norman if it was Wolfe. Norman said yes. Wolfe was standing at the bar, and I grabbed him by the shirt and said: "My name is Jose Torres. Do I look like a fucking pet primitive to you?" He didn't have a response, wouldn't talk to me, so I said: "Fuck you", and walked away.'

Despite this, Wolfe emerged from the seventies with a deep interest in the sources of male courage. It became the subject of his non-fiction account of the race for space, *The Right Stuff*. 'What is it,' asked Wolfe, 'that makes a man willing to sit on top of an enormous Roman candle, such as a Redstone, Atlas, Titan, or Saturn rocket, and wait for someone to light the fuse?' The book that attempts to answer that question is a very brilliant one – brilliantly made, beautifully worked.

There is energy all the way through *The Right Stuff*; if there is patriotism at its heart, there is also drama, pattern, precision. The book sold millions of copies. Wolfe had found a subject worthy of the schism at the back of his talent; he could record the lot with his eye, his ear, his social nose and he could gloss it wise with conservative thinking.

No longer was he mixed up in a counterculture that he could describe very well, but never believe in. He'd arrived in the American mainstream.

'Forgive me,' Wolfe says, 'for saying so, but America really is a wonderful country. It's truly democratic. If you have the numbers, and some semblance of organization, you could take political power.'

Wolfe's wife, Sheila Berger, came into the room while we sat there. She's a smiling, nice-looking woman, who does the covers for *Harper's Magazine*. They have two children, Thomas and Alexandra, both quite young. Their photographs are all round the room, on the piano, on side-tables, sometimes with each other, their parents, or horses. Wolfe says he spent a year designing the cornicing in his living room. It's a bold, many-layered affair, and we sit below among pretty cushions, vases, and walls of books. Some of Wolfe's friends believe he's become reactionary.

'It bothers me more to be called reactionary than conservative,' he says. 'I mean, what is my agenda supposed to be? I just think the political arm of this country has bent over backwards to help the downtrodden. I believe what the blacks need is strong, bourgeois role-models. It's strange. If Ronald Reagan's name was mentioned at a dinner party in the eighties, you were expected to snigger. I didn't feel he was a comic figure. I think he was one of the great presidents.'

Bonfire of the Vanities was the sonic boom novel of Reagan's eighties. Its author, who has always been interested in the character of decades, showed himself to be the funniest and most entertaining anatomist of eighties greed, opportunity and status-bedlam. And the book was a product of the age it described: gaudy, fast-moving, introspection-free, and ripping with bad money. Manhattan was shown in all it glittering dankness. 'Boys on Wall Street, mere boys, with smooth jawlines and clean arteries, boys still able to blush, were buying three-million dollar apartments on Park and 5th.'

If Wolfe has none of Fitzgerald's interest in the real sources of power, and none of Don DeLillo's talent for capturing a mental atmosphere, he does have a talent for hacking into the lingo of a period, for bringing a host of urban entities together on the page, for showing how different sorts of people organize their resentments. *Bonfire of the Vanities* is a kind of *Vanity Fair*, but with far better jokes. It sweeps up and down society in a way it is hard to imagine any British novel doing nowadays. The novel brought Wolfe to the place he'd always been heading towards – realism – achieved not by bringing the techniques of fiction to the writing of journalism, but by bringing the techniques of journalism to bear on the writing of fiction.

The best critic in America, Harold Bloom, says that Wolfe's novel brings some of the lustre back to the great tradition of the American realist novel. 'To me it's been a goldmine,' Wolfe says, 'the fact that no one is doing this sort of book. It follows the form of nineteenth-century realism. I've been calling out for it since the New Journalism. But very talented American novelists have followed the doctrine of disengaged, self-conscious, "pure" writing. Not for me.'

Tom Wolfe has grown into himself. 'I'd be kidding if I said I hadn't enjoyed my success,' he says, 'and all the attention.'

'A lot of his early writing was about being obsessed with age,' Lillian Ross says. 'Anyone over the age of thirty-five was a sinner. Being young was the only thing to be for Tom Wolfe. He'd make a fool of people's wrinkles, and how they dressed, what make of shoes they wore.'

And though he will still notice the make of shoes, the colour of a lining, his new novel, *A Man In Full*, is a novel which, in several senses, is the product of sixty-eight years. It is the darkest of his books, the most spiritual, and the least fashion-conscious. It is billed as a novel of the nineties, but that doesn't mean much. It is a good novel – one with nerve, with personal grist – and it finds the pulse of the modern American South. Charlie Croker, the book's main event, is a troubled tycoon, devoid of hope and romance, a kind of anti-Gatsby, a man whose pain is not just social, but personal, and physical.

Wolfe says he doesn't see the world as his characters do. His aim is to see everything, and conclude nothing. You might say he has a liberal's eye, but a conservative heart.

Speaking of which, how is his heart? 'I feel quite well now,' he says. 'I had a really rough time in 1996. I'm now on a regular diet and exercise regimen. Like most men who have heart attacks, I was taken completely by surprise. I had felt invulnerable. When I'd walk the streets and see a fat man, I'd think: "Uh! Your days are numbered, but not mine."'

A woman who used to live in Wolfe's block used to see him taking his daughter to the bus stop each morning. 'Always poised, always dressed,' she says. 'He was such a strange sight on 79th Street. So elegant. So mannerly. Just like a Southern gentleman taking the air.'

31 October 1998

Life at a glance

THOMAS KENNERLY WOLFE

Born: 2 March 1931, Richmond, Virginia.

Education: Washington and Lee University, Yale University.

Married: Sheila Berger (one son, one daughter).

Career: Reporter, *Springfield Union*, Massachusetts (1956–9); reporter, Latin American correspondent *Washington Post* (1959–62); reporter, magazine writer *New York Herald Tribune* (1962–6); contributing editor *New York* magazine (1968–76); *Esquire* magazine (1977–).

Select bibliography: *The Kandy-Kolored Tangerine-Flake Streamline Baby* (1965); *The Electric Kool-Aid Acid Test* (1968); *Radical Chic and Mau-Mauing the Flak Catchers* (1970); *The New Journalism* (1973); *The Right Stuff* (1979); *In Our Time* (1980); *From Bauhaus to Our House* (1981); *Bonfire of the Vanities* (1987); *Ambush at Fort Bragg* (1996); *A Man In Full* (1998); *Hooking Up* (2000).

Awards: Front Page awards, Washington Newspaper Guild (1961); Virginia Laureate for literature (1977); American Book award for general non-fiction (1979); Columbia Journalism award (1980); John Dos Passos award (1984); Washington Irving medal (1986).